BRITISH FILM INSTITUTE

bfi

BFI PUBLISHING

First published in 1993 by the
British Film Institute
21 Stephen Street
London W1P 2LN

This revised edition published in 1996

The British Film Institute exists to promote appreciation,
protection and development of moving image culture in and
throughout the whole of the United Kingdom. Its activities include
the National Film and Television Archive; the National Film Theatre;
the Museum of the Moving Image; the London Film Festival;
the production and distribution of film and video; funding and
support for regional activities; Library and Information Services;
Stills, Posters and Designs; Research; Publishing and Education
and the monthly *Sight and Sound* magazine.

British Library Cataloguing-in-Publication Data
A catalogue record for this book is available from the British Library

ISBN   0-85170-573-1

Cover design by Mark Goddard

Typesetting by D R Bungay Associates, Burghfield, Berks.

Printed and bound in Great Britain

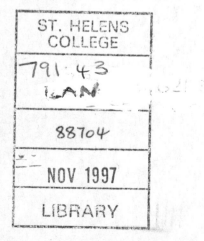

CONTENTS

ACKNOWLEDGMENTS

The author would like to thank: Dinah Caine, Director of Skillset, the Broadcasting, Film and Video Industry Training Organisation, the Industry Lead Body for Broadcasting, Film and Video; Stuart Conway of High Peak College, Buxton, Derbyshire; Janet Couzens, Recruitment Co-ordinator, BBC Network Television; Irene Ibbotson, Julie Evans and Liz Simpson of BBC North; Anne Fleming of the National Film and Television Archive; John Mundy, Richard Hines and Ian France of the University College, Warrington; David Martin of ft2; Al Garthwaite of Vera Productions; Bill Curtis of Ravensbourne College of Design and Communication, School of Television and Broadcasting Short Course Unit; Martin Brown of Equity; Alistair Fell of Cosgrove Hall Films; Richard Holmes and the New Producers' Alliance. They gave their time in personal interviews or long telephone conversations or checking up on facts; they answered queries either about the industry or about the impact of new developments in education and training. While every effort has been made to check the facts reported in this book, the opinions expressed remain the author's own. I would also like to thank Bill Byers Brown and Christine Upton for their help and support.

INTRODUCTION

In the three years since the first edition of this book the film, television and video industry has undergone a period of massive change thanks largely to the impact of electronic technology. This has, in turn, contributed to continuing changes in the ways in which people enter the industry and in patterns of training and employment. In 1993 I wrote that the previous decade had been one of upheaval, that technological change, political attack, the decline of union power, the rise of the independents, had all blurred the lines between the various sectors of the industry. I predicted then that the industry would be increasingly easy to enter and there would be more mobility, but that employment conditions (in terms of salaries and perks) would be less attractive, freelancing would be endemic and permanent jobs a thing of the past. This prediction has proved to be true but at a rate and pace that has astounded and confounded most observers of the industry, including myself.

The rapid advance of multi-media, a somewhat enigmatic term which describes the convergence of all forms of electronic communication into digital mode, is having an increasingly important effect on the landscape of the film, television and video industry and also on training and education. When digital signals can be used to represent text, graphics, still and moving pictures, and sound it means that old boundaries, which once completely separated the different sections of the media industry from each other, are rapidly disappearing: the concept of multi-media renders them meaningless.

However, it is not only the traditional boundaries of the film, television and video industries which are being eroded. On the larger scale, as the 20th century draws to its close, the frontiers between the huge, formerly distinct businesses of computing, cable, telecommunications, television and entertainment are all collapsing to create a single communications industrial giant. When everything from television to telecommunications can be transmitted in binary code – the language of computers (and the human nervous system!) – it means convergence at a rapid rate on a global scale. Most experts predict that the communications industry will be one of the largest in the world by the 21st century. The marrying of the cable converter box and the computer, the turning of television pictures into compressed digital form, the introduction of fibre optics and the linking-in of personal computer software permits access to, and the interactive manipulation of, a wealth of information and informational products. Goldman Sachs, the investment advisors, have called this new world the 'Communacopia'. Elsewhere the process is referred to as the onset of 'the information age' which, it is alleged, will be as significant in terms of human society and economic development (and as important in terms of human history) as the Industrial Revolution.

In 1993 I wrote that the film, television and video employee was in the vanguard of economic, social and industrial change. Everything has confirmed this. A roller-coaster atmosphere of continual transformation and shifting uncertainty is today a fundamental fact of life for all employees in the workforce, but in this industry more than most. Young people embarking on their careers at the present time will need emotional stamina and flexibility to accept the uncertainties that rapid economic and technological change increasingly dictates. They will also need to recognise and understand that future employment prospects are wrapped up with consumer demand and political and economic decision-making. Business analysts, for example, suggest that the new digital television hardware is central to the take-up and use of the information superhighway. It will be customer demand for entertainment which will be a central factor in the extension and exploitation of the superhighway technology and its capacity for interactivity etc. Supplying the consumer thirst for entertainment will be a dynamic factor in the wiring of homes in preparation for the information age and those employed in doing this will be key players in the predicted expansion of the information society.

Any lecturer or teacher of media at the present time (myself included) has had to become accustomed to persistent and hostile attack from the press and from the public about the current popularity of media courses. We have to inure ourselves to supercilious sniffs about 'hordes' of students embarking on media degrees and qualifications, the implication being that this is, at best, an easy option or, at worst, a complete waste of time. In fact, however, in acquiring knowledge, understanding and basic skills in the communications industry young people may be wiser than their elders because they are equipping themselves for the next century. The media/entertainment/information industry will be one of the powerhouses of the future and instinctively, perhaps, young people understand this better than the older generation who have little comprehension of the scale of change over the last few years.

This edition like its predecessor is divided into four parts. The first part of the book describes the state of play in the film, television and video industry for those who want an overall picture; the second section describes education and training; the third and fourth parts describe the process of production and the actual jobs. Three years ago I advised readers who only wanted practical information to skip the first part and begin on the second section. Today, by contrast, I would suggest that the first part, which sketches out the history of the industry, the contemporary landscape and possible future developments, is by far the most important.

In the preparation for this new edition I spoke to many young people who had been in the industry for two or three years. Time and time again they said that they wished they had had more knowledge of the overall picture, that they felt themselves being hurtled along at tremendous speed but they had no signposts to guide them. If they had known more about, for example, globalisation and the move towards the information superhighway, they would have understood more about what was happening to them in the world of work and may have taken more sensible decisions about their own futures.

This book, like its predecessor, attempts to describe the various jobs in the industry in the context of the economy of the industry as a whole. It is principally intended for young people leaving school, college or university who are interested in working in film, television and video but who know little or nothing about the industry. It is also intended as a resource book for educators and career counsellors who wish to advise the many students who are interested in working in the media industry but who have no first-hand experience of their own to offer them. It is also aimed at young people who have secured their first job in the industry but who are bewildered by the pace of change and may be frustrated by the lack of training opportunities to help them surmount the technological challenges. They may have also have heard of the National Vocational Qualification and the industry training body, Skillset, but they are not really sure about its role or about what it is intended to do.

The communication industry is a growth area. Working in the film, television and video sectors today should provide young people with the basic skills to surf the media landscape of tomorrow and secure for themselves interesting, stimulating (and continuously evolving) jobs. I hope this book will help them to gain employment in the first place, to understand the environment once they have a job and to orient themselves to an ever shifting industry which, although unpredictable, rarely falls short of being totally engrossing and enormously exciting.

Good luck!

PART ONE
THE INDUSTRY

I

TERRESTRIAL TELEVISION
The Onward March of the Market

During the 80s the film and television industries, which historically had been somewhat hostile and competitive towards each other, began to draw closer together. The economics of film and television became more closely intertwined and the border between the two became blurred: today film companies produce films for television, independent film and video companies produce television programmes and television companies finance feature films. In addition, with the decline of the unions and the ending of the closed shop, people working in film, television and video move freely between what were formerly three highly separated sectors.

The following four chapters will look at the implications of these developments for people contemplating a career in the audio-visual industries as the century draws to its close. The discussion will begin with television because it was the television industry which bore the full brunt of the many shifts in political and economic philosophy and it was also television which experienced the main impact of the new technology.

At the beginning of the 80s the television industry enjoyed a unique position in Britain with a worldwide reputation for quality in content and technique. This was true for both the public (BBC) and commercial (ITV) sectors. Earlier in the 80s most people would probably not have considered British television to be an 'industry' at all, certainly not in the sense of the chemical industry or the engineering industry. Television carried a varied set of programme genres and was a 'mixed bag', partly in the public and partly in the private sector. It consisted of a huge organisation, the BBC, which had long dominated British broadcasting, and a group of highly regulated commercial companies linked together as independent television (ITV). The majority of employees in television, to a greater or lesser degree, were sheltered from the full force of the cold winds of market reality. Producers and directors had little direct involvement with finance as an aspect of programme planning. The name of the game was creativity: producing good programmes was the prime motivation. Financial responsibility was the task of upper management.

By 1991 much of this had changed. The 1990 Broadcasting Act ushered in a franchise system for ITV, the initial intention of which was to sell independent television licences to the highest bidder. Although this was eventually modified by an emphasis on a 'quality' threshold (see below), the new system of granting ITV franchises meant that, in principle, British commercial television faced, for the first time, the full force of the market-place and a reduced legislative obligation to maintain public service broadcasting, thereby conforming at last to the economic and political trends of the previous decade. Furthermore it seemed likely that, as the 90s wore on, the BBC would be forced to follow suit. The renewal of the BBC's licence to broadcast due in 1996, provoked much talk of changing the licence fee system which had financed the Corporation since the 20s. To understand the dramatic implications of all this, especially for those employed or wishing to be employed in the industry, we must briefly examine British television in its historical context.

Public Service Broadcasting
In the 20s, when broadcasting began as a mass medium, it was characterised by two different philosophical models. In the US broadcasting from the first was part of the marketplace and was seen mainly as a medium of entertainment to be paid for commercially through advertising. In Britain (and to a greater or lesser extent most other European countries) broadcasting was regarded as a public service, paid for by public funds (through the licence fee or, in some European countries, by a charge on the electricity bill) and untainted by any form of commercialism. In Britain the government was involved in broadcasting almost from the first. It had legislated into existence the British Broadcasting Corporation (BBC), an institution which under threat of legal sanctions had to abide by certain basic principles.

The purposes of British broadcasting were repeatedly declared to be information, education and entertainment. Any inspection of BBC radio and television archives before 1955 (when ITV began) leaves an abiding impression of an upper middle-class Establishment institution more concerned with a lofty mission of informing rather than entertaining the British masses. For many years most BBC broadcasters believed they were in the business of 'improving minds' and they turned up their noses at American radio and television with its crude, commercial attitudes that resulted in poor programmes characterised by cheap quizzes, inane game shows and melodramatic

4

soap operas. The British congratulated themselves on their vastly superior system exemplified by high-minded programmes and high-quality production standards.

Behind the British and most European governments' traditional attachment to the concept of public service broadcasting lay the belief that broadcasting had enormous power to influence people's minds. It was definitely not an industry like any other and it had to be carefully controlled and supervised. Governments feared the possible negative influences of broadcasting on their citizens through propaganda and demagoguery and, concomitant with this, they also believed in broadcasting's ability to mould public opinion in a positive direction and raise the general level of education.

In Britain this approach has been dubbed Reithian, after the first Director General of the BBC, John Reith, who conceived of the Corporation as a mean of promoting national, social, religious and democratic integration. It was Reith who laid down the principles that the BBC should inform and educate as well as entertain and that it should be funded by a licence fee and not by advertising. Reith was suspicious of popular culture and, as a Scottish Presbyterian, did tend to imbue the Corporation with a sense of moral obligation. Reith insisted on the necessity for 'the brute force of monopoly', that the BBC should have no rivals, and under him the Corporation developed into what Raymond Williams called an 'authoritarian system with a conscience'. Reith gave much time to religious broadcasting and under his prodding there were so called 'closed periods' when no programmes could be broadcast in order not to compete with churches. Even though Reith had resigned from the Corporation in 1938 his influence was felt as late as 1959: until that time no television programme could be transmitted for one hour on a Sunday evening to give people time to attend Evensong. Reith was utterly confident of the superiority of the BBC's public service monopolistic system and spoke scathingly of American broadcasting which functioned 'on a cash basis [and] operated irrespective of any consideration of content or balance'.

For a quarter of a century the BBC held its monopoly over broadcasting but, after the Second World War, the consensus about the superiority of the British system began to crumble. Many business interests in Britain began to cast envious eyes westwards to the United States where commercial broadcasting, closely linked to the advertising industry, was making huge profits. A campaign began for the introduction of commercial television in Britain, and in 1955 the monopoly of the BBC with its metropolitan bias was broken with the introduction of independent television (ITV), a commercial television system which was regionally based.

The introduction of ITV, however, was a typical piece of British compromise. Although the system was financed by advertising, the idea of television as solely a money-making industry was still unacceptable to most British people, especially to those in power. Various Royal Commissions and government legislation insisted that both the BBC and ITV had to provide a high-quality public service, and the commercial television companies were also put under an obligation to produce programmes which were educative and informative as well as entertaining. This public service element in commercial television was supervised by an organisation called the Independent Television Authority which eventually, after the introduction of commercial radio, became the Independent Broadcasting Authority (IBA). For the next thirty years a dual system (sometimes called the 'duopoly') of the BBC and the IBA, with a strong public service ethos, characterised British television.

Channel Four

The idea of public service broadcasting reached its apogee in 1982 with the introduction of Channel Four which, although it showed advertisements, was obliged under the jurisdiction of the IBA to take account of minority interests and transmit quality programmes. Channel Four was protected from the market-place: it was financed by levies on the advertising receipts of the ITV channels, which had the right to sell advertising time on Channel Four transmissions in their regions.

The establishment of Channel Four apparently confirmed the public interest nature of the British approach to broadcasting. In fact, however, it also presaged a momentous change. Channel Four, unlike the BBC and ITV, was a 'publisher-broadcaster' rather than a 'producer-broadcaster' company. It made hardly any programmes in-house; it commissioned them from outside. This was an enormous boost to the so-called 'independents', small, usually struggling, production companies making films and videos. Such companies had always found it difficult to broach the ramparts of the monolithic BBC and ITV to enable their programmes to reach the screen.

Here a word of caution is in order: the term 'independent' can lead to considerable confusion since ITV is itself often referred to as independent television. In the 80s, however, 'independents' became the current term for describing small production companies which had no part in the transmission of programmes but which sold completed programmes to mainline broadcasters or co-produced programmes with them. Channel Four was the great stimulus to the growth of this sector because, as a commissioning company, it placed contracts for programmes with independent producers (it also placed contracts with ITV itself). *Brookside*, commissioned from Phil Redmond's company,

Mersey TV, was a typical case in point. By 1984-5, 313 independent companies contributed 690 hours of television to Channel Four. By 1995, despite the recession (of which more below), there were calculated to be around 1024 independent companies producing programmes and feature films for British television. The independent sector has now become a very important production force in the UK. It is expected that the expansion of satellite and cable (see Chapter 3) will stimulate even more business for this sector whose interests are represented by the Producers Alliance for Cinema and Television (PACT).

Channel Four quickly established a reputation for innovative programmes which expressed radical political and social views. If asked, most people would have identified the Channel with the political left rather than the right. In fact, the principle behind Channel Four was, to a degree, an expression of the classical liberal economic theory which was to become so fashionable in the 80s and which laid emphasis on competition in the market-place. Channel Four challenged the cosy duopoly of the BBC and ITV/IBA and liberated British broadcasting from an organisational strait-jacket. In opening up the airwaves and allowing more access to the screen for the products of small companies it heralded a massive shift in the system which had governed British broadcasting for more than thirty years.

Deregulation
Between 1982 (when Channel Four was founded) and 1996 the whole landscape of British television has undergone a vast and rapid upheaval. The reasons for this can be traced to two main influences: politics and technology. In the United States and Europe the 1980s saw the election of many right-wing governments committed to so-called deregulation. This meant, in practice, freeing business from what was considered by economic conservatives to be the undue and excessive restraint imposed by government 'over regulation' and the restrictive practices of trade unions. This so-called 'Reaganomics' (after President Ronald Reagan of the United States) had a worldwide impact and led in broadcasting generally to the dismantlement of many of the public service regulations that had previously governed radio and television. This had less impact in the United States, where broadcasting had always been less supervised and more commercial, than in Europe, where it led to dramatic change. In many European countries in the 80s there was a stampede to adopt the free-market model for broadcasting. The public service broadcasters' monopoly of the airwaves was broken and a tidal wave of privatisation hit European broadcasting. European countries, which had never had any form of commercial television before now, permitted private commercial stations to exist: new television

(and radio) companies sprang up all over the place challenging public service values. Many experts predicted the end of public service broadcasting and its replacement by the market system.

One of the first results of all this was a boom in advertising. Television enjoyed a halcyon period, with entrepreneurs making huge profits. Most of the private channels accepted that television was basically an entertainment medium. Under the slogans of 'choice', 'freedom' and 'democracy' power over broadcasting content was said to be handed over to consumers. The days of the rather grey, preachy, government-run systems which had typified television in some European countries were numbered. Advertising money flooded in and by the mid-80s the entertainment programming schedules of Europe's television systems had brightened considerably. With much more money slopping around, the future seemed rosy, especially for employment.

Conservative Policies
In the UK Margaret Thatcher and the Conservative Party came to power in 1979. The Thatcher government had many ideological strands but one of the most significant was a passionate desire to loosen economic regulation. The Prime Minister believed in a rugged free-market individualism and was determined to push back the frontiers of state intervention. She was particularly hostile to what she referred to as the 'nanny' state which, in her eyes, the mandarins of the BBC and the IBA exemplified. The state, she believed, meddled far too much in the affairs of the individual. Moreover, she was deeply suspicious of some British broadcasters who espoused liberal views and cultivated a 'lack of bias', an attitude which was out of tune with her own conviction politics.

The Thatcher government was also predictably hostile to any form of protectionism, especially as exemplified by trade unions, which were very strong in certain sectors of the broadcasting and film industry. With the Prime Minister gunning for the unions it was inevitable that broadcasting fell within her sights. The first round was with the BBC. In 1986 the Prime Minister ordered an inquiry (the Peacock Committee) into the financing of the BBC where many wet liberals were supposed to lurk. This aroused widespread fears in the Corporation about the survival of the licence fee. Peacock proposed abandoning the public service requirements of the BBC in a general sense: programmes which appealed to a minority audience (basically cultural ones) were to be financed through a pay-as-you-view system. The Committee also proposed that by 1996 the proportion of independent programmes on the BBC and ITV should reach 40 per cent; the government in November 1986 decided that 25 per cent should be the aim by 1990.

8

ITV, with its powerful unions, could not hope to escape from the government's reforming scrutiny and, in the end, it was probably ITV which bore the full brunt of the free-market fervour. The 1990 Broadcasting Act abolished the IBA and the protective shield which it had erected to secure public service broadcasting on ITV. The IBA was replaced by the Independent Television Commission (ITC) which has a much less interventionist mandate. The Broadcasting Act also altered the way ITV franchises were awarded. However, it was in her attack on the broadcasting unions that Thatcher's economic philosophy was most in evidence.

A basic principle of the Thatcher government was a supreme confidence in the business ethic and the virtue of competition, which the Prime Minister saw as the basis of the world's most successful economic system, capitalism. Capitalism, for Thatcher, was an agent for good and the guarantor of liberty. One of her most widely quoted remarks, 'There is no such thing as society', summed up her hostility to mutually protective groups, especially those which acted together in such a way as to thwart the 'healthy' self-interest of the individual businessman or woman. According to this world-view, men and women pursuing their own self-interest would bring great wealth to the whole nation. At the time there was much talk of the 'trickle-down' effect; as the top earners in society became richer, the theory ran, wealth would eventually seep down to those at the bottom: less has been heard about this in recent years.

The Thatcher government consistently expressed a strong philosophical opposition to 'socialist' ideals, and particularly those which the union movement represented. According to this view, traditional British corporatism and craft protectionism, closed shops, union 'tickets' and all types of restrictive practices had been the main reason for Britain's lacklustre economic performance since the Second World War. Throughout the 80s, therefore, the Conservative government launched a series of onslaughts against British trade unionism which left the movement reeling. New labour laws effectively broke union power. All this affected many British industries but the impact was very acute in television, notably in ITV.

At a notorious meeting with representatives of the television industry in September 1987, Thatcher declared ITV to be the 'last bastion' of the most severe restrictive practices. They had contributed to a fat-cat, mollycoddled industry which the government was determined to wean away from its cream. The government believed that ITV did not really function in the free market and that it had been grossly over-staffed and protected for many years. This had resulted in a virtual closed shop, soaring labour costs (in part owing to very generous overtime agreements) and expensive programmes.

Technological Change

In addition to the philosophical and political turmoil that hit British television in the 80s, the industry also found itself disturbed by rapid advances in the so-called new technologies. Television since its beginnings has always been the mass-communications medium most closely linked to technological advance. Throughout its history the development of television has been furthered by many scientific and technological disciplines including mechanical and electrical engineering, electronics, optics and acoustics. During the 80s, however, the pace of technological change accelerated thanks to advances in semi-conductors, lasers, fibre optics and space technology. Semi-conductors gave rise to integrated circuits ('chips') and to microprocessors, and these devices rapidly achieved higher and higher levels of performance in television thanks to their capacity to store data, their computational speeds and their complexity. Digital data processing became increasingly important and this, combined with integrated circuits and microprocessors, quickly revolutionised every aspect of television technology including production, processing, storage, transmission, broadcasting and the receiving of audio-visual information. The end result was an explosion in audio-visual technology and a spectacular multiplication of the number of television channels that could be transmitted, especially through the increasing development of the cable and satellite industries.

In the past, television, with its terrestrial broadcasting transmitters, was easily controlled by national laws. The airwaves were regarded as a scarce resource. In the era of satellites, the notion of spectrum scarcity began to lose its meaning. Direct broadcast satellites (DBS), and the services that cable could provide, cut right across national boundaries and made government regulation much more difficult and problematical. Technological change, therefore, provided an encouragement towards deregulation throughout Europe and further prompted the loosening of the noose of state regulations, the weakening of the concept of public service broadcasting and the move towards privatisation.

Advances in television technology increased the versatility of the medium. A greater variety of production methods was possible and the process of making programmes was simplified. Costs of equipment were reduced and the whole industry became much more accessible. The result was a boom in the independent video sector; the technology of television was no longer the fiefdom of the 'experts' at the BBC and ITV. Companies were formed to produce programmes for television, pop videos and publicity for the corporate and public sector. Every business wanted to market itself and the corporate video became the mark of a company which was doing well. This created an expanding video production industry with new opportunities for producers and freelancers: even experienced television personnel with secure jobs began to 'moonlight' in the video sector to supplement their salaries.

The old system whereby an intellectual and craft elite, working within the framework of large institutions such as the BBC and ITV companies, monopolised a complex body of knowledge (lighting, sound, camerawork and so on) and therefore power was eroded. So too was the protection from competition which the closed shop had ensured. Thus technological advance, combined with the deregulatory approach and anti-union legislation, split the industry open. The heyday of the energetic and talented freelancer on the way to making a fortune was at hand: everything was possible, or that was how it seemed ... at first. Then the recession hit and the pound notes fluttering before entrepreneurial eyes suddenly became fewer and farther between. The brave new world of freelancing suddenly looked very insecure and not very well paid besides.

The Recession
By the end of the 80s the world economy had slowed down; the advertising industry was one of the hardest hit and the market model for television looked somewhat tattered. This was especially so in Europe, where a decline in programme standards and a slackening of the specifically European dimension of television (and film) under the impact of American imports became a matter for concern. As the decade ended, and the recession deepened, it was not clear that the money available for home-grown television production was actually going to increase. It seemed far more likely that the now heavily fragmented European television industry would be colonised by cheap American products; that the result of deregulation was going to be more of less – more slick internationalised and homogenised programmes and fewer stimulating, innovative ones that expressed national or European identity.

The heady roller-coaster days of the mid-80s were over and Europe began to count the cost of deregulation: the dominance of the American imports (often dubbed 'Dallasification' after the hugely popular American import), the increasing number of repeats and, in countries such as Italy, a sleazy home-grown commercial system which hit the lowest common denominator of public taste. No wonder the European Community began to take note, and no wonder many British legislators also began to view the future with alarm and to back-pedal on some of the more extreme free-market views.

The Impact of the 1990 Broadcasting Bill
The Broadcasting Bill of 1990 was a curious piece of legislation from many points of view. It dealt with the BBC hardly at all, even though it

11

was obvious that the future of the BBC was a crucial issue which would have to be addressed well before 1996 when the BBC's Charter was up for renewal. In this it was similar to the Peacock report of 1986 which was supposed to be looking into the financing of the BBC but largely confined itself to proposals for restructuring ITV.

The Bill, as originally drafted, had very much expressed the free-market views contained in the 1988 White Paper 'Broadcasting in the '90s: Competition, Choice and Quality'. However, as the debate in parliament and the country went on, some of the hardest free-market edges were knocked off and replaced with what was called the 'quality programme threshold'. This was designed as a means of excluding porn merchants and other undesirables, as well as those who might bid too much money and thereby undermine the viability of their own business plans with a consequent knock-on effect on the quality of programmes. The principle that the market should be the sole arbiter of the winner was therefore, to a degree, subverted since an exceptionally 'high quality of service' bid could outdo the highest monetary bid. This at least was a token return to some of the principles that had governed British broadcasting throughout its history.

The Broadcasting Bill did help the advance of the independent sector with its provision that 25 per cent of all new programmes shown on the BBC and ITV (which the Bill renamed Channel Three although, in the event, the Companies have preferred to stay with the name ITV) had to be supplied by independent producers after 1992 (when the Act came into force). This provided independents with access to an additional minimum of 5,000 programming hours per annum. Independent production companies, mainly working in video but also in film, thus received a tremendous boost and became a fast growing and influential sector of the UK audio-visual industry (see Chapter 3).

However, in making provision for Channel Five and for satellite and cable television, the Broadcasting Bill also gave an impetus to the further fragmentation of television. In the views of some critics at the time this would have a very detrimental effect on programming because it would limit the pool of available revenue. Money coming from advertising sales, licence fees or subscriptions would have to stretch further and there was a prediction that there would be a definite decline in the quality of programmes on offer: a prediction which many people believe has come true.

The BBC, it was feared, with a smaller proportion of total broadcasting, could also find the universal licence fee increasingly under threat. People who have many channels to watch, it was argued, would resent being forced to pay for the maintenance of the Corporation and the British tabloid press would certainly be willing to load the cannons:

newspapers have never had much love for television, which they see as their greatest rival. As it turned out, dire warnings that when the BBC's licence came up for renewal the government would attack its funding base and the licence fee would be abolished have proved to be unfounded. In fact, it is generally recognised that the BBC has managed to survive the winds of change with a fair degree of success. The same can not be said of ITV in the fall-out from the auction of the TV franchises for Channel Three.

The Franchise Auction and its Consequences

The impact of the Broadcasting Bill has been particularly dramatic for ITV. The auction of the new Channel Three broadcasting licences during 1991 caused considerable anxiety, and four incumbent TV companies (Thames, TVS, TSW and TV-am) lost their franchises. Eight of the licences, however, did not go to the highest bidder, as the original legislation had planned, because of the quality programme threshold. Eleven bidding groups failed to pass the threshold and were therefore rejected on these grounds, and three bids were rejected by the ITC because their quality promises were judged to be unsupportable given the cash level of the bid. The wide variation in the cash bids offered caused considerable concern, especially in the case of those companies which bid huge sums (Yorkshire bid £37.7 million and Carlton Television, the newcomer which defeated Thames, bid £43.17 million), because, in addition to the annually index-linked cash sum, winners also had to pay a fixed percentage of revenue predetermined by the ITC. All this engendered fears throughout the industry that financial problems would produce even more pressure to reduce costs (in 1993 ITV gave £300 million to the Treasury) enforcing economies of scale which would have a depressing effect on programme expenditure, particularly in a period of declining revenues from advertising.

To a large extent these fears have proved to be justified. The new licence holders have had to concentrate on cost effectiveness and all Channel Three companies have shed staff and, although there has been much more commissioning of material from independents, this has not compensated for the loss of jobs in ITV. Since 1993 ITV companies have also been subject to potentially hostile take-over bids (which in former days used to be blocked by the IBA): this has led to further cost-cutting in order to increase the company value on the stock market. Indeed, what is happening in ITV has aroused concern about media concentration (see Chapter 4).

In the 90s all the terrestrial channels are having to compete for audiences with the new delivery systems of cable and satellite. Although the BBC has a certain level of fixed funding, guaranteed by the licence fee, the financial basis of ITV is much more volatile because it is in competition with, for example, BSkyB to deliver large audiences to advertisers. The increasing fragmentation of the audience, because of the proliferation of channels, means that fewer people today watch ITV, and, as a result, its advertising rates have declined – with a consequent loss in both the quality and range of its programmes. Yet, unlike its cable and satellite rivals, ITV is obliged by Parliament to maintain informational and educational content in its programming as well as a proper balance and wide range in subject matter. This handicaps the ITV network in the competitive market-place which is why there are constant rumblings about moving *News at Ten*. ITV wishes to shift the national news so that movies can be shown without the half hour break but the politicians have resisted this fiercely.

During the summer of 1995 ITV's ratings fell disastrously and the network recorded a very low share of viewing (33 per cent). Advertisers bombarded the channel with demands for more airtime for commercials and more investment in programmes. An additional £13 million was added to the network budget for 1996, but ITV's troubles are likely to worsen when the new Channel Five comes on air in January 1997.

Channel Five
The 'quality not price' debate that was such a feature of the debate over the Channel Three franchises was highlighted once again in October 1995 with the award of the ten-year licence to 'Channel Five Broadcasting', the company which the ITV judged to have passed the quality threshold (unlike its rival UK-TV which had bid more). Channel Five will not be a national station: reception problems will limit Channel Five to 70 per cent of the country and also require millions of video recorders, satellite receivers and computer game consoles to be retuned (because otherwise their owners would suffer from picture interference whether or not they actually watched Channel Five).

While the new channel aims to provide a popular service for a variety of tastes it is on a smaller scale than ITV. Its organisers plan to spend £100 million a year on programming (a third of the budget of Channel Four and one-seventh that of ITV). Channel Five's evening schedule will start with quiz shows and comedies at 6 pm followed by a daily soap. There will be entertainment shows at 7 pm and the main evening news, which will be supplied by ITN, will be at 8 pm followed by a ten-minute current affairs show. At 9 pm like ITV it will show feature films and drama series but without the obligation of having to break them up for a *News at Ten*. The impact of Channel Five on the other terrestrial channels is still uncertain but it will further fragment the audience and may have particularly severe repercussions as far as ITV is concerned.

The BBC: Producers' Choice and the Renewal of the Licence

For many years the BBC enjoyed substantial increases in income as the number of TV households in the UK rose and as more and more viewers switched from black and white to colour sets. Eventually, however, most homes had colour sets and the number of households buying TVs had reached virtual saturation point. This meant the value of the income from the licence fee was flattening while costs were rapidly increasing. Greater competition for sports rights and audience-pulling entertainers, for example, all drove up costs and the Corporation began to feel financially pinched especially as new technology was proving to be expensive.

In addition, the emphasis on market forces also prompted a great deal of analysis and heart searching at the BBC. How was the public service mandate to be interpreted in the new era? The Corporation had to find a new role in an expanding broadcasting market-place. Major shifts in culture and ideology are never an easy matter to negotiate for a traditional institution but one significant response by BBC managers was the launch of a project called 'Producers' Choice' in the early 90s. 'Producers' Choice' was designed to increase internal competition within the Corporation. BBC producers were given control of their own programme budgets and were allowed to shop around outside the Corporation for cheaper facilities.

This was tantamount to a revolution for the BBC which had always prided itself on the self-sufficiency of its organisational structure. Producers were now expected to buy in the services they needed (scenic design, costumes, studio space, graphics and post-production) from wherever they could secure the best deal. BBC resources departments, which had previously always supplied services, could only earn income if they could sell their services to programme-makers. Producers were now charged a share of overheads, such as accommodation and capital costs, in the same way that independent producers were charged for the use of BBC facilities. This all helped to produce programmes more cheaply and efficiently, but it has also meant a drastic reduction in staff. On the positive side, on the other hand, it has generated greater expansion in the independent sector.

On 31 December 1996 the current Royal Charter, the formal document establishing the Corporation, its constitution and its overall power, ends. Despite the fears of many, the government has proposed renewing the BBC's Charter for another ten years until 2006. The draft of the new proposals was issued in November 1995 and it confirmed the public service and programme priorities that had been laid out in 1992 in a BBC document called 'Extending Choice': the universal licence fee was confirmed, as was the BBC's obligation to

15

provide services of 'information, education and entertainment'. The main changes referred to the Government's intention of privatising and selling off the BBC transmission network and the clarification of the role of the governors in dealing with issues of impartiality and taste and decency. The Charter was said to build for the BBC a major role in the multi-media world of the future.

Impact on Employment

For the thirty years of the duopoly from 1955 until the mid-80s BBC and ITV producers were virtually a protected species. Their main obligation was to make good programmes; the system was 'ideas-led': it was for others to worry where the money was coming from. That protection has now gone. In the harsh climate of the 90s British terrestrial television industry is more like the British film industry and is dogged by financial problems. It is no longer enough to be a talented television producer: financial acumen is as much in demand as creative and artistic ability – but more of that later. Many of the small companies which have sprung up to produce films or programmes for television since the establishment of Channel Four (and the legislative obligation on the BBC and ITV to buy in 25 per cent of their programmes) have not survived the harsh financial climate of the 90s, although others, often equally short-lived, have sprung up to take their place. The ability to raise money from co-production sources and programme distribution, and to save money in operating overheads, has become an increasingly highly valued skill. As the independent television sector matures, take-overs, mergers and bankruptcies are becoming as common as they are in other British industries. Attracting investment and income in the harsh, unprotected, competitive corporative climate is crucial if a company is to survive.

Television (henceforth closely linked with film and video) is becoming an industry much like any other except, perhaps, less stable than most. If, in the old days, producers made programmes to impress their peers, they now make programmes to impress their backers (that is to say, programmes that sell). The idea of the broadcaster as a figure apart, high on a pedestal above ordinary mortals, well-paid, admired and virtually untouchable, has gone for ever. In future most people working in television will no longer be employed in secure jobs. The development of more terrestrial channels and the growth of satellite and cable-delivered services, plus the likely impact of the information super-highway, have opened up opportunities for employment but most of the new employees are freelances working across the film, television, video and other media sectors. Some veterans of the British television

16

industry even doubt that the BBC will survive as a production base in the long term.

Summing Up
The traditional economy and culture of the terrestrial television industry has been irrevocably altered in the last few years and employees are far more subject to fluctuations in the market-place. Newcomers to the industry should be aware of this.

2

FILM

Will Everyone Be Working for Uncle Sam?

Prior to the 80s film production was an industry apart, with its own culture, traditions and working practices. It held itself aloof from television which historically had been its main rival for audiences. In the 50s the popularity of television had almost killed the British film industry and many old film hands really despised and resented the 'Little Box in the Corner'. Film people regarded the BBC in particular as too establishment-oriented and television in general as too down-market and populist, without any true lasting cultural value. The fact that the British film industry was often in financial difficulties increased the sense of alienation between employees of the two industries.

During the 80s, however, the film and television industries drew much closer together. Increasingly the same 'products' were seen on cinema and television screens. As we have seen, political, financial and technical pressures brought about a revolution in television and this in turn altered its relationship to film. There had always been some overlap: many prestigious television drama productions were filmed (the BBC at one time had its own film studios out at Ealing) and a number of independent companies produced high-quality filmed commercials for ITV. As a consequence, although the film industry did not experience the same degree of upheaval as did television during the 80s, increasingly there were shared issues of considerable significance that had an impact on employment especially in the feature film sector.

Feature Films
'Features' are those films intended for release in the cinema. They usually run between 90 and 110 minutes and generally tell stories. Documentary films intended for distribution in cinemas are relatively rare in the 90s, although they used to be popular, especially in the 30s. Today documentaries are mainly a television genre; the cinema is virtually exclusively devoted to feature films.

The basic fact about film which everyone who wishes to enter the industry has to grasp is that it is a very expensive medium indeed (especially as compared with video), but it has a special mystique because of the beauty and accuracy of the images it produces and the hands-on immediacy of its traditional editing techniques (digital technology has meant great changes in editing but purists insist the old methods are best – see Chapter 15). It is the visual quality of film which cinematographers and all lovers of the cinema enjoy, an attribute which the video image (until recently) could not even approach. For many years the practised eye could tell immediately if a television programme had been recorded on film or video.

Costs of feature film-making can be very high indeed, especially in Hollywood: Kevin Costner's *Waterworld* cost a reputed $180 million to produce. To recover such sums a great deal of effort has to go into marketing and distribution because profits are recouped at the box-office (and increasingly in the video sell-through and rental market). Television programmes (at least until the development of pay-TV) have not been directly financed by the numbers of people who watch them whereas films always have been. Since a film's success is largely determined by the number of people who buy tickets at the box-office it is important to gauge the mainstream market accurately. The American film industry is geared to this and American films are marketed and distributed brilliantly. From the idea for a film to its eventual release in the cinema, Hollywood films are subjected to the most skilled promotional strategies of a market economy (about 70 per cent of the cost of a Hollywood film go to distribution and advertising while the figures for European films vary between 2 and 30 per cent). For the Hollywood studios film as art is an incidental pay-off: film as a profit-making activity is always the main concern. 'I make films', Alfred Hitchcock once said, 'If it turns out to be art that's fine with me.'

Even in Europe, where cinematic film was invented, the big distributors are American and they have a tight grip on the films which are given priority distribution. Europe's own national films thus have difficulties getting into first-run cinemas even within their own countries, a situation which causes much resentment. Over 95 per cent of British commercial, non-art house screens now show only American films, and the same is true for Germany and Italy.

Money has always been a problem for the British cinema and one of the persistent cries of the industry has been for some form of government aid, through tax breaks and so on, to protect British film from American domination. These pleas have usually fallen on deaf ears.

The British government has always been far less bothered about film than television. Film, although a mass medium, has never engendered

19

the fear in politicians which broadcasting has always evoked. Film, in its theatrical setting, did not enter the home and it does not deal, at least directly, with political matters. The British Parliament has therefore never been much troubled about its impact. Indeed, non-interference (even malign neglect) could be said to characterise the attitude of most British politicians towards the film industry. Campaigns to protect the British film have usually met with the lukewarm response that marks the British attitude to most cultural issues – an attitude incidentally which has often been in sharp contrast to other European countries, notably France and Central and Eastern Europe (before the collapse of communism).

British Screen Finance, however, a private company aided by a government grant, does exist to support new talent in commercially viable film productions which might find difficulty in attracting mainstream commercial funding. Between 1986 and 1993 British Screen Finance invested in eighty-seven productions including *The Crying Game*, *Orlando* and *Scandal*. There are also plans for the British film industry to benefit from the Arts Council's National Lottery Funding to the tune of £75 million pounds over a five-year period. It is likely that Lottery funds will be used for popular features rather than 'art-house' projects. Less encouragingly, in November 1995 the British government cut its £2 million grant to Eurimages, a Council of Europe project which had funded about fifty-six British films.

The American Giant

The experience of the European cinema industry, including the British, cannot be separated from the pervasive presence of American films. While European broadcasting developed along its own particular path, constantly monitored by anxious politicians, European film-makers were left largely on their own to wage a monumental struggle with the American giant. In the early days of cinema history the Americans quickly established an expertise assisted by the natural benefits of weather and light which Hollywood in California provided. In addition, the First World War decimated the European film industry and in its place European audiences grew accustomed to the new American 'feature-length' films with their Hollywood 'stars'.

The large American domestic market meant that production costs were usually recovered at home before the films were marketed abroad. In this way foreign and overseas exhibition charges were comparatively low, a situation which benefited the American industry. The advent of the 'talkies' in the late 20s probably helped the non-English-speaking European cinema to survive, but for the British film industry the difficulties were only compounded. The sharing of a common language

20

made the British particularly vulnerable to the American cultural invasion. Since the British government was usually uninterested in protecting its own, the American film entertainment industry met with a free run – a situation which still persists today.

British Cinema

Nevertheless the story was not entirely bleak: British cinema did survive over the years thanks to the unsung heroes who were passionate about keeping it alive. In the 30s, for example, British film-makers carved out a splendid reputation for high-quality documentaries and British technicians were admired for their consummate professionalism. In the 40s and early 50s the British feature-film industry beat off some of the American competition and the lively Ealing comedies enjoyed vast popularity. By the 50s, in fact, films were being produced which actually reflected the reality of British provincial and working-class life and the cinema was becoming a genuinely popular art form.

Then, in 1955, the establishment of ITV brought about a shift of the audience away not only from the cinema but also from the sober programming of the BBC. Television suddenly became a 'popular' medium. Even the stately BBC, which had tended to be very middle class in its orientation, began to entertain (rather than instruct) viewers. All over the country, cinemas closed as the British stayed home in droves, glued to the novelty of the 'Box in the Corner'.

By the end of the 50s the British feature film seemed in terminal decline, with no hope of recovery in sight. One of the interesting features of the history of British cinema, however, is the frequency with which the industry has been written off and the equal frequency with which the supposed corpse has revived. In 1963 *Tom Jones*, a British film financed by the American studio United Artists, was an international success. Other famous 60s successes included *A Hard Day's Night* (1964), *Nothing but the Best* (1964) and *Morgan* (1966). Britain in the 60s was 'swinging' and one of the main beneficiaries of the new fashion for all things British was film. Soon 'The name's Bond, James Bond' was a phrase which reverberated round the world, and British cinema became a popular international success.[1]

These so-called British big-budget films were, however, almost always financed by American money. Although the film industry in Britain was superficially doing well and employment was booming (many American companies had realised that production costs were low and the workforce highly skilled), it had lost its financial independence and most of its essentially British character. The themes, the actors and the technicians may have been British, but the money, treatment and marketing were American. British cinema by the late 60s was

21

becoming part of a transatlantic movie culture. It had lost the authentic British voice which films of the late 50s and early 60s such as *A Taste of Honey*, *The Loneliness of the Long Distance Runner* and *Saturday Night and Sunday Morning* had expressed.

During the 70s there were good British film-makers around who were not tied to American financial apron-strings. John Schlesinger, Richard Lester, Ken Russell, Ken Loach, Peter Watkins, Ridley Scott and Alan Parker were all making low-budget British films. Some of these film-makers had come up through television and others through advertising, where the technical excellence of British film craftsmanship and invention still flourished. On the whole, however, the work of British film-makers did not appeal to mass audiences brought up on a diet of American films, though they were popular with a minority audience of the young educated middle class, who wanted something more from the cinema than pure entertainment and had a feeling for film as an art form. By the end of the decade, however, some of these directors, weary of the financial struggle which working in British cinema demanded, had emigrated to America in search of the 'big bucks' necessary to make films which would appeal to an 'international' audience. Commentators began to remark that the British film industry was alive and kicking and living in Hollywood!

In the early 80s the British picture seemed to enjoy something of a revival with the huge worldwide success of such films as Hugh Hudson's *Chariots of Fire*. The early 80s saw a boom in British film-making and hopes were suddenly raised for the expansion of the industry. There was, in addition, a host of well-financed British companies willing to risk money in films, among them HandMade, Hemdale, Virgin, Goldcrest and Thorn EMI Entertainment. Today, however, no such British companies exist (unless one counts Polygram which strictly speaking is Dutch). It was the collapse of Goldcrest, a prestigious British film company, which put an end to this period of optimism and seemed to confirm that British film-making was doomed. Financial insecurity seemed endemic – at which point, enter Channel Four.

British Cinema and Channel Four
The year 1982 saw a surprising new twist in the convoluted history of British cinema. Channel Four, the new commercial television channel with its guaranteed income and its remit to cater for minority interests, had a dramatic impact on British film and can be credited with creating a mini-boom in British cinema. Television, the historic enemy, was galloping, it seemed, to the rescue as Channel Four's commissioning editors began to put money into the industry. A deal was negotiated which permitted films financed by Channel Four to have a six-month

showing at the cinema, after which they could be transmitted on the small screen.

For years television had been viewed as hostile to film; now it became its patron and a whole series of successful, low-budget and well-received films were produced, including *Letter to Brezhnev*, *The Ploughman's Lunch* and *The Draughtsman's Contract*. The film industry perked up tremendously and began to make quality films for television as well as for theatrical release. American 'made for TV' films might still dominate the television market-place, but the British, thanks to far-sighted managers at Channel Four, had found a novel way of providing an alternative to the American presence on the small and large screens. British film-makers carved a niche on British television's minority channel and when the BBC also began to put money into British films a beneficial symbiosis was apparently under way. Everything looked set for a revival of the British film industry.

The Recession
By the late 80s, however, optimism had faded again. There were two reasons for this: American dominance and the world recession. It soon became apparent that deregulation and the emphasis on the market had actually benefited the giant of the film entertainment industry, the United States. By the end of the decade this had become a matter of grave concern, not only in Britain but also in those European countries which took film very seriously. It was suddenly apparent that the indigenous European film and television industries (by now usually linked together and referred to in Europe as the 'audio-visual' industry) had been adversely affected by the internationalisation of the money markets and the decline of public service broadcasting. As American influence increased unemployment also began to grow alarmingly. As far as the entertainment industries were concerned, it was abundantly clear that the main beneficiaries of the free-market orgy had been the American moguls and the American studios

The European Dimension
Trouble with the American film industry was not a new phenomenon for Europe but it became more acute in the 80s and seemed likely to worsen as the increasing privatisation of television provided even more outlets for cheap American films (and programmes) which became one of the most popular forms of programming on the new commercial channels. Certain European countries had, over the years, developed aid schemes to protect their national film industries against American encroachments but subsidies too fell out of favour as economic liberalisation and deregulation tightened their ideological grip. The situation

became even more dire from the employment viewpoint when, all over Europe, public service broadcasting with their long-standing emphasis on national productions came under consistent and concerted attack.

Eventually, however, the European Community (which after the 1991 Treaty of Maastricht became known as the European Union) awoke to the danger and to the realisation that film and television were important components in Europe's cultural heritage and identity. The idea that entertainment was 'an industry like any other' suddenly sounded rather hollow when European film companies began to collapse and people woke up to the cultural threat this represented. Europe might be a giant in general economic terms, but the highly efficient and profitable American film and television industry was the market leader in entertainment. In comparison with America, Europe's film industry appeared to be a dwarf and a rapidly shrinking dwarf at that. The imbalance was acute: in 1993 American film and video sales to Europe were $1,159 million while Europe only exported $256 million to the US.

Yet the European film industry overall produces more films than the American (about 500 plus a year to 400). However, Europeans spend less money on making each film (the total of European budgets is less than half of that for American films) and the European film industry is fragmented by language and also by different approaches to culture and copyright. In most European countries the home-produced film industry represents no more than 20 per cent of the films shown. The rest of the exhibited films are mainly American. The American film industry also benefits from the fact that films are released in the States ahead of their European premiere and this provides advanced 'hype' to prime the European cinemagoer to want to see the American product. In addition, European distribution companies are mainly American-owned and they favour American films: there is no true pan-European distributor.

The huge volume in American film sales means that the Hollywood majors and the independent film companies can make a bad film and survive. The American majors make between fifteen and twenty films a year and the American independent studios produce around ten to fifteen films. By contrast, production companies in the fragmented European film industry are small, making between one and three films a year with a average budget of $2.16 million (the average cost of a 'mostly' British film in 1993 was £1.32 million, about one fifth of the average cost of Hollywood movies made in the UK). Consequently, European film-makers do not have enough resources to take risks: they cannot survive a box-office disaster. This is not good news for European employment.

Some observers suggest that the reason for American success is that the Americans have managed to develop a universal film language and mode of storytelling that is acceptable worldwide. The States, according to this argument, is a country of great ethnic and cultural diversity so what appeals to an American mass audience is likely to appeal elsewhere. Critics of the European industry argue that Europe's financial incentives and structures are not actually geared to the production of films that audiences want to see. European producers have little regard for consumers; the gap between Europe's producers and their audiences is too wide. Research does indicate that Hollywood serves the mainstream, young-adult audiences which go most often to the cinema.

The MEDIA programme

It is now generally agreed that the European film industry needs to put money and resources into popular movies, but there is considerable debate about how this should be done. One of the key elements is the European Union's support programme for the European film industry which is called MEDIA II. On 21 June 1995 the Council of Ministers decided to put 310 million ecu into MEDIA II which concentrates on three main areas: training, development and distribution. Its projects include support for feature films and animation, and it encourages distributors to play a direct role in financing productions in the initial stages. Loans are also available to encourage television companies to co-produce works with independent production companies and for the broadcast of such material widely across the European market. The MEDIA I programme (which predated MEDIA II) laid great emphasis on co-production and supported 781 feature films and 178 animated films and series but some commentators were critical of the co-production emphasis asserting that, although in theory co-produced European films were international, they were a conspiracy of nationals pretending to address international audiences but actually meeting restricted domestic objectives. In addition, co-productions have sometimes been dubbed 'Euro-puddings' because of the way cultural elements are mixed and stirred together to create a product which lacks authenticity and is weighed down by the effort of appeasing varied national sensitivities. Critics of MEDIA I and II also think they fail to match the scale of the problem because the sums of money involved are very small, especially in comparison to American distribution budgets.

France versus the US

The European country which has most concerned itself with responding to American dominance is France. The French government has always been anxious to maintain French language and culture and has always valued film's significance as an art form. The French tend to reject the American idea that films are primarily goods and as such not much different from wine or cheese or lamb. In France Hollywood films represent about 60 per cent of the total shown (but even this is rising, a few years ago Hollywood films were only 45 per cent of the French total). The French concern about films is why the French refused to sign the General Agreement on Tariffs and Trade (the GATT Treaty) in 1993 and argued for a cultural exclusion clause on the basis that industries to do with culture are different from other industries. France limits non-European programmes on its television screens and diverts some box-office proceeds, including those collected on US films, to subsidise its film industry. It has also lobbied consistently within the European Union for the establishment of strong quotas limiting the amount of non-European programming on Europe's television.

This French attitude is resented by the Americans especially because the audio-visual industry is the second largest overseas money-earner for the States (after the aerospace industry). The reaction of Jack Valenti, President of the Motion Picture Association of America (MPAA), is typical. Europeans, he said, should 'do what Americans do, make films that people want to see' (*Guardian,* 6 September 1994).

It is certainly the case that on television stations in Europe American imported films and programmes dominated the early phases of privatisation. In the start-up phase US programmes were 80 per cent cheaper to buy than the home-grown product. The much-vaunted international programme flow (which free marketers talked so much about) largely flowed one way – from America to Europe. However, as the private stations have become more established there has been a move towards more locally commissioned productions including films and more expensive television programmes.

American domination, however, still provokes anxiety from both the cultural and employment viewpoints. Perhaps as a result, at the end of 1995 the Americans and the European Parliament came up with an initiative to head off the French-led campaigns for quotas to limit the Hollywood presence on Europe's screens. Certain American studios have agreed to put $2 million into a scheme to train young European directors and technicians in film-making. They will go to California for courses in script and project development, production, marketing and distribution. American money will also be spent on the European Film College in Ebeltoft in Denmark. The project is intended to improve transatlantic links in the industry (*Guardian,* 28 December 1995).

Regulation?

This, then, is the picture of the film industry in Europe: one of American domination with the native European film industry struggling to survive. Is the picture, therefore, all bleak? Not quite. One of the positive results of the recession at the end of the 80s has been a realisation that, as far as Europe is concerned, deregulation and market forces might not be the ideal solution for the cultural industries. This is particularly the case on the Continent where, as a reaction to what has been going on, a certain amount of re-regulation has begun.

The national cultures of Europe do seem determined to resist domination, and the European Union, in particular, has become very concerned about the film and television industries and has launched a whole series of initiatives to protect the European market. Laissez-faire economics have proved dangerous for the European film industry; moderate and imaginative interventionism now seems to be the name of the game

The British Connection

In 1989 the United Kingdom experienced its lowest level of theatrical film production since 1981. In 1993, however, there was a dramatic and unforeseen increase in the number of feature films made in the UK: sixty-nine compared with 1992's total of forty-seven. A major reason for this was the increase in the number of British films with substantial foreign (mainly European) creative or financial input. Since 1990 the investment by non-US foreign investors in British film has increased. Of twenty seven co-financed or co-produced films in 1993, nineteen had European partners and the leading partner was France which invested in eight films, followed by Germany (seven) and Ireland (four). In all, companies from twenty one countries (fifteen of them in Europe) contributed to the production of British films in 1993. The total expenditure on British films also went up by 19 per cent from £184 million in 1992 to £220.4 million in 1993.[2]

In addition, the US market, while it is effectively closed to most European films (because Americans reject dubbing and subtitling), has not been so resistant to English-speaking films. In recent years *The Crying Game, Much Ado about Nothing, Remains of the Day, Four Weddings and a Funeral, Sense and Sensibility* and *Trainspotting* have all done well and boosted British (and Irish) morale. It is for this reason that the British were less than enthusiastic about the EU's desire for quotas.

Indications are, however, that even the British government, the arch upholder of the free-market system, may have begun to moderate its approach and to have woken up to the potential importance of

27

the British film industry. Politicians are realising that Britain occupies a key position at the crossroads between Europe and the USA and that the skill of British technicians and the facilities of British studios have been utilised for a number of American blockbusters, especially in science fiction, thereby making a sizeable contribution to the British economy. As an English-speaking country, with access to a potential North American market of 260 million and a European market of 325 million, the opportunity exists for the UK to become a major film and television base. The government, it is rumoured, is finally beginning to realise that it may pay economic dividends to support the film industry. It was perhaps in the light of this that some modest assistance was offered in the March 1992 budget.

Another cause for moderate optimism is the fact that the audience for films is growing. The popularity of cinemagoing as a leisure activity is increasing and in Britain the decline in audience figures that took place in the 80s has been reversed. This is especially the case for the 15-24 age group who, having formed a habit of cinema attendance, may continue to go in the future. The problem here is that the young-adult mainstream market likes American films and if there is to be a resurgent European or British cinema perhaps it will have to challenge Hollywood on its own ground. Many in the industry, however, now believe this goal to be both unrealistic and unnecessary. Some experts argue that mainstream movies are global in nature and Hollywood is the marketplace in which rights, talent, and finance for such films are bought and sold. They point to the example of the film *Cliffhanger*, which many regard as a quintessential Hollywood product but which was entirely financed by European money, made by a European director and crew, shot on location in Europe and with post-production also in Europe. Yet the film was American in subject and supposedly set in the Rockies. In view of this, ideas about a specifically British, Italian, French or European cinema appear irrelevant.[3]

Advertising

One area of British film-making that retains its national character is advertising, an area where, in the past, the film and television industries met. British commercials are often of a very high quality and were (and are) traditionally recorded on film because of its visual superiority. Generally, more money is spent per second of screentime on a commercial than on a feature film. To be fair, however, that is somewhat a function of the fact that often the same size of crew has to be assembled even though a commercial is much shorter (the average length of an advert is thirty seconds). Advertising is also a sector where film meets computing – commercials have been an area of extensive experimentation with new technology and film-makers in this sector often work with state-of-the-art equipment and high budgets.

There has always been a great deal of talent around in British advertising and this is reflected in television commercials, which have an international reputation for originality and humour. Many producers and directors in this field are now treating commercials as mini-dramas (Renault, BarclayCard) and are honing their storytelling skills in ways that are more characteristic of the feature film.

Companies specialising in commercials are exceedingly professional and the technical standards extremely high. Many young, talented film-makers with feature film ambitions start in the advertising industry. The commercials are the training ground for the big commercial films they hope to make in the future (Alan Parker and Ridley Scott 'cut their teeth' on commercials). Film-makers with international reputations also make commercials: Peter Greenaway, Federico Fellini and Woody Allen are just three examples. Unfortunately this section of the industry was particularly badly hit by the recession and the resultant decline in advertising budgets.

In 1996, however, a revival is beginning to take place and a group of young British film-makers have established a company called Impossible Impact. They are making commercials that challenge the stereotypes of the traditional advertising industry and are working for agencies who want adverts with a grittier, more realistic, bent.

Technology
Film is also experiencing the impact of the digital revolution (see Chapter 4). The increasing use of computer-generated special effects in films is increasing all the time. Facilities houses, which used to be mainly occupied with video work, are increasingly working with film-makers. The divide between video and film work has become increasingly blurred, especially in post-production. This development does not meet with universal approval. According to some commentators there is still a profound difference between the culture of film and video: film necessitates a sense of pictorial quality which video does not; video, they say, requires shorter cuts and is more highly stylised.

The cost of digital effects in movies can be very high but in a production such as Mel Gibson's *Braveheart* they can save thousands of pounds. Fewer extras have to be hired because a few actors can be made to look like a huge horde. Computer/video technology can also save money in landscapes: inappropriate pylons and aircraft in backgrounds can be simply removed in post-production. Understanding the potential of computer techniques is increasingly important for young film producers and directors. Digital technology is already significant in picture and sound editing and even has a role on the performance side. Stunts, for example, are increasingly reliant on computerised visual effects rather than on the skills of individual stunt men and women.

The Future

Assessing the overall picture, it looks as if the demand for feature films will increase, although the main outlet will no longer be cinema but also television and video. It is also interesting to note that important television programmes are now often filmed in 35mm instead of video. This is the result of a number of factors including an economic system that favours market-oriented, large-scale production, the convergence of the film and television industries, and especially perhaps the prospect of high definition television. In some quarters there has been a revived interest in film, despite its expense, partly for its quality and partly for its instant widescreen superiority.

Feature films are expensive to produce and their exploitation on television and video, and via satellite, cable and pay-TV is now a key factor in the economic viability of the industry. Feature films have become a central element in the schedules of satellite and cable television and on privatised commercial channels, and the video and television industries are increasingly dependent on the publicity which a film generates in its theatrical showing.

Recent research indicates that television funds about 25 per cent of cinema production in Europe and now more funding comes from private than public TV. Television managers are also moving beyond purely monetary considerations and are involving themselves in long term creative decision-making in order to protect their investment. As a result, the economics of film, video and television, as pointed out in Chapter 1, have become so closely intertwined that it is now quite correct to think in terms of one industry rather than three.

Employment

Feature films will survive and so will jobs in the industry, but it will require energy and far-sightedness to resist the Americans. Pessimists believe that if something is not done today, in twenty years time all films could be American in the same way as today most video recorders are Japanese. Workers in the British film industry will be working in branch plants of the American industrial entertainment complex. Jobs may be there, but an authentic British (and European) cinema will have gone. This is, however, the worst scenario. It is more likely that film production in Europe will increase by the end of the century, in part thanks to the rise in co-production, trans-European (and American) financing and the European Union's commitment to a policy of moderate protection and regulation. It will, however, be an extremely tough battle.

Central and Eastern Europe
From the employment point of view, the collapse of communism in Central and Eastern Europe was a severe blow for the European film industry. Socialist states, until the Berlin Wall came down, heavily subsidised their film industries as part of their country's cultural profile. As long as film-makers toed the party line, both documentary and fiction film-makers received a great deal of support. Today, however, all the film and programme industries in Eastern Europe are in difficulty. This is the case even in Poland and Hungary which have, in the past, won international reputations.

Summing Up
The future of European film might lie with politicians. While the quality of scripts and of production is of course central in the whole film-making process, the quality of political leadership is also important. The sector will only boom if the conditions it needs to thrive internationally (and resist American domination) are agreed and adopted by the European Union and the Council of Europe. The truth is that, with production, distribution and exhibition so difficult for Europeans in the global market-place, many film-makers are either making films with no regard whatever for box-office appeal or simply giving up and working in television. Increasingly, however, there is some evidence that very young, very enterprising film producers, directors, actors and technicians are beginning to make headway in a commercial environment.

An important point to remember is that, when a film is released, theatrical showing in the cinema is no longer the only viewing arena. Today a film's financial success is closely linked to its transmission on television and video. In business terms, it is increasingly important to shoot a movie that will look good on TV. The exploitation of films on television and video, and via satellite, cable and pay-TV is now an important factor in the economic viability of an expensive medium. It is no longer sensible to speak of several moving-picture industries because all sectors are 'converging' into one – the giant audio-visual 'entertainment' industry.

The moving-picture landscape has changed in the last decade. In terms of access, television and film are more open than they ever were before, and newcomers, without connections, have more chance of breaking in (see Chapter 5). To an extent this has been the result of technological advance, which promoted the video revolution. Video, together with the new delivery systems of cable and satellite television, have brought long-established barriers tumbling down. It is time to examine these developments more closely.

Notes

1. For a discussion of this period see Robert Murphy's *Sixties British Cinema* (London: BFI, 1992)
2. For a further discussion of this issue see the *BFI Film and Television Handbook 1995* (London: BFI, 1994).
3. For a further discussion see the *BFI Film and Television Handbook 1995* (London: BFI, 1994).

BROADENING THE LANDSCAPE
Video, Satellite and Cable

Chapter 1 looked at the impact of technological and political change on the traditional landscape of British television. Chapter 2 surveyed film, which did not experience the same upheaval as television, but, from the point of view of employment, moved towards greater integration with the television sector. This was largely because of the decline of union power in both sectors and the problems presented by the increasing strength of the US film industry. This chapter will examine some of the newcomers to the industry and the impact they have had, and will continue to have, on the broad employment picture. Video technology, satellite and cable have all contributed to a change in the nature and pattern of employment in film and television over the last few years. This has drastically altered the outlook and the working practices of the two traditional sectors.

The Video Revolution
Video was the big story of the 80s and, as we saw in Chapter 1, it rapidly brought about change in aspects of television production. Lightweight cameras and instant playback facilities revolutionised news coverage in television. Where picture quality was less important than topicality and immediacy, Electronic News-Gathering (ENG), or video recording, quickly replaced film as the favoured method of news-gathering. The old method, whereby cans of films were dispatched, usually by motorcycle, to laboratories for development in time for editing for the evening news, disappeared almost overnight. Film camera crews attached to news production in television companies had to swap to video (which actually was very simple to use) or else retire!

In employment terms, video made its greatest immediate impact on the non-broadcast section of the industry. The great virtue of video is that it is quicker and cheaper than film to use and the technical equipment is lighter and more portable (though its actual technology is far more complex). Once the quality of the image improved enough to rival (although not equal) film, independent entrepreneurs saw possibilities in video and independent production companies sprang up to exploit new business opportunities.

At the start of the video expansion most of the companies were very small, many of the staff were inexperienced and, because of low profit margins, freelancing on very short-term contracts became the main mode of employment. Initially these video 'freebooters' in the non-broadcast environment were looked at askance by the well-trained and heavily unionised employees in broadcasting and film. But the advance of the non-unionised freelancer in the small video companies has been quite unstoppable and has eventually spread to the older industries. Today virtually 60 per cent of all the estimated 209,500 employees across the film, television and video industry in the UK are freelance, and this percentage is growing all the time. Moreover, numbers employed in video are estimated to be equal in numbers to those employed in television (about 41,000).

The great attraction of video as far as employers were concerned was that it did not require large crews and this cut costs. One person could do several different tasks and, since unions made little headway in the independent sector, there was no strict division of labour according to function. What came to be dubbed 'multi-skilling' developed. Instead of separate people being employed to write scripts or do research or handle lights, cameras and so on, everything could be done by one person. This, aided and abetted by government policy, was to drive a nail into the coffin of the old specialised craft unions which had dominated film and television (at least ITV) for so long.

In its early days the independent video industry was not involved in creating material to show either in a cinema or on television. The two highly prestigious industries were essentially closed to outsiders. The BBC and ITV tended to look down on non-broadcast video production as a 'mickey mouse' sector, full of inexperienced, second-rate 'amateurs', notable only for their lack of professional finesse. Most independent video companies produced an inferior product in broadcasting and film terms (while both British film and television were known for their high technical standards) and, as far as mainline production was concerned, were therefore irrelevant. Small-time video producers and their employees would never, it was thought, darken the doors of any established British film or television studio. They were merely involved in the decidedly inferior, and rather sordid, commercial activity of making half-baked productions for the assorted clients who commissioned them. They were record companies wanting to publicise a singer or a song; local authorities wanting to extol the virtues of their area or give out health information to the public; multinational corporations

34

that wished to promote products, illustrate their contribution to scientific research or provide safety instructions for their employees. In any event, whatever or whoever they were, as far as mainstream broadcasters and film-makers were concerned, they were of no importance at all. Certainly, the work of video companies who serviced such clients could not be compared to the important business of broadcasting high-quality, public service programmes of information, education and entertainment to the great British public.

How quickly circumstances can change! The pop music and non-broadcast corporate sectors quickly proved to be huge money-spinners, especially by the mid-80s. In addition commercial businesses, corporations and local authorities were beginning to fancy the idea of advertising themselves through a prestigious up-to-date medium and were beginning to put big money into promotional videos. Moreover, the significance of the video sector was not purely commercial: training videos (especially interactive training videos), a neglected sector of British educational provision, quickly became a growth area. John Cleese made a fortune through humorously teaching people about management techniques.

Fairly swiftly, technical and production standards improved in the non-broadcast sector. This was particularly because, unlike broadcast programmes, a corporate video was destined to be seen over and over again by highly critical and often expert audiences. Scientists invited to watch a chemical company's video were unlikely to be fobbed off with generalities or poor production techniques. Polished presentation and up-to-date information were essential, and the old days, when a boring elderly managing director in a conservative suit spoke direct to camera, were left far behind. Professional presenters, graphics, 'paint-box' techniques (another offshoot of the microchip/computer revolution) soon made their mark.

Although some video companies became multi-million dollar businesses, the employee base was usually still kept very low, with staff used on contract for individual productions. Consequently it was (and still is) much easier to break into the non-broadcast video world than into television or film and, in some ways, it provides an excellent training-ground for all facets of production. The mainly freelance staff have to be capable of turning their hands to anything and, in pop video companies especially, directors and producers were sometimes very young indeed, often in their late teens and early twenties, a situation which used to be unthinkable in the hierarchical traditions of conventional film or television. Moreover pop video producers proved to be inventive and imaginative, undercutting some of the more conservative and traditional ideas of the rather stuffy light-entertainment producers at the BBC and ITV. Pop videos took the teenage market by storm and made conventional television seem old-fashioned.

Gradually, the fact that a lot of money could be made in video attracted the attention of the creative and technical staff in mainline films and television. The improving technical quality of video production also changed minds. The best corporate productions began to compare favourably with broadcast television and many 'professional' film-makers and television producers and directors began to freelance in the independent sector. Working in video was no longer regarded as 'slumming it'.

The walls between the various sectors of the audio-visual industry were beginning to crumble and it became clear, even to the dinosaurs of the film and broadcasting world, that the video industry might be around for a rather long time and was actually becoming respectable. More significantly, it was also finding government support: small entrepreneurial companies of the independent type fitted in well with a prevailing Thatcherite philosophy that was hostile to restrictive practices in the film sector and in ITV and also to the public service ethos of the BBC.

By the end of the decade, independent video companies were making programmes and video 'films' for television. Former employees of the BBC and ITV and the film industry migrated to the independent production sector, often attracted by the lack of bureaucracy and the entrepreneurial atmosphere. This trend was encouraged by the government's insistence on the so-called 25 per cent quota. Legislation was introduced which guaranteed that by 1993 at least 25 per cent of programmes on the new Channel Three and the BBC would have to be made by independents.

Today there are many independent companies producing material for broadcast and non-broadcast purposes. For newcomers to the industry the openness of the independent sector has triggered endless possibilities. The video revolution has broken down union barriers and the broadcasting elitism which once seemed insurmountable. For years film and television were difficult to break into: video has made the technology, and therefore the industry, much more accessible. Many people can now enter the industry though the non-broadcast sector and those with experience cross freely between film, television and video as they gain in knowledge and technical expertise.

The decline of public service broadcasting has also benefited the non-broadcast sector. In the future, BBC and commercial television will probably make fewer educative and documentary programmes. Specifically educational programmes could be pushed off the mainstream channels and into an independent educational video market. Already the decline of programming for children on television has meant an increase in the sell-through market for children's videos. Of the top twenty video titles in 1993, ten were for children. Educational video may become a boom area for many independent companies as encrypted learning and satellite educational channels increase and as educational programmes on broadcast television diminish. In addition, the pace of change in all employment will, by the year 2000, make training and retraining a vital aspect of educational provision (this will be discussed in more detail in Part Two). Every individual with a desire to succeed will have to cope with a world in which technological change puts an increasing onus on the employee to learn new techniques and to constantly update his or her skills. Educational videos will obviously find the market expanding to meet this needs. Many people who have trained and worked in video are now moving over to the new media and producing the software for the increasingly sophisticated interactive training programmes being developed on CD-ROM and CD-I (see Chapter 4). This is becoming more and more a significant area of employment.

The Workshop Sector
One interesting non-commercial area that has provided many opportunities for newcomers, and has also been an excellent source of training over the last decade, is the so-called 'workshop' sector. Workshops actually encompass both film and video, but the ease and cheapness of video in particular stimulated an expansion in this 'alternative' sector. 'Independent workshops' are small production groups many of which were established in the early 80s as a result of political pressure for more open access to broadcasting. Workshops are usually non-profit making and often have a specific political, social or sexual orientation. They are often set up to give space to those film- and video-makers who wish to challenge the attitudes and ethos of the mainstream industries, and are usually subsidised, often by the unions, the British Film Institute (BFI) or Channel Four. Lists of workshop groups can be found in the *BFI Film and Television Handbook* available from the BFI (for more information see the Appendix).

Many of the existing workshops are involved in training people who would not normally have access to film and video equipment enabling them to make videos and films for themselves and their organisations, many of which are voluntary. Many people have become enthusiastic about film-and programme-making through their workshop experiences and some of them have entered the commercial side, often initially in the non-broadcast video sector. This has brought a broader social and political outlook to more conventional areas of the industry.

The Home Video Software Industry

In addition to the production of videos for broadcast and non-broadcast purposes, the video revolution has had another very important and largely unforeseen effect. This is the impact of the home video recorder on public interest in feature films. Ownership of video recorders boomed in Britain in the 80s and 78 per cent of British homes (by far the highest percentage in Europe) now possess this heavily used and much-cherished piece of high-tech equipment: around £1.2 billion a year is currently spent on buying or renting video cassettes.

Although initially the video recorder probably had a negative effect on cinema attendance, it eventually provided a secondary and increasingly important source of revenue for films: the growth of the video rental market almost certainly helped to develop an appetite for films among young people. At first the major distributors of films were wary of, and indeed hostile towards, video; increasingly, however, they began to appreciate the financial benefits that could accrue from its exploitation and large film companies have gradually moved into the video market-place which has become an ever more significant element in the calculation of production profits. The great advantage of the video outlet for the American motion-picture industry is the extremely low distribution costs

In 1992 in Britain the video rental market, mainly dominated by Hollywood films, seemed about to decline, but this setback proved to be only temporary and by 1993 recovery was underway. The sell-through market (the purchase of videos over the counter) has continued to be buoyant – the public's interest in Hollywood film seems insatiable. The sell-through video market also provides children's programmes, music titles and television comedy compilations and these have proved to be a particularly rich source of income for the BBC which can draw on its large library and archival resources.

In recent years cinema admissions in Britain have risen (albeit rather slowly) and it appears as if the feature film and the home video rent and sell-through markets now feed on each other to their mutual benefit. Many young people who purchase films on video watch them over and over again and there is a growing impression that this has produced an increasing fascination with, and knowledge of, film techniques. The rather short-lived development of the laservision market in the United States, where classic films were reissued on videodisc with additional material such as interviews with directors and actors about the making and editing of the film, was an expression of this trend.

Certain genres of films seem to thrive in video; more horror movies are now being produced largely because of their guaranteed success on video. Critics of the trend towards video movies point to what they call the consequent 'televisionisation' of the film industry whereby a number of today's theatrical movies leave the impression of being photographed almost entirely in close-ups and medium shots because these register best on television. Film directors are accused of shooting action only in the central area of the frame in order that the film will transfer well to television where it has to be cropped for the smaller and squarer screen. This, according to some critics, alters the integrity and mood of film medium. It can also destroy a scene. In the film *The Graduate*, Dustin Hoffman and Anne Bancroft take off their clothes, each at either extreme of the screen. It was impossible to get both stars in at the same time on video. 'Televisionisation' has also been criticised for destroying the subtle lighting nuances of film when it is transferred to video. Film buffs tend to dislike the idea of films being watched in the busy domestic environment of the average living-room and agree with Stephen Spielberg who said: 'Movies should be seen in dark and hallowed halls.' The director of *Nightmare on Elm Street 4*, however, has defended the video industry, 'Today's young audiences have grown up with TV and they watch a lot of videos. So its important to shoot a movie that will look good on TV.'[1]

The future of the over-the-counter video trade, however, does appear uncertain at the present time because of the impact of the new technologies, especially the internet and the information superhighway (which will be discussed in Chapter 4). Video-on-demand, delivered down telephone lines or via cable and viewed at leisure without the necessity of going out to a shop to pick up a videocassette and then return it the next day, could easily spell disaster for the rental and sell-through video market.

Satellite Television

Another sector that since 1989 has had an impact on employment in the traditional British film and television industry is satellite television. Technically, when people talk about satellite (and cable) television they are talking only about a *delivery* system. Careers in satellite and cable television, therefore, often have more to do with sales and marketing than with the actual production of films and programmes, the *raison d'être* of the traditional industry. In fact, for old-timers in film and television, satellite and cable television are not really bona fide sectors at all, because the focus of activity has shifted from programme-making to profit-making. Traditionalists see satellite (and cable) as brash new phenomena, illegitimate offspring of the new technology and the market-place, feeding parasitically on the creative talents of the traditional workforce. This attitude does not endear them to satellite and cable employees who, in their turn, view

39

traditional employees as elitist, feather-bedded hacks out of touch with modern reality.

BSkyB, which dominates the British direct-to-home satellite market, is a particular target for the enmity of the traditional broadcaster and film-maker. The company is in broadcasting to make money and this point of view is ultimately reflected in its programming and policies. For business-oriented people, BSkyB represents the broadcasting model of the future. Its supporters are excited by the limitless business opportunities and untold riches that the company may have in prospect.

Satellite and cable television bring into focus the distinction between broadcasters who are channel operators and broadcasters who are programme producers. Channel operators are concerned with 'packaging', scheduling, transmission and marketing of programmes but not usually with their production: most programmes are 'bought in'. Satellite and cable, on the whole, *consume* programmes and films already made for other outlets. Programme producers are concerned with the creative activity of programme-making, which inevitably dictates a different set of criteria and motivations. The clash between satellite and cable broadcasters on the one hand and traditional programme-makers on the other is a clash of cultures that derives from their different perspectives. (Although the publisher-broadcaster mode of some of the ITV stations and Channel Four is not production-oriented, there is a strong interest in programme-making because of the channel's commissioning activity: companies in ITV that won their franchises as publisher-broadcasters have increasingly involved themselves in programme-making and the same tendency may be developing at BSkyB.)

The start-up costs for satellite broadcasting are extremely high and, partly for this reason, the development of a satellite service in Britain has been immensely fraught, a situation that gave considerable pleasure and solace to its many critics. At the beginning of 1990 it looked as if there might be two competing companies broadcasting direct-to-homes via satellite: Rupert Murdoch's Sky Television and British Satellite Broadcasting (BSB). Sky Television was first into the field and launched its four-channel network in February 1989, using the Astra satellite.

BSB, Sky's rival, had a more up-market image and very glamorous headquarters in the Marcopolo building, south of the Thames. BSB's services were scheduled to be transmitted via the Marcopolo television satellite and, unlike those transmitted on Astra which was categorised as a telecommunication satellite, had to abide by a European Union Directive on technical standards. These gave better sound and image quality and more secure encryption but unfortunately were much more expensive to run. BSB services were originally scheduled to be launched in the autumn of 1989 but the start had to be postponed to the spring of

1990, a fatal delay: its receiver, the so-called 'Squarial' (because of its shape), encountered design and production problems. This delay gave Sky time to build up an overwhelming lead, assisted by publicity in the Murdoch-owned press.

However, 1990 was not a good year for investment in any business venture, and especially not one on the scale of satellite television. BSB and Sky were launched as the recession began to bite and advertising revenues began to fall. It was a nightmare scenario for a new television venture. Satellite dish sales failed to take off, despite a marketing blitz; BSB began by losing £30 million a month while Sky lost £10 million a month. Finally, amid much controversy over the issue of monopoly, in November 1990 Sky Television and BSB 'merged' into BSkyB ('A fight to the finish had become a shotgun marriage'). This stopped the haemorrhaging of money and ITV suddenly had a very real competitor for a share of the advertising pot. Moreover, BSkyB television had the advantage that its hands were not tied by the programme obligations of informing and educating which were laid upon ITV and Channel Four. The vigour of BSkyB's presence pushed up the prices for film, television series and sports rights just at the time when the recession hit and the advertising revenue boom ended.

The new company, however, still faced financial difficulties. To counteract these, the staff of the two combined stations were cut from around 4,500 to fewer than a thousand and the nine existing channels were rationalised into six. Programme resources were also cut from £5.1 million to £2.9 million. Opponents of satellite immediately charged that the result was a decline in programme quality, that the emphasis was on what was cheap to do rather than what was worth doing. Over the next eighteen months BSkyB struggled on, losing money all the time. Dish sales, however, eventually began to take off. By 1992 BSkyB had reached 2.9 million homes (13 per cent of total) and dish sales were about 70,000 a month. In March 1992 BSkyB was technically in the black (except for paying off interest on loans) and was beginning to win favour in the City. In the same year the company announced plans to spend £175 million on programming, two-thirds of which were to go on its two movie channels. (In comparison, ITV planned to spend £540 million on programming for one channel during 1992.)

BSkyB movie channels are paid for by subscription and are encrypted so that only subscribers can have access. For a while four-fifths of sales income came from subscriptions to the two movie channels. 70 per cent of people who purchased dishes subscribed to a movie channel and 80 per cent of these took both – which helped to boost revenue. By buying up the exclusive right to films from a number of Hollywood studios BSkyB increased its subscriber base, and it was argued that the movie channels on satellite television would act as a stimulus to the film industry – in rather the same way as the home video recorder has made young people more knowledgeable about, and interested in, the cinema.

However, although all the Hollywood studios are committed to supply films to BSkyB until the year 2000 at least, there is now some evidence that movies are losing their attraction for viewers on pay channels. Movie channel subscriptions are said to be faltering and movie watching itself is in decline in multi-channel homes. In 1991 viewers in multi-channel homes spent 1 hour 26 minutes watching the Movie Channel but the figure had fallen to 53 minutes by 1993. In part this is because ITV has strengthened the movie scheduling on terrestrial television. Despite a slight dulling of the gloss on the Sky movie sector, the company is now investing money in British films thus following in the footsteps of Channel Four, ITV and the BBC. This is a development to watch.

By 1995 BSkyB's marketing strategy was shifting to sport. Through such coups as the acquisition of top events in boxing and the signing of Premier League Football clubs, Sky has managed to pull in new subscribers to its two sports channels and pushed up its revenue. It is estimated that BSkyB now has about £400 million a year in subscriptions to spend on sports rights, thus making the company an increasingly important competitor in the bidding battle against terrestrial television. No true sports fan can now live without Sky television but the company's contribution to sports programming is extremely controversial – as its proposal for a world wide Rugby League indicated. While coverage of sport has expanded and improved and sporting bodies have gained financially from pay-TV, critics assert that sporting traditions have changed for the worse. Critics also focus on the fact that, while sports coverage has expanded greatly for those who subscribe to Sky (20 per cent of households), it has declined for the other 80 per cent who rely on terrestrial television. Moreover, costs are going up all the time: in 1992 the cost of subscribing to Sky Sports was £72 a year; by 1995 the annual fee was £180.

The important point about BSkyB, however, is that it has emphatically proved that viewers are willing to pay for their television. Although the company still tends to be regarded with disdain by the traditional broadcasters, it tries to counteract criticism by providing 24-hour news coverage on Sky News. BSkyB is not obliged to provide news by law at all but Sky News helps to reject claims that the company is in the market solely to provide the audience with junk TV. In February 1995 BSkyB announced a deal whereby Reuters, the news agency, would supply and manage the channel's news coverage. During the same year Sky News provided live coverage of the O J Simpson trial. Critics of Sky pointed to this, however, as an example of the so-called 'tabloidisation' of news values.

The main entertainment channel for Sky is Sky One: Sky Soap and Sky Travel are also available. In addition, BSkyB movie subscribers also have access to other channels being beamed down from the Astra satellite including the Discovery Channel, Shopping Channels such as QVC, the Disney Channel, Children's Channel and many others.

The financial future of satellite television used to be a matter of controversy, but by 1994 it had become profitable and there was much more optimism about it in the City. By 30 June 1995 BSkyB had proved itself a goldmine and become one of the most profitable businesses in Britain. It raises more revenue through subscriptions than any other television company in the world. Turnover rose 41 per cent to £778 million and operating profits went up 44 per cent to £237 million. Many people in Britain say that they will never get satellite television, or that they will wait until cable brings it in unobtrusively (see below), with the added benefit of cheaper telephones. Where viewers have the choice of satellite or cable they tend to opt for the cable. On the other hand, some media consultants suggest that satellite will control a fifth of all the television advertising budget by 1998. Advertising is a problematic area because many experts query whether advertisers will be so interested in television as a medium once the audience becomes heavily fragmented. In New York (where there are many television channels available) advertisers appear to be switching to newspapers that have large readerships. There is certainly some evidence that advertisers are becoming disillusioned with terrestrial, cable and satellite television now that the era of huge mass audiences for a very restricted number of channels is over.

Increasing revenue has meant that BSkyB now spends more on programming so that it can attract new viewers and advertisers. This in turn may help to increase employment. One of the great unknowns is how the rivalry between satellite and cable delivery systems will eventually work out. Satellite television allows for cheap access to many channels. Although it is more complicated than cable in the sense that, in addition to acquiring a satellite receiver, a dish has to be attached to the house, the dishes will eventually become much smaller and, once the equipment has been acquired, viewers will have a very wide freedom of choice as the dish can be pointed at any satellite within range. Satellite reception systems also tend to give users complete anonymity concerning the programmes watched. There is no possibility of controlling who is watching a given programme and when. On the broader European front, satellite television is always a good solution for remote and fragmented populations that can not access the mainly urban cable networks.

Whatever the future and profitability of satellite television, however, it has had an impact on the general employment picture. BSkyB has provided an alternative theatre and 'culture' of work rather as the video industry did in the 80s. Initially there was a period of ruthless cost-cutting at BSkyB, but the company does employ technical, engineering, journalistic, administrative and sales staff and, although most of its programming is bought-in, BSkyB does increasingly produce its own programmes. Sky News, for example, employs journalists, presenters and scriptwriters.

Compared to traditional broadcasting companies, programme production at BSkyB is said to be more informal. Multi-skilling is everywhere and there is little evidence of the rather hierarchical broadcasting 'culture' of the BBC or ITV. It is probably easier for inexperienced newcomers to break into satellite television than it has ever been for them to break into the BBC, ITV, Channel Four or the film industry. However, experience still counts and some broadcasters from the BBC and ITV have moved over to Sky. Many of the staff at BSkyB are quite young. The company takes on 'runners' who are similar to runners in the film industry (see Chapter 2). Runners do various low-level production chores but are also given the opportunity for hands-on experience: they can then work their way up into other jobs. BSkyB will also sometimes offer very short periods of work experience and work placements to young people during school and college holidays. Employment opportunities in satellite television, however, will inevitably depend on the market-place and on the rise and fall in profits.

The broadcasting industry was taken by surprise by the spread of satellite television. This was largely because at the beginning of the 80s there had been many predictions about the quick take-over by cable (see below) and the confident assertion that terrestrial television would quickly lose its dominance. When this proved not to be the case many people thought that satellite television would experience the same slow start as cable. In fact satellite television sales accelerated rapidly.

Cable
Satellite television is one illustration of how the industry has become more 'permeable' for outsiders; cable is another. Cable, like satellite television, is basically a delivery system (although it also produces some programmes). Cable too is paid for largely by subscription. In addition to the provision of television and radio, cable is also important because of the prospect it holds out of interactivity. Cable can

provide interactive telephone and communications services – home shopping, home banking (tele-banking), electronic mail, remote meter reading and security and alarms services. Cable technology has the ability to deliver digitally compressed signals over fibre optic networks which can provide customers with pay-per view, digital audio and video-on-demand services: these will be the driving force for the establishment of the information society (see Chapter 4). If all goes according to plan the 'wired' world will create a unique home and office environment centred on interactivity.

Cable made great headway in Canada and the United States from the 70s onwards and was much vaunted in Britain in the late 70s as *the* system of the future. Cable was supposed to be the harbinger of the 'wired society', gaining much support in government circles and there were all sorts of projections for phenomenal growth. In 1981 Margaret Thatcher set up a panel to look into information technology issues and in 1982 this produced a key report called 'Cable Systems'. The report stressed that cable should be developed by the private sector and that it should be entertainment-led; in other words popular programming on cable would eventually lead to a communication system as other components were bolted on to the technology acquired to view television.

For various reasons, however, cable penetration in Britain proceeded at a snail's pace for most of the 80s. Since the financial outlay involved was huge, cable tended to be regarded as a risky investment: no-one knew how many subscribers it would attract or how it would fare in competition with satellite. This remained the case for a long time even though the Thatcher government did not allow British Telecom (BT) to wire up Britain in order to allow the cable companies – mainly North American owned – a free run and promote more competition and market forces. BT built up an impressive national grid of optical fibres but did not embark on the expensive task of wiring the grid up to homes because the Conservative government had banned BT until 2001 from sending television down line (which would have provided BT with income to recoup its investment).

BT can send television pictures down ordinary telephone lines but, because of these legal restraints, must offer these as video-on-demand. The viewer dials up a menu and selects a movie or special event which is sent down the line to special order. Thus BT is a monocaster and not a broadcaster. Between 1995 and 1996 BT pioneered video-on-demand and transactions services in 2,500 homes in the Ipswich and Colchester area. Homes began receiving five services from the BT interactive systems – movies, television, music, education and home shopping (including banking) which were all delivered down standard copper-wire telephone line.

Eventually, by 1989, there was a huge influx of cash from US and Canadian cable and telephone services into Britain (when restrictions on non-UK shareholding in cable companies were dropped) and, by the beginning of the 90s, the progress of cable had quickened considerably. By April 1995 cable had 'passed' nearly 4.5 million homes and in July of the same year cable had signed up 1 million users. The industry was turning over nearly £250 million a year and beginning to pay back the £10 billion already invested in digging up roads to lay the high-tech cable to homes.

According to the Independent Television Commission, which is the public body responsible for licensing and regulating cable, cable systems in Britain are almost always installed in ducts below roads and footpaths. They radiate from a central control point (called the head-end) to home and businesses or, in London, to groups of boroughs. Optical fibre, coaxial cable and copper wires are all in use in the cable system.

The so-called 'broadband' cable (sometimes referred to as 'wide-band') is the one that matters. Broadband cables are the modern, multi-channel, interactive system carriers now being installed in most areas of the country. They can provide a full range of new television channels, telecommunications and interactive services. In April 1995 there were eighty-six broadband cable systems operational and they are the base on which the optimistic forecasts for the cable industry rely.

Readers should note that 'narrowband' is sometimes used in opposition to broadband but is a relative term without explicit definition. The telephone system is sometimes referred to as narrowband to distinguish it from the system that is also capable of carrying television signals. At other times older television cable systems are referred to as narrowband because they are capable of carrying only four to six channels as opposed to the new broadband systems which can carry thirty or more. The older television cable systems can not offer telecommunications or interactive services.

'Local delivery franchises' are similar to cable franchises, though the licensees may utilise not only broadband cable but Microwave Video Distribution systems (MVDS) and Satellite Master Antenna Television (SMATV). MVDS (sometimes called 'wireless cable') is a technique not so far used in the United Kingdom because it is still under technological development. SMATV are smaller systems, sometimes servicing only specific blocks of flats, which have been built to deliver a range of satellite television channels to the homes connected to them. The important point about these two forms of local delivery is that they permit the speedy introduction of choice for the viewer without the expense of installing a broadband cable system.

In addition, there are 'broadcast relay cable systems', sometimes called 'communal aerial systems', and these do not have to be licensed. They exist to provide broadcast television (BBC, ITV and Channel Four) to a number of homes from a master aerial. There are also 'Up-grade' cable systems initially installed for broadcast relay purposes and then 'upgraded' to provide new programme services such as cable television. Upgrade cable services have a limited capacity and are likely to be replaced in time by broadband cable franchises.

Cable is carried to viewers' existing television sets usually through a set top box provided by the cable operator: the television channels provided include those from a number of satellites as well as from other sources. In addition to supplying the BBC, ITV and the Astra channels (including BSkyB channels), cable-exclusive channels included the Travel Channel, the Parliamentary Channel and SelectTV. Cable systems currently being built can carry between thirty and forty-five channels but these will increase when digitisation gets firmly underway. Because a cable connection avoids the need for a viewer to have satellite dishes, receivers and decoders, cable provides an easy way of delivering new television choices. Cable subscribers are not limited, as are British satellite subscribers, to what is available on the two Astra satellites or Marcopolo. Most cable companies pick up and relay services from other satellites. Cable does not have any obligation to carry educational programmes: its niche in the television market-place has been compared to the role of magazines in the print market.

Cable systems in the UK have also been encouraged to provide telephone services, and where this is done a separate wire is usually provided, pending the full development of the technology for integrating voice, video and data and routing them in different ways (see Chapter 4). The UK was the first country to promote convergence of television and telecommunications and this part of the cable business is extremely popular. Subscribers tend to feel that they can off-set the greater expense of cable television versus satellite by cutting down on their telephone bills. It is an interesting to note that despite the fact that cable television is more expensive than satellite, where both are available, cable is more popular. Research indicates that subscribers like the fact that cable companies are local employers: this wins favour.

Although cable, even more than satellite, is about delivery rather than programme-making, a few cable companies do have small-scale studios where local programming is produced. Some of the broadband cable systems run a local channel for news and information plus special features: this provides some community access and minority programming. It used to be said that, in the future, local programming would be the surprising success story of cable, although it is comparatively insignificant from the point of view of revenue (unless local advertisers use it extensively). Local programming on cable was very successful in North America, supposedly recreating something of the community atmosphere of the proverbial 'conversation around the village pump'. However, local and community programming has never made the same impact in Britain. The 1984 Cable and Broadcasting Act did require all cable operators to provide local programming, but the 1990 Broadcasting Act removed this obligation because the government wished to attract overseas investment. This has undoubtedly reduced the cable companies' interest in making local programmes.

Nevertheless, people do apparently like seeing themselves, their neighbours and their dogs on television! When Granada Television ran its so-called Television Village experiment in 1990 (in which it provided the village of Waddington in Lancashire with access to all available television channels), it was the local programming which proved most popular. In the last week of the experiment only 3 per cent of viewers were not watching it.

Most of the jobs in cable involve marketing and sales, and it is mainly people with these skills who will find employment in the sector. However, in North America, many people who later worked in mainstream broadcasting had been introduced to the industry initially by producing local television programmes on cable. The community element of local cable programming, should it ever take off, may prove to be a useful training-ground for people who wish to know more about how a television studio functions.

The Role of the ITC

Before leaving satellite and cable it should be pointed out that the Broadcasting Act of 1990 gave the new Independent Television Commission (ITC) responsibility to license and regulate all non-BBC television services, whether terrestrial, cable or satellite. In its first year the ITC was principally concerned with terrestrial television because of the importance of the Channel Three franchises. Since then the role of the ITC's Cable and Satellite Division in the development of satellite and cable has been increasingly significant. Previously, programme channels carried on cable systems were regulated by the Cable Authority (which ceased to exist on 1 January 1991 when the 1990 Broadcasting Act brought the ITC into existence).

Summing Up

In the past decade the British film, television and video industry has experienced a period of massive upheaval. Cable and satellite have spelt the end of the old notion of spectrum scarcity in broadcasting while technological change, political attack, the decline of union power and the rise of the independents have all blurred the lines between once highly distinct film and broadcasting sectors. From the point of view of employment the industry has been transformed. Opportunities have expanded, and will continue to expand; at the same time, however, career security has diminished and unemployment has increased. The recession hit the advertising industry particularly badly and this affected ITV. ITV was also damaged by the franchise auction and there has also been large-scale unemployment in companies that lost the franchise race. For the first half of the 90s redundancies and retirements were the order of the day. The recession also halted the expansion of the independents (despite the legislated 25 per cent rule), and even the monolithic BBC in the face of organisational change cut jobs or offered employees only short term contracts.

In the 90s the industry has become easier to enter, thanks to video, satellite and cable, and there is more mobility. Employment terms, salaries and perks, however, are far less attractive (except perhaps for the extremely talented or the unusually skilled). The whole industry is more diverse, insecure and hazardous. Freelancing has become the main mode of employment and permanent jobs seem a thing of the past.

Anyone who wants a career in film, television or video in the 90s must understand the new structure (or lack of structure) in the industry and the implications of the changes for employment opportunities. Above all, they must have some grasp of the impact of technology and the fast pace of change expected in the future. During the 90s a career in film, television or video demanded great resources of emotional stamina to accept the uncertainty and even enjoy the roller-coaster atmosphere of an industry increasingly subject to rapid change. Many older people in the industry were perplexed and disturbed by the way in which established working practices became increasingly outmoded. Young people proposing to enter the industry today, however, must embrace change, not fear it. In any case, what is happening in the communications industry today will happen in all other industries tomorrow. More than ever, intelligent understanding of the issues and flexibility of approach are essential for survival

Dominating the future is the question of technological change. The film, television and video industry are in the vanguard of that change and anyone entering the industry today must understand contemporary developments and be prepared continuously to assess their significance. No would-be employee of the entertainment industry can afford to bury his or her head in the sand and fail to see the larger picture. All

49

employees, if they wish to be successful, must have some grasp of the significance of the multi-media revolution and the impact this is having on the landscape of work. and the changing nature of the media business. From the employment point of view the name of the game today is globalisation and behind this lies a political issue, that of media concentration. Chapter 4 attempts to provide some insight into the technological issues and sketches out some of broader themes to do with the directions in which the industry might be going. However, it is only a guide. As with all crystal-ball gazing the future itself may confound all predictions.

Note
1. Janet Wasko discusses these developments in detail in *Hollywood in the Information Age* (Oxford: Polity Press, 1994).

4

DIGITISATION,
MULTI-MEDIA AND CONVERGENCE
What Does It All Mean?

The audio-visual industry today is on the threshold of dramatic change thanks to two factors: the development and impact of digital technology and the convergence of the formerly highly separated industries of computing, telecommunications and telephony. The first three chapters of this book have examined the way film, television and video are merging into a single audio-visual entertainment industry, but beyond this there is an even more significant convergence taking place. The technologies behind television, telecommunications and computers are merging to create a giant global communications industry which is almost certain to become one of the powerhouses and largest employers of the 21st century.

A central factor in all this has been the extremely rapid introduction of digital technology. Any would-be entrant into the media industry should have a basic grasp of that new technology and an understanding of its impact on the industry, the economy, society and, therefore, on their own future careers.

Going Digital
Digital technology used to be associated entirely with the highly distinctive computing industry. Information expressed in the mathematical binary code of two basic digits – zeros and ones (for example, 01101) – was processed and then displayed in words, figures and graphs on computer screens. In the past fifteen to twenty years computers have made an enormous impact on business, commerce, record keeping and scientific research – on everyone in fact who, at home or at work, deals with facts and figures. Today, however, sound, music, video and sophisticated graphics, as well as text and data, can all be expressed in binary figures and 're-created' by computer speakers and screens. As a result the whole notion of 'information' is changing and broadening. The term now encapsulates all the various forms of the communication media that can be expressed in binary code (that is, digitised) – a development usually referred to as multi-media.

Multi-media and multimedia are enigmatic terms which confuse many people. Multi-media with a hyphen is mostly used simply to mean the bringing together of the television, film, video, radio and music industries. Multimedia without a hyphen is used in a related sense in the computing industry to mean the bringing together of texts, graphics, music, animation, video and publication-quality capability on computers. All multimedia really means is that data of all sorts can be expressed in a common language – the binary code – in which the basic *bits* of information can be stored in innumerable sequences and at enormous rates and mingled and mixed together. The computer screen, which once displayed only facts and figures, can now also produce voices, music and moving pictures. Not surprisingly, this development is having an enormous effect on the audio-visual industry which, through film, television and video, used to be the main providers of entertainment. For simplicity's sake this chapter will stick to the term multimedia in an overall sense to refer to the whole digital revolution, but readers should take note that in the digital and information revolution the terminology has not yet completely settled down.

A key element in the digital revolution, especially as far as television is concerned, has been the evolution of digital compression technology. This 'compresses' the raw digital forms of sound and pictures, which are extremely large, by removing intrinsic redundancies and repetitions. Compression technology means that only the moving parts of a picture are updated with every frame. Anything which has not moved is reused from the previous frame. When a television picture is sent out, the entire first frame is transmitted for broadcast but the second frame only contains the changes while the same background as frame one is reused. In this way essential space is saved in the recording medium (tape, disc) and in the bandwidth needed to transmit the TV signal, thus permitting the creation of infinitely more television channels (see below).

In 1996 it is now possible to compress and decompress, encode and decode 'information' inexpensively, at an incredibly fast rate and with high quality results. This development is very significant, and a point to grasp is that compression technology has been achieved much more quickly than people expected. In 1993 when the calamitous European Union's High Definition Television (HDTV) policy was finally abandoned, experts were still arguing that digital/compression technology would not be a reality until the 21st century. Instead the digital revolution is virtually complete.[1]

For the audio-visual industry the digital revolution has enormous implications in all sorts of areas. For a start, the television set, which today is viewed as the provider of one-way broadcast entertainment to the home, in the future will become another means of delivering a large range of information to homes and businesses. When computers can play moving pictures and television sets can carry out computing functions, the distinction between them dissolves – the teleputer perhaps? To date 'multi-media' has generally been associated with the computer screen (see above), but as computers and television screens converge (that word again!) our notions about the distinctiveness of entertainment and knowledge, broadcasting and computer processing, will also shift as the frontiers between the sectors disappear.

Fundamental to the success of the digital revolution is the convergence of the technologies of telephone and cable, and the fact that telecommunications have been revolutionised by the possibilities inherent in fibre-optic cable and its superiority over the old metallic wires. In the future cable, with its ability to deliver digitally compressed signals over fibre-optic networks, will be a driving force pushing the entertainment and information revolution forwards.

Interactivity on the Internet
The outstanding characteristic of the telephone is its interactivity: we talk to each other over phone lines, we interact verbally. At the present time telephone lines not only connect people across the globe, they also connect millions of computers to each other via devices called 'modems'. This is the much-hyped 'Internet' which allows computer users to 'talk' freely to each other. The 'wired' world of the future will create a home and work environment centred, according to the enthusiasts, on interactivity. (Note that the word 'wired' nowadays implies either electronic or optical connection.)

At the present time the Internet is about computers talking to computers over telephone lines. The technology that made this possible was used by the military as early as the 50s when, with the introduction of modems, a computer's digital signal could be translated into analogue form, sent down a telephone line and translated back again at the other end. By the 70s financial institutions and universities were using the system to transfer data rapidly from one computer to another and journalists began to find that it was far easier to write a story on a portable computer (fitted with a modem) and send it down the telephone line than it was to dictate the same story to their editors over the phone.

Telephone companies realised that the transfer of data had commercial possibilities and began to encourage the use of their lines for data transmission. When the telecoms systems themselves went digital, and institutions such as British Telecom moved from the public to private sector, the companies became much more aggressive in their sales and marketing strategy.

Meanwhile in the computer industry computers were shrinking in size and cost and becoming more powerful. The desk-top computer had quickly become the norm and computer companies began to realise that they could make more money by being less exclusive. In the 60s anyone who bought a particular company's computer had found it difficult, if not impossible, to transfer data to another company's make. By the 80s IBM's personal computers were being copied ('cloned') around the world and the Microsoft operating system (MS-DOS) worked on the vast majority of them.

The commercial interests of the computer and telephone industries were beginning to converge and, eventually, the idea of the 'Net' developed in which a network of desktop personal computers could interact with each other across the globe by telephone lines. One of the earliest 'nets' was Janet which connected university computers around the world so that at first the Net appeared to be the preserve of high-flying academics who 'understood' computers and could use the system to swap equations and rarefied scientific and technical information. However, by the mid-90s, as ownership of desktop computers in offices and homes burgeoned, more and more people discovered that it was useful to have instant access to vast amounts of the 'free' information that had become available.

Remarkably quickly the Net became a democratic free-for-all, where people could browse for information on the World Wide Web, send E-mail messages, make friends and even, reportedly, fall in love! One of the great attractions of the Internet is its individualistic, anarchic culture. In the beginning 'wired folk' were not Establishment types; they were democratic, multiracial, egalitarian and indifferent to conventional aspirations. Perhaps the most alluring aspects of the Internet was that individuals could both provide and consume information. There was a two-way flow which appeared to open up all sorts of exciting possibilities in terms of personal and political global interaction.

The Information Superhighway – Communacopia?
The forthcoming marriage of personal computers, cable and telephony through the use of fibre optics (watch out, though, for the re-emergence of radio waves!) and the turning of television pictures into digital form (and their compression) are developments that allow access to, and manipulation of, a bounty of information and informational products, paving the way for the 'information society' or 'Communacopia'. This development will arguably be as important in the history of civilisation as the Industrial Revolution.

The huge flood of information on the Internet has an important characteristic. It can flow directly from person to person, bypassing social classes, race, gender, political borders and governments. It is making the world a smaller place and the 'globe' is shrinking a little bit more every day. All this has implications for those contemplating a career in film, television, video and the entertainment industry because some experts predict that television, in particular, is destined to play a central role in the development of the information society. In a market economy the thirst for home screen entertainment will be the dynamic factor in encouraging people to go out and buy the hardware. Television hardware could be a central factor in the extension and exploitation of the technology, paving the way for the building of the fibre-optic cable infrastructure – essential to the much vaunted information superhighway.

Unsurprisingly, given the cost, scale, scope and potential impact of the superhighway it soon attracted the attention of politicians and media entrepreneurs who, in the past few years, have been busy developing policies and strategies for the new age.

The Internet versus the Information Superhighway

In March 1994 Vice-President Al Gore of the United States made a speech to the International Telecommunications Union in Buenos Aires, in it he spoke of the marvellous and endless possibilities of the global information superstructure – what has come to be called the information superhighway. Gore, who recognised the possibilities inherent in the new technology relatively early on and who has been described as an ideologue of the information superhighway, declared that the global information superstructure could bring huge benefits in terms of education and democracy to 'all members of the human family'. It will bring everything from early warnings of natural catastrophes, improved health care and resolution of environmental problems to economic competitiveness and international co-operation!

Gore's utopian vision of the possibilities inherent in the development of the information superhighway has not met with universal approval. Many people are sceptical of the rhetoric about democracy, individualism and the advantages flowing from a world of easily accessible information. Critics of Gore point out that it is a mistake to think of the information superhighway as just a faster, more powerful version of the Internet. The data on the proposed information superhighway will be delivered through the expensive fibre-optic, broadband cable systems presently being built and speculators will want a healthy return on their investment. A crucial difference between the Internet and the information superhighway is that Internet users usually pay a flat fee to join the network and from then on all information is free, while the information superhighway is likely to be based on a pay-per-use model. This will make a profound difference.[2]

A flat-fee system encourages play and exploration. Users can wander through the webs of information and make discoveries. Pay-per-use forces users to be more focused because browsing will be expensive. Global media companies will be able to meter the information they provide because digital documents can report back to their owners and this endows them with great power. Haunted by fears of expensive monthly bills, searchers on the information superhighway will tend to rely on certain 'reliable' information providers, government summaries for example, instead of searching documents for themselves. Cost will force people to accept 'information packages' provided by information suppliers. Consequently, material available today on the Internet for 'free' may well be a source of profit for the superhighway owners. This will narrow down users' options.

It follows that there are two key questions for the future: who will own the information superhighway cables; and, perhaps more significantly, who will own the *information* on the information superhighway? Most experts believe that copyright will be a key factor in determining the costs. According to John Naughton of the *Observer* the United States is already in the process of giving great power to copyright owners (the large corporations) through a proposed National Information Infrastructure Copyright Protection Bill. As a result, says Naughton, users will be delivered 'neatly trussed into the clutches of Murdoch, Time-Warner, Disney and all the other multi-media conglomerates who view the information superhighway not as a Jeffersonian tool for liberating mankind but as a firehose down which they can pump lucrative pap and from which nobody will be allowed to drink for free.'[3]

The Media Industry: Gold Rush Fever
Certainly, the idea that it will be entertainment which will prompt consumers to wire up their home has, in the last few years, encouraged feverish activity in the businesses associated with entertainment and communication technologies. The tempo in the economic competition between all sectors and the market has speeded up. Mergers, buy-outs and take-overs in cable, telecommunications, computing and large entertainment companies are taking place virtually every day, especially in the United States where the entertainment industry is immensely powerful: all the major players are rushing to secure a dominant position for themselves.

Until the early 80s the American government regulated broadcasting relatively strictly: there were laws against cross-media ownership and Hollywood production houses could not own national broadcasting companies. As we have seen, however, Reaganomics favoured deregulation and in the 90s the laws controlling the activities of trusts in the media industry were relaxed, allowing the Disney Company, for example, to buy up the American Broadcasting Company (ABC), a national network, in 1995.

Technological change has driven the entertainment market mania forwards, and the United States, which has acquired a strong lead in digitised products, is believed in some quarters to be using the technology to create a new level of competition in the global market-place.

There is concern too about a process known as 'media concentration' whereby huge media conglomerates appear to be falling into fewer and fewer hands: those of the so-called 'media moguls' such as Rupert Murdoch of News International. Murdoch has suggested that all media are one, a remark which worries those who still see definite distinctions between the cultures of film, television, the press and so on. Some experts now predict that at the beginning of the next century there could be as few as five companies controlling all the world's entertainment and information on a global superhighway. Young people entering the film and television industry today can not afford to ignore what is going on at the global level. It is *their* jobs, *their* conditions of work – *their* futures – which are at stake.

The Death of Television?
The merger mania in the media industry is fed by the belief that consumer demand for entertainment will be a central factor prompting the construction of the information superhighway. There are, however, opponents of this view who argue that the television and film industries, as we know them, are about to die, that the information superhighway will be mainly driven by the computing culture of the Internet which is individualistic, interactive and creative. These commentators suggest that television, with its allegedly couch-potato culture, is about to crumble and disappear.[4]

Recent reports indicate that by 1997 Americans will be able to download feature films from the Internet in a fraction of the time it takes now. Since legal controls on the Internet are, at present, virtually non-existent, the film industry fears that this development could lead to a boom in the piracy of copyright material on a global scale thus depriving the big companies of their profits; it would also give the advantage to the computer in the television-versus-the-computing-screen rivalry. No-one really knows for certain what will happen. It is all a question of wait and see.

Winners and Losers
From the point of view of the business world the great problem with technological systems is predicting which are going to dominate and

who is going to pay. Fortunes can be made and lost on backing the right or wrong technology. Every one is haunted by the way the technically superior video format of Betamax was beaten by VHS in the 80s (many commentators see the same scenario in the way Microsoft has currently outstripped Apple Macintosh). Large international corporate forces want to take advantage of rapid technological change, as do the politicians, and they are all anxious to bet the right way.

In this connection the whole evolution of High Definition Television (HDTV) is instructive. In the early 90s all hopes for the television industry in Europe focused on competing systems of HDTV. When this book first appeared in 1993 all the experts were predicting that HDTV was the television technology of the future. Extraordinarily rapidly, however, digital technology has tended to shunt HDTV into a siding. However, since the prospect of improved television picture quality is still an issue, some understanding of the HDTV question is important.

HDTV – A Cautionary Tale
In the 80s the world's television market had virtually reached saturation point and it seemed that the industrial economies would benefit if a new television system could be developed that, because of improved picture and sound quality, would persuade people to go out and buy new television hardware. Consequently, a great deal of research and development effort focused on HDTV: it seemed to offer a way to boost the worldwide market in electronics and could even affect the positions, share and balance of power of the advanced nations in the world economy.

Today's television standards date back to the 60s. The oldest television standard is the American NTSC (National Television Systems Committee) which has a 525 line picture. It is also used in Japan but not in Europe, which is divided between two systems: the German/English PAL (Phase Alternation by Line) and the French SECAM (SEquentiel Couleur à Mémoire). Television screens do not produce a high degree of picture resolution; the quality is nowhere near that of 35mm film. In addition the shape of the TV screen is boxlike, with an aspect ratio of about 4:3. Films shown on television have to be transmitted in a letterbox format or cropped to fit the smaller screen, or panned and scanned by a human operator who attempts to catch the most relevant parts of each scene (some film-makers such as Woody Allen do not permit this). There was clearly room for improvement in television receivers and by the 80s this was a much debated issue.

The Japanese had been researching the next level of television hardware since the 60s and had invested about a billion dollars in HDTV. By the 80s they had developed a system called Hi-vision, and in 1986,

when the International Telecommunications Union met in D
(in the former state of Yugoslavia), the Japanese tried to :
adoption of their system (based on 1125 lines) as the world
Americans at that point were not particularly concerned a
have agreed, but the French rallied the Europeans to resist an
the Japanese from dominating the world HDTV market. Sinc
anese had largely taken over the world's video-recorder m
French were anxious that they should not do the same with
The Europeans, therefore, pressed ahead with their own re
HDTV.

The purpose of HDTV, with its larger number of line
improve the televisual experience. With HDTV the picture is
clearer and contains more information (pixels). The detail and
its high resolution made it of obvious interest to people who r
quality of the image (in the same way certain visually oriente
uals have always preferred film to video). HDTV packs a m
dramatic visual punch: viewers have a greater sense of imme
involvement in what is happening on screen because it feels
are 'inside the picture', an experience akin to seeing a film in th
Certain types of programmes were said to particularly be
HDTV: films, drama, sports events, wildlife programmes and
of all sorts. It was, however, by no means clear that consum
go out and buy the new systems, so HDTV was always a gam
ers are astoundingly tolerant of bad television pictures and p
quality). Only if HDTV were available at a reasonable pric
ever be successful.

Once it was clear that the world would not accept the
standard, the Japanese moved quickly to commercialise their
tem and steal an advance on the market. By 1989 they had a
analogue HDTV system based on 1,125 lines which broad
hours a day. By January 1991 Toshiba began production
called MUSE HDTV sets. However, development was handic
the high cost (about £6,000 per set) and by the fact that very l
esting programming existed for the new sets. The Japanese
HDTV system to record sports events such as the 1988 Seou
Olympics and the World Cup (just as the Europeans used th
Olympics at Albertville as a showcase for their HDTV system
The purchase by Sony of the Hollywood studio Columbia in
Matsushita's acquisition of Universal studios in 1990 were :
associated, in part, with the desire of these Japanese compani
vert Hollywood studio film libraries into their version of HD

After Dubrovnik the Europeans pursued their own policy
on, and research into, analogue HDTV. The defining moment

59

in 1986 when a European Directive made Multiplexed Analogue Component (MAC) technology (an intermediate stage paving the way for HDTV) compulsory for all Europe's transmissions via television satellites. Between 1986 and 1993 the European Union spent a great deal of money to support the MAC initiative and to assist the development of a European HDTV system based on 1250 lines. Both Thompson Consumer Electronics of France and Philips in the Netherlands eventually came up with working HDTV systems. However, the EU support project was always controversial and eventually proved somewhat fruitless. There were many reasons for this including the fact that multinational, private media companies such as BSkyB were opposed to the EU policy and evaded the regulations on the introduction of MAC technology. BSkyB was supported in its resistance by the British government which was lukewarm about the EU policy.

American Screens versus European Screens

Both the European and Japanese HDTV systems were 'analogue' which means the signal is sent in the form of an electromagnetic wave of rapidly changing amplitude or frequency (AM or FM). Both systems were very rapidly, and very suddenly, outstripped by American digital technology. In 1988, after the Dubrovnik meeting, the United States backed research into a digital HDTV system which, while it seemed likely to take longer to effect, seemed to have more potential. In fact it developed at an extremely rapid rate and soon rendered the analogue system virtually obsolete.

It seemed that both the Europeans and Japanese systems were superseded by a superior technology. Yet it is not quite so simple. Supposedly, the crucial point about American HDTV was that, in being digital, it was compatible with computers and telecommunication systems. Digital HDTV offered the prospect of uniformity in operating methods right across the board (television, film, photography, the press, computerised graphics, data processing and so on). However, the fact that an HDTV picture is digital did not turn out to make it more appropriate for multi-media since most computer screens are analogue. In addition, HDTV requires greater bandwidth which could make it more difficult to send information. Early in 1994 the Americans announced that they had settled on a standard for digital broadcast high-definition television. What this could mean is that the United States, where the current NTSC 525-line picture quality is lower, will move towards HDTV, while Europe, with higher picture quality systems (PAL and SECAM), will not follow suit.[5]

Negroponte in *Being Digital* is interesting about the HDTV question. He suggests that the basic mistake of the Japanese and the

Europeans was to think of the next evolutionary step in television in terms of improvement in the hardware, i.e. increased resolution and better colour. This merely emphasised picture quality rather than content when there was no real evidence to suggest that consumers were particularly bothered about picture quality. In any case increased image enhancement is no longer a central issue once television's technology becomes digital because high picture quality and flexibility is inherent in digital technology.

In other words, digital television has much more to offer than just high resolution ... which is not to say that digital television will not offer HDTV. The then Heritage Secretary, Virginia Bottomley, specifically mentioned HDTV when, in 1995, she announced the government's plans for digital broadcasting.

Widescreen Television

At the present time the main marketing focus centres on widescreen television, which though not HDTV, does provide stereo sound and enhanced picture quality due to the fact that the picture scanning speed is twice that of today's sets. This does not increase the picture resolution, nor does it allow for large flat panel displays, but it does make the normal television picture more stable with less flickering. It also has the advantage of not making existing receivers obsolete, yet at the same time it provides consumers seeking better picture and sound with a new type of set.

Widescreen TV changes the present picture shape from the aspect ratio of 4:3 to a ratio of 16:9, about one-third wider than at present for the given picture height, but not as stretched as the cinema screen. When television first began, films were also shot in a format of about 4:3 but then changed to widescreen because the shape is a better match for the human field of vision. We see more horizontally than vertically (because we have two eyes spaced horizontally). Therefore the brain registers a widescreen picture as being more like a scene in real life. With the introduction of the widescreen system television is finally beginning to catch up with film.

Widescreen sets have been available for several years but sales were slow owing to the lack of programmes that could do the sets justice. This is no longer the case and programmes are now being made in the widescreen format, thus enhancing the attraction of the widescreen receivers.

Digital Television

The planned introduction of digital television over the next few years is of immense significance, and Europe's television companies are already racing to offer digital services and equipment. Only viewers who equip themselves with digital decoders will be able to receive digital services on their existing sets. BSkyB has invested heavily in the decoding technology required by the new system.

European satellite, cable and terrestrial broadcasters will all soon be offering a huge array of digital television channels and services (although the lack of standardisation at the present time means that home televisions will need several set-top boxes to receive the variously transmitted services). The first digital services will be on satellite television via the Astra satellite. Eutelsat, an organisation owned by a consortium of European telecommunication companies, is planning to offer digital television services on its new series of Hot Bird satellites, the first of which will be launched in 1996.

Digital television transmitted by satellite will have the capacity to offer up to 200 channels. Cable television companies using fibre-optic broadband cable will eventually offer even more and are well-placed to exploit the digital revolution since they already have the capacity to provide two-way interactive services on their hundreds of channels. Satellite and cable together could supply an additional 400 channels by the year 2000.

Digital systems are particularly important for the terrestrial television industry. Since the television signal can be compressed, several television channels can be offered on a narrow frequency or bandwidth. This could mean an increase from the four terrestrial channels of today to around eighteen, and even forty, channels in the medium term, with four or more digital channels carried in a space currently occupied by a single analogue channel. HDTV of a very high quality would require more bandwith space and would therefore reduce the number of services available. Viewers, however, may opt to use HDTV for some programmes and not for others.

Digital television also means the viewer can be offered improved programming facilities as well as technical quality. In sports coverage viewers could opt to be on the centreline of a football match or behind the goal and they could change ends at half-time! This type of option would also require a greater transmission capacity and more production resources at the match. It would also have an impact on the way producers and directors work in television, which again has implications for careers in the industry.

Government plans for digital terrestrial television (DTT) in the UK have proposed a new idea for blocks of channels known as 'multiplexes'. While in analogue television each programme service required a single channel, in digital TV the multiplex combines a set of services in a single frequency. Companies will have to bid for a licence to run a multiplex and it is likely that telecommunications groups, broadcasters and electronic organisations will all be interested.

Although DTT can never compete with satellite or cable, in terms of numbers of channels offered, it does have certain advantages. It can offer a universal service and will reach places not easily or cheaply accessible by cable or satellite since it will use existing aerials and will not require satellite dishes or expensive cabling. It will also be more suited to portable reception and allow for regional programmes. The first digital terrestrial channels should be available by 1997.

The Future

It is pretty clear that the entertainment industry is undergoing a multi-media revolution and that this is affecting the economy, politics and the stock market. *Toy Story* (1995) earned a place in film history by being the first full-length feature film to be entirely generated by computer. Broadcasting has been working with a single technology for seventy years: analogue. Now it is entering into the digital age and this is going to have a big impact both on the way programmes are distributed and on virtually every single piece of equipment associated with programme production and reception.

Computing technology has already had an impact on how programmes and films are made (this will be discussed more fully in Parts Three and Four); now the technology of digital compression is expected to revolutionise the UK broadcasting sector in the next century. It will result in a multiplicity of commercial, subscription-based, conditional-access channels and permit a more direct relationship with the viewer. It will allow subscription and pay-per-view services on mainstream terrestrial television and create room for new channels which can be used for a system known as near-video-on-demand (NVOD). With this system the same movie is broadcast on several channels but the start is staggered by around half an hour on each channel so the viewer is never further than half an hour away from start of the movie. The picture is scrambled until payment is made, probably by an electronic smart-card system.

Digital systems, of course, mean that transmission signals can carry other forms of data such as computer games, text, credit-card transactions, and so on. Pictures will be clearer too (which is why the concept of an HDTV receiver is now of less central concern). Digital television means no 'noise' where off-air reception is poor and no 'ghost echoes' from hills and buildings.

At the present time the digital revolution is providing a huge headache for managers in television. With the technology of the industry about to change on such a massive scale, millions of pounds are at stake. As far as equipment is concerned broadcasting companies have to decide which of the various competing systems are the most attractive. At the present time, for example, there are, three main digital camera formats on offer to replace Sony's Betacam which is currently the industry standard, and computer giants like Sony, Avid, Quantel, Tektronix, BTS and Panasonic are all fighting to develop a complete computer system for the newsroom of the future.

No-one so far has studied the effect of all the digital technology on traditional broadcasters and their programme suppliers, although there is some evidence that many practitioners have found the changes deeply disturbing and frightening. Some quarters of the broadcasting industry wish that digital technology had never been invented because it has brought so much expense and uncertainty in its wake. Young people who are new to the industry, and less afraid of change, should, however, monitor and face up to the economic implications of technology; otherwise they will be manipulated by those who control it.

According to some experts, however, digital technology is not just another technology. It could, for all sorts of reasons, change our conceptions and perceptions of the world around us and alter our mental landscapes. The industry has tended to concentrate on the nuts and bolts: that is to say, how much will it all cost. But the broader question of the impact on the imagination has at last attracted attention and 'the future' has suddenly become a central focus of debate. Some experts think that the essential interchangeability that digitisation provides will alter our perceptions, attitudes and expectations. In the 60s, the philosopher of the media, Marshall McLuhan, suggested that there are subtle effects of the medium which influence what we can know. To put it another way for the 90s, digitised media could change how we know what we know.

Mass Media or Personal Media?
Historically British and European television was a mass medium shaped by two factors: first, there was the perceived shortage of frequencies imposed by analogue technology (spectrum scarcity) and, secondly, there was the Establishment fear that television was too powerful a tool to be left solely in hands of practitioners causing it to be heavily regulated and supervised by the State. The first idea is now outdated and it is increasingly difficult to argue for the second.

When everything from sound broadcasting to telecommunications can be encoded in digits there is an enormous extension of choice. According to some commentators, this will lead to a move away from the concept of a mass media to one of personal media and individual choice. Certainly, our own age may be the last in which a whole nation shares in a common mass experience of watching the same television broadcast.

According to the optimists the information age will mean a massive increase in the individual's power to access services tailored to his or her specific wishes and needs and this will make global communication much more difficult for national (or international!) politicians to monitor and control – the new era will be all about individual choice, democracy and freedom. As far as television is concerned, for example, the concept of 'a channel' will dissolve because all individuals will be able to access a favourite programme at any time of his or her choosing, becoming, in fact, their own programme scheduler.

Other observers are more cynical. They point out that ownership is critical. If the mega media companies have built the information super-highway then people will be relegated to the role of information consumers and the interactive role allotted to them will be very narrow. The Internet of today may be about information reaching a single individual, about browsing and choice, but, on the information super-highway of the future, global multi-media companies will want to reach tens of thousands of users to justify the costs of offering services. In the end this will almost inevitably result in a shift away from the Internet's orientation towards the individual and niche interactive audiences and back towards the old formula of mass audiences – albeit with the time-access staggered for the sake of convenience. This shift will bring homogenisation and standardisation in its wake because mega media companies will inevitably favour uncontroversial programming and inoffensive information with mass appeal and little diversity and all of this on a global scale. Little of the anarchic, egalitarian atmosphere of the Internet will remain because the big media companies, in the thirst for profit, will have pushed aside the interactive individuals in favour of relatively passive mass audiences who will happily pay to consume their entertainment and information packages.

Some Points to Think About
According to some experts, computing facilities built into the television set will, in the future, filter, sort, prioritise and manage multi-media on our behalf so that, where today's television allows the viewer to control lightness/darkness, volume and channel, in the next century the computerised screen 'appliance' will select programming from millions of sources of information according to the consumer's specific interests. The television 'experience' of the future will be more like the newspaper experience of today and viewers will be able to browse and skip through all the 'information' available and 'interact' if they wish to do so. With all the hype it is perhaps sensible to ask what the viewer will

really make of all this. There are only a limited number of hours available to watch television and there is only so much cash to spare to pay the viewing bills. Advertisers, too, will only have a certain amount of money to spend on commercial television and, as viewing choices widen, the audience watching any given programmes is bound to fragment.

Supposedly, 'interactivity' is the name of the game on the Internet and even to a degree on the information superhighway, and complex programmed interactivity is already part of CD-I, but the average TV couch potato may not be as enthusiastic about all this activity as those who promote the information society assert. Will viewers really use the new technology to become smarter, richer and more productive? Will the interactive Internet culture actually diffuse downwards and outwards through the general population of TV watchers (indeed, even kill off television itself)?

As far as television is concerned, all 'interactivity' seems to mean at the present time is a phone call from the viewer to the TV presenter or the use of a computer terminal to send money to a shopping channel or a charity. This is probably what the mega media companies prefer. Certainly there is very little chance to genuinely interact on more subtle questions (is it even possible to bargain for a better deal with the shopping presenter?).

For the believers in the future of the digital world, however, this argument is irrelevant. We are only seeing, they say, the very primitive beginnings of a huge revolution. They point to the huge interactive forums on every conceivable subject on the Net, the so-called World Wide Web (WWW). Who could have foreseen in the 18th century the invention of the motor car and the freedom it brought. Who would have predicted how many people would have cars and learn to drive them? Human beings, according to the prophets of the information age, are about to embark on the process of learning to drive along the entertainment/information superhighway of the future.

Summing Up
The digitisation of the electronic media is bringing together the formerly separate spheres of broadcasting and telecommunications. Satellite, cable and wireless delivery will connect to home telecommunications and broadband networks and be processed by powerful home computers to bring new programmes and services to the consumers. In theory, the result will be a world of communication where all citizens are connected and may have access to whatever information or entertainment they choose.

At the beginning of this chapter it was pointed out that the digital revolution is nearly complete. Providing interactivity is really now only a question of economics, of return on capital invested. What will consumers want? What will they be willing to spend on having more programmes, more choice and faster delivery? Can the new services be profitable? Will the big companies dominate? These are all uncertain areas. The City seems to be backing the new giant media companies, cable and telecoms operators presently in the process of merging. Nobody really knows, if and how, these mergers between culturally and organisationally very different companies are going to work out in practice.

Young people entering the media business today will experience an extraordinary, and perhaps unique, time in the industry when everything is in a state of flux. New employees will enter a workforce in a state of upheaval. They must expect constant variation as a fact of life and be prepared to keep up with emerging technologies and periodically retrain. In corporate terms, the Net, in providing easily accessible information, rendered superfluous a whole layer of information managers and staff. *Time* magazine estimates that by the year 2001 only one manager in fifty will be promoted compared to one in 20 in 1987 (15 April 1996). The multi-media revolution means that no-one has a secure job anymore and no employee can expect to work in one sector all the time. Film, video and broadcasting employees must be prepared to move in and out of jobs as employment opportunities in one area wax and wane. The barriers between all sectors are crumbling and those people who can accept, manipulate and cope with all forms of media will be the most employable.

The question is; how can the individual secure some protection in today's very exposed competitive global environment? The answer is to be well-informed (reading a popular scientific journal such as the *New Scientist* is a good idea) and flexible and to embrace retraining and versatility as a fact of life.

Notes

1. Popular accounts of the digital revolution include: Nicholas Negroponte *Being Digital* (London: Hodder and Stoughton, 1995); this (rather aptly) is also available on tape; also David Bowne, *Multimedia* (London: Bowerdean Publishing Company Ltd., 1994).
2. See Howard Besser, 'From Internet to Information Superhighway', in *Resisting the Virtual Life* ed. James Brook and Iain A. Boal (San Francisco: City Lights, 1995).
3. 3 March 1996
4. For an account of this issue see George Gilder, *Life After Television* (London: Norton & Co., 1994).
5. Bowen, *Multimedia*, p. 67.

PART TWO
EDUCATION AND TRAINING

THE TRAINING VACUUM

By the early 90s training had emerged as one of the main problems facing the industry. How were the increasingly prevalent freelances to secure the necessary skill base which would maintain the industry's high standards? For thirty years the BBC and ITV had trained their own highly efficient staff, but their role was now diminishing in the totality of broadcasting. In the film industry the unions had protected the skill base but now this too had been eroded with the decline in union power. It was clear to everyone that there was a severe and growing skill shortage in broadcasting and film and that the training systems which did exist were not in tune with the pace of change. A crisis situation had arisen and there were many questions to be asked: How was the industry to train people for the future? What did the industry really require? What sort of people would the industry need? New systems had to be developed, new approaches explored.

For young people entering the industry in the 90s the future opened up many possibilities. The dead hand of tradition had loosened its grip with the decline of restrictive practices and there were more opportunities available. It was the old who were to find the pace of change difficult, the young accepted it, but, because the audio-visual industry was becoming more complex, the young had to prepare themselves – the question was where when training provision seemed so piecemeal and uncertain?

The Broader Picture
The 80s had witnessed important changes in the British approach to education and training. Politicians had begun to realise that in the 21st century employees would have to be highly educated and possess marketable skills in order to cope with the pace of technical change. In response to this the government embarked on a series of reforms in education and training designed to prepare the British workforce for the brave new world of the year 2000. New systems,

new qualifications, new methods of assessment were introduced. The next section of this book will discuss these developments in more detail, looking in particular at the effect of the changes on higher education and vocational training and at how the new ideas are having a practical impact on the broadcasting and entertainment industries. But first some explanation of the terminology in education and training is in order.

Until the age of sixteen formal full-time education is compulsory in Britain. The minority who choose to go on after sixteen used to have two very different paths ahead of them: they could opt either for education or for training. Education usually meant academic courses – theoretical in approach and competitive, and open-ended in the sense that they are (or were) in many cases not directed towards a specific goal (a skill or job of some sort). The subject-matter of education was broad and general rather than narrow and skill-based. Students who opted for full-time education usually did A levels and then, if they were selected, went into 'higher education' to university or college to gain a degree or diploma in Higher Education (Dip HE).

Training used to be thought of as very separate from education and was sometimes referred to as vocational training. The term implies learning that is practical, work-related in the sense of the job market, and with definite goals in view, usually the acquisition of a specific craft or skill. Training was often short-term (one-day training courses were not uncommon).

Training courses are often linked together under the heading of 'further education'. On the whole, training is not competitive but directed instead towards the acquisition of 'competence'. You can either do the job or you can't: there is no competition with other candidates to secure higher grades. Traditionally, higher education in Britain was full-time and training, both full-time and part-time.

In Britain there used to be a very sharp division between education and training. Post-sixteen students were sorted into appropriate learning slots and considerable class snobbery attended the chosen path. Higher education was for the clever and the few, further education and training for the less intelligent and more numerous. Those acknowledged to be 'bright' rarely opted for vocational courses because these courses had more than a whiff of inferiority about them: training was down-market. The only real exceptions were degrees in medicine and law; even engineering at degree level was regarded as somewhat inferior. In short, training in Britain lacked prestige and was usually deemed 'lower class'.

Britain's economic competitors did not share this bias. In West Germany vocational courses (and engineering) were held in high esteem and, as has often been pointed out, this is not unconnected with the country's economic success. The link between skill-based knowledge and the high quality of services in countries such as West Germany and Japan eventually impressed itself upon the attention of British legislators. Evidence accumulated that effective training increased a state's productivity and profits. Rather belatedly, the British began to take this point of view seriously. The increasing impact of technology on Western society obviously meant that a much higher proportion of the workforce had to be highly skilled. This would be even more the case in the future: an untrained workforce would equal widespread unemployment and low productivity – in other words – economic disaster.

In 1984 the British government commissioned a report entitled *Competence and Competition*. This emphasised the lack of training and skills within the UK as compared to other European countries.[1] In 1988, 63 per cent of the British workforce had no vocational training at all; this compared with 38 per cent of the Dutch, 26 per cent of the German and 53 per cent of the French workforce. More than 70 per cent of British workers who would be in the workforce in the year 2000 were already in employment and most of them were unskilled. They were, in other words, totally unprepared for the market of tomorrow.

The government needed to act, and act quickly, and the improvement of the vocational skills of the British workforce became an increasingly important emphasis in public policy. This will be discussed in detail in Chapter 6. Suffice it to say here that employers, employees, educationalists, trainers and the government all agreed on the need for action to improve the nation's skills, and in the last decade an effort has been made to increase access to further (and higher) education.

People now talk of 'education and training' in the same breath and accept that the enduring division in standing and prestige between them has had an injurious effect. Of course there is still a residue of innate conservatism. Britain is singularly resistant to institutional change. It has been suggested, for example, that if Britain is really serious about educational reform and a higher evaluation of training, then A levels should be abolished altogether. Critics have argued that it was ridiculous to make the A-level system the academic gold standard.[2] The Major government has taken some of the criticism of A-level elitism aboard and the recent Dearing report recommended that an 'applied A level' should be introduced to replace the GNVQ (Advanced Level).[3] The Dearing report seeks to bring the A levels and the General National Vocational Qualification (GNVQ) into close alignment.

What is certainly true is that, for the first time in Britain, the characteristics of college- and university-based higher education and of work-oriented further education and training are beginning to converge.

Higher education is increasingly oriented towards the workplace which, in turn, is more alert to the need for some form of qualification system for skill-based tasks.

Education and Training in the British Audio-Visual Industry – How It Used to Be Done.

British film and television have always been a mystery to those seeking to work in the industries. There are roughly five main strands to working in television and film: *creative production* (director) with creative support (for example wardrobe designer); *technical* (engineer) and technical/operational/craft (vision mixer, camera operator); *journalistic* (journalist or researcher); and *administrative/management* (production manager, facilities manager, financial support services, etc.). In the past it was always difficult to break into film or television, particularly at producer or any managerial level. Opportunities for employment were scarce, mainly because until the latter part of the 80s there were only three places where film and television people were employed: first the relatively small film industry where experienced unionised staff worked on feature films and commercials, then the BBC, and finally ITV and Channel Four.

How then did people train to enter the film and television industries? The answer is that they mostly didn't: in the arcane way of many British institutions there was virtually no formal method of education or training which was recognised by the industry as preparation for a job in film and television. Training did not precede entry into the profession; rather, it followed it. The main problem was always and, in fact, remains 'getting in'.

Film

'Getting into film' was especially difficult. Degrees cut no ice; indeed they were largely irrelevant. The film industry and the universities had nothing to say to each other: you were either in film or out of it and having a degree made no difference. Further education, with, for example, a City and Guilds qualification, was a little better for the craft grades but not much. The main way in was either 'luck' or 'pull', and 'insiders' had it easier. On both the craft and the production side the main way in was through 'contacts': a mother or father who worked in films in any capacity was a definite asset. A word in the ear here, a tip-off about a vacancy there, was the way the industry worked. There was hardly anywhere specific to go for practical information and for many years no independent or academic institutions provided education or training acceptable to the film unions, except for a few art colleges offering foundation courses in film and programme production.

A craft job in the film industry was almost a family inheritance, handed down from father to son (rarely from mother to daughter). Of course people complained about the outrageous unfairness and the Catch-22 situation: without a union card people could not work and without a definite job there was no union card.

The restrictiveness meant in practice that many people (even sometimes those with Oxbridge degrees) entered the film industry as 'runners' or 'gophers'. This was (and is) a 'dogsbody' job. It involved doing errands for the production team and only the incredibly persistent were taken on and survived. It meant long hours, low pay and hard work. It was a grind and it could lead nowhere, but it offered the potential recruit an opportunity to gain knowledge of the industry at the ground-floor level. Runners often ended up doing tasks quite unrelated to film-making. They could, for example, find themselves taking the director's car to the garage to be repaired or his coat to the cleaners. Running errands showed willing and was thought to be character-forming, and it allowed people in the industry to assess the suitability and aptitude of the would-be recruit. In any case, despite its oddity, the system had a sound logic behind it. As many people in film can testify, having the appropriate skills or training are all very well, but the qualities which matter most are dedication, determination and imagination (this will be repeated often in this book), and these attributes are difficult to quantify by any examination system.

'Film people are different' is still a truism (despite the way the lines between the film and television sectors are blurring), although defining their particularity is difficult. It certainly includes an obsessive fascination with film and a willingness to work long hours. In a world of fanatics, academic degrees and even vocational qualifications were (and still are to a large extent) beside the point. What mattered in the industry was enthusiasm and, certainly in the past at all craft levels, being a union member. If you had a union card then you could certainly do the job. In the rather macho world of film-making, academic qualifications could even be a handicap.

Union Membership

For many years the main aim of the would-be recruit was to get into the appropriate union. The main film union used to be the ACTT (Association of Cinematograph Television and Allied Technicians), which effectively operated a closed shop in the film industry (and also in ITV). It recruited about 1800 members a year with a total membership of about 21,000. If you wanted to work you had to be a union member; an application to join a union had to be signed by a group of members who were willing to support you. Initially, new employees with a union card had to stay on the same grade for two years.

This created in the young unionised trainee a high degree of loyalty towards the union sponsors and encouraged from the outset a corporate and communal feeling about the union and the job. After two years the trainee could move to new employment or go freelance. It required patience to progress through the union grade structure and the whole system fostered a sense of brotherhood (less often sisterhood!). Rampant individualism was not admired; in any case, it was inappropriate since the technology of film and, in its early years, television called for team effort.

Best Trained Technicians in the World

There is no doubt that the whole system was far removed from the ideal of equal opportunities and indeed was irrational, restrictive and unfair. The fact is, however, that it worked very effectively. The slow pedestrian grind through a union apprenticeship produced some of the most skilled technicians in the world. Film is an extremely expensive medium and mistakes can be disastrous. Trainees started at the very lowest levels where they could do no harm. Promotion was slow and most people were exceptionally well-trained in how to do the job above them before they were ever promoted to do it.

The union structure, for all its faults, ensured excellent on-the-job training. No further education college or film studies course could offer better. British film-makers and technicians consistently won more than their fair share of Oscars (32 per cent of American Oscars including the technical categories were won by the British in the two decades between 1973 and 1993). Top jobs in the film industry (producers, directors, cinematographers) usually went to people who came up through the union ranks. A few very talented directors might move across to film from the stage or television (and vice versa) and many of these would have degrees, sometimes in drama in the case of theatre directors. As far as the film industry was concerned, however, academic qualifications were irrelevant.

Television

In television the situation was different: in most areas formal education could be very significant and a degree mattered, especially at the higher levels. The conventional high road into programme production was via the BBC, which was part of the British cultural élite. To get into the BBC management or top levels of production, a degree was (and still is) very useful indeed. Recruits did not need to know much about television, since the Corporation itself would train them, but the creative side of programme-making was felt to be the domain of the exceptionally clever. A degree, especially from Oxbridge (preferably in some thing esoteric), was taken to indicate intellectual superiority and a common point of entry for the graduate trainee was as a 'researcher'. BBC News Traineeships, for example, were much sought after and the scheme received thousands of applications every year for very few places, most of which went to high-flying graduates.

The Corporation was not totally degree-oriented. One route in as a producer was (and is) via journalism. Working on a local newspaper often led into local radio, and radio, especially in the regions, could, in turn, lead to a post as a researcher or journalist in television. From there, if the recruit had the ambition and energy, he or she could move up through the internal training schemes of the Corporation to reach producer level. Entry into sports broadcasting could be particularly idiosyncratic, since many reporters came in via their own enthusiasm for a particular sport.

BBC Engineering was similarly prestigious and highly competitive, although in the early years a degree was not necessary. The Corporation was expensively equipped and at the forefront of technological experiment and research. BBC engineering entrants were usually school-leavers on the science side with excellent A level passes (usually in physics and maths), and with good references. An interesting development in recent years (would-be recruits should take note) is the increasingly high level of ability demanded by the engineering side of television. As broadcasting equipment has become more complex and sophisticated, engineers have to be well-qualified in electronic communications. Over 95 per cent of engineering entrants now have degrees – today's engineers have to have theoretical understanding in addition to practical skills. However, it is still possible for technicians without degrees to be recommended for engineering training from within the Corporation.

On the whole engineers at the BBC were, and are, a special breed. They had (and still have) a separate career and training structure within the Corporation and they could be quite scornful of more obviously 'creative types'. Few engineers were impressed by the idea of directing or producing and they were rarely interested in moving over to the programming side of television (or radio); it was the technology that fascinated them. The attraction of the job was the opportunity it provided to work with equipment at the cutting edge of the communications industry. Retraining on new equipment was part of the normal career process and job satisfaction was always high.[4]

Other technical/operational/ craft posts in television, such as camera operators, sound technicians, and lighting specialists, were filled by recruits with some form of technical training at the tertiary level. Until the 90s it was not common for technical trainees to hold degrees, they held instead a BTEC qualification or something similar. Today, however, more of them have degrees and they are usually expected to be multi-skilled. In the past, candidates were taken on for a six month probationary period, after which, if they were suitable, they would be considered as a trainee within a particular specialism. The BBC then provided a full training through their own internal courses.

There used to be a strict hierarchy in television, but an ambitious recruit could move, thanks to the various BBC training courses, from the lower technical/craft levels through to the higher, and then on to the creative side as a producer or director. In the early days, directors with this type of background occasionally had an advantage over the non-technical recruits from the universities because practical know-how was then a more necessary component of programme-making. There was, however, a persistent bias in the BBC towards people with degrees and, generally, it was harder for those who had taken the technical/craft route to reach the higher levels of management.

A BBC job was much sought after. Recruitment took place through outside 'competitions' and only 'the brightest and the best' got in. Once in, however, all sorts of opportunities were available for those who wished to advance. In the past most people entering the professional grades were white, Anglo-Saxon males, but women graduates were often recruited at the secretarial and support staff level, and a few of them did clear the hurdles and make it through to producer level (especially if they had charm or good looks, a situation which, while unfair, was typical of an industry which still places a premium on physical attractiveness). Women, however, rarely became directors: this used to be regarded as a technical position for which they were not suitable. Even more rarely did women break into the higher echelons of BBC management. They came up against what has been called the 'glass ceiling' – senior management was assumed to be a male preserve. Recently, thanks to considerable pressure, the BBC has made a concerted effort in the equal opportunities area, but for most of its history the ethos of the Anglo-Saxon, Oxbridge-educated, white middle class male permeated all levels of the Corporation's culture.

For many years the system resulted in a highly skilled, professional but narrow and inward-looking workforce. (The narrowness was usually vigorously denied, but there was an out-of-touch quality about the BBC which was damaging when it came under political attack.) A job at the BBC had extraordinary cachet. 'I work for the Beeb' was a phrase liable to provoke envious intakes of breath on social occasions. This probably gave some members of the Corporation a rather exaggerated idea of their own importance and made them ill prepared for the brutal changes of the 80s and 90s.

For years television training and the BBC were virtually synonymous. The Corporation's internal schools had an international reputation and people from broadcasting systems all over the world came to take courses. Whether in management, engineering, journalism or presentation, the training was of a very high quality and one of the basic principles, whatever the level or speciality, was that employees should be provided with an overview of the whole programme-making process. The emphasis was on 'on-the-job' instruction combined with formal teaching.

By contrast, in the early years of television training in ITV lagged behind the BBC. However, the BBC trained staff beyond its requirements and many qualified people moved from the Corporation to the higher salaries of the commercial sector which consequently was often accused of 'poaching' the best people. The 'production-process-as-a-whole' nature of the BBC training system colonised ITV and the outward flow of creativity probably provided, at one time, about half the senior posts in the rest of the industry. It also contributed to the consistency and uniformly high quality which characterised British television. This is part of what is meant by British broadcasting 'culture'.

As ITV grew in stature and wealth, however, its training programmes expanded. These were usually organised on a company basis with certain companies specialising in particular areas: Thames Television had a technical trainee scheme; ITN had an editorial trainee scheme; and Granada had a course for trainee researchers (which was advertised externally every year and led to thousands of applications for six places). ITV also developed a close relationship with Leeds Polytechnic and Ravensbourne College of Art and Design, both of which were well-equipped and ran courses in television. ITV employees were frequently sent to Ravensbourne for updating and retraining. In addition, the IBA had formidable engineering responsibilities and its engineering department, based mainly at Crawley Court near Winchester, became a byword for technical excellence.

For many years the hands-on side of television technology was complex. Operators of equipment had to be highly skilled because the mistake of the uninitiated or the inexperienced could be expensive. No wonder, therefore, that the BBC and then ITV were prepared to pay for their own in-house training rather than trust it to an unknown agency. The system was inward-looking and autonomous (and very frustrating to those who wished to train in television yet who could not find employment with the Corporation or the ITV companies), but it worked. If it irritated outsiders who failed to break in, if it appeared cliquish and élitist, the main argument in the system's defence was the high quality of the programmes. British television was reckoned the world leader.

The benefits and job satisfaction in television were high. Union power was entrenched (especially in ITV) and although this made it difficult for outsiders to get in, standards were maintained. A job in the media bore no relation to life on the assembly line. The work was highly skilled with a glamorous component and would-be recruits clamoured at the doors all the time. This produced a somewhat smug attitude in those who had the jobs and perhaps an overweening pride (and greed). Union agreements frequently led to inflated overtime benefits which were reported in the right-wing press with hypocritical indignation (journalists on newspapers were not exactly paupers). Nemesis, however, in the guise of Mrs Thatcher, was at hand.

The television industry had already come under attack in the 70s. At first this was mainly from radicals on the Left and the most obvious manifestation was a campaign for more 'public access'. Critics wanted to see more programmes made by non-BBC, non-ITV staff that reflected working-class, ethnic minority and community concerns. Why, they demanded, was it assumed as a God-given right that only employees of broadcasting organisations could make programmes? The BBC especially was accused of being monolithic, self-contained and difficult to penetrate. Over the long haul this left-wing attack may have weakened the Corporation because, in the 80s, the BBC proved somewhat unequal to the task of repulsing the more orchestrated onslaught from the Right that attacked its unwieldy bureaucratic and financial structures. As a national institution the BBC had been inclined to believe in its own immortality, an attitude which left it ill-equipped to deal with the ideological changes of the 80s and the animus of the Right towards 'inefficient' public service institutions that were 'unresponsive' to consumers.

As we saw in earlier chapters, in the 80s the industry underwent a period of upheaval: video technology made the industry more accessible and permeable, the equipment was increasingly 'user-friendly', craft unions no longer had a monopoly of the skill and knowledge that gave them power and the Conservative government launched an attack on all restrictive practices which especially affected ITV. With deregulation, and the advent of satellite and cable, the number of broadcasting channels increased and the 25 per cent quota encouraged the formation of many small companies which meant that the BBC and ITV were no longer dominant. The 1990 Broadcasting Bill thrust ITV firmly into the competitive market-place and the BBC found itself reeling under attacks over the cost of the licence fee.

Financial pressure on all sides led to cutbacks and training was a major casualty. Training was an easy target for cost-cutting managers at the BBC, more concerned with short-term solutions than long-term benefits. Similarly ITV, faced with a drop in advertising and with the franchise auction, had little energy or money to 'squander' on training. (The failure to award Thames Television a franchise was a disaster from the training viewpoint because the Company had been very training oriented.) The government's onslaught on the unions meant in practice that there was no longer any major group or body devoted to stressing and preserving craft skills. By 1990 the mysterious and haphazard system which had trained British film and television personnel for years was falling apart. Some provision still existed but it was insufficient to cope with the scale of the problem. Training, virtually unnoticed, had fallen off the agenda. Suddenly, virtually overnight it seemed, the industry awoke to a skill shortage.

It was the burgeoning of the small independent companies and the expansion of the freelance market which brought the problem into focus. New recruits sometimes had no training at all and had to pick up skills and knowledge as they went along. It is difficult to convey how much of a shock this was to old-timers with a tradition of rigorous and thorough apprenticeships behind them. Craft unions that had protected high-level skills no longer had the authority to insist on anything. Moreover, craft technicians with years of experience were retiring and there were no replacements.

What was alarming was that standards did drop. The British began to lose their reputation. Production mistakes that would never have been tolerated in the past cropped up more frequently, especially on the small screen. Retired television hands watching live programmes were often appalled at what they saw and were heard to mutter about 'things being different in the old days'. They were right. Suddenly the industry that had considered itself the best in the world had a large pool of young, inexperienced and untrained personnel and a severe shortage of the high calibre staff. The training 'system', illogical and irrational as it had always been, was rapidly unravelling.

Something had to be done but what? Training was expensive and it required organisation. There was no longer any dominant agency which could provide a training service, the unions had lost their teeth and the BBC and ITV were under financial pressure. It was time for the industry to look beyond itself. It had to turn its attention to the new thinking about training which was beginning to penetrate government circles. There were courses in television and film provided by higher and further education but traditionally these had been rather despised. Perhaps, after all, they had something to offer? Perhaps they had to be taken more seriously? A major adjustment and transition was under way.

Notes

1. *Competence and Competition: Training and Education in the Federal Republic of Germany, The United States and Japan,* a report prepared by the Institute of Manpower Studies for the National Economic Development Council and Manpower Services Commission (London: MSC, 1984).
2. Employer, quoted by Sir Christopher Ball in his interim report, *Learning Pays, the Role of Post Compulsory Education and Training* (London: Royal Society of Arts, April 1991 p. 41). Sir Christopher's report is a powerful argument in favour of training and points to the economic advantages which could ensue if Britain developed an efficient training system.
3. Ron Dearing, *Review of Qualifications for 16-19 Year Olds Summary Report* (Middlesex: SCAA Publications, March 1996).
4. It should be noted that, at the time of writing (1996), the Industry Training Organisation, **Skillset** (see Chapter 8), is carrying out a survey of employment patterns and training needs of Broadcast Engineers.

6

MEDIA DIPLOMAS AND DEGREES

Are They Any Use?

Young people who want to enter the industry often ask: Should I take a degree? Will I have a better chance? Well, yes and no. The answer has to be: It all depends. Since 1990 a shift has taken place in the way education and training are viewed by the audio-visual industry. There has also been a corresponding shift in the way that 'higher education' institutions view training. Many people are still unaware of the implications of all this. This chapter will examine the situation in detail.

The American and European Model

In some ways the problem with education and training in the audio-visual industry in Britain in the late 80s was unique. Other European countries managed the change in employment patterns brought about by the decline of public service television, and by deregulation, more smoothly. One of the main reasons was that their skill training provision was better organised and more widespread.[1] In the United States, where many more people go to university, students who wished to get into the industry did degrees in film, communications, journalism or the media business and part of the degree often involved an element of training. Remember that television in the United States, unlike European television, did not function according to a public service ideology; it was firmly in the market-place, and there was little industry-based training available on the scale of that developed by the BBC. People with degrees from American universities did not expect to enter either the film or television industry at the top level: many of them went into the craft and non-professional areas or into the business side and sales. In Britain people who wanted to get into film rarely went to university, and those with degrees who went into television had rarely followed any relevant or immediately useful course. At university they were likely to opt for classics, politics, history, modern languages or English literature.

The Traditional Inferiority of Media Studies

It was a fact of British life that industry and university were worlds apart. Since education was seen as totally separate from training, the universities had little interest in industrial skills. This was particularly the case for the audio-visual industry. For many years British institutions of higher learning did not offer media or communications studies at degree level at all. Such courses were viewed as frivolous and 'American' and consequently, television, one of the most important mass media of the 20th century, was, until recently, scarcely examined or studied by British scholars. Film was slightly more acceptable because it could be regarded as an art form, but graduates recruited by the BBC were still likely to know more about *Beowulf* than Bergman.

Journalism was a similar case in point. Television news relied on journalists, but for years British universities regarded a degree in journalism as a peculiar American aberration. Until 1991 there were no undergraduate degrees in journalism offered by any British university or polytechnic, although a number of polytechnics did offer journalism as part of a three-year course in communications or media studies, or as a postgraduate degree. In September 1991 the London School of Printing, City University and Lancashire Polytechnic all began to offer BA degrees in journalism.

Industry Suspicion of the Media BA

The blame for this bizarre attitude, however, cannot be laid entirely at the doors of higher education. Film, broadcasting and newspaper personnel were for different reasons all equally suspicious of media degrees. Workers in creative and technical areas were unimpressed by ivory-tower academic study. For years journalists believed that the best way to train was to start at sixteen as a cub reporter with minimum qualifications and 'work your way up'. Indeed the new BAs in journalism have been regarded with much suspicion. Keith Hall of the National Council for the Training of Journalists has declared that the impetus for such courses has not come from the industry and that graduates won't be regarded as having the training required. Brian Hitchin of the *Daily Star* was reported as saying: 'BAs in Journalism? They don't turn me on. I've only met one graduate in journalism who was any good. Most of them are appalling. There's only one way to learn journalism and that's starting at the bottom' (quoted in Nick Turner, 'Newshounds on Course', *Guardian*, 30 September 1991). Film people at all levels had similar attitudes and sniffed at impractical theorists from academic institutions. 'They don't even know how to thread a Steenbeck' was a familiar cry. Graduates who entered the BBC showed a similar disdain for media degrees. Any academically 'respectable' degree

84

(usually a First in Sanskrit perhaps or Theology) proved intellectual worthiness. This then merely had to be 'topped up' or 'finished off' with professional in-house training. In short, the working world of British film, television and journalism was just as wary of educational qualifications in media studies as universities were suspicious of media studies as a valid intellectual discipline.

The industry was (and still is) strongly biased towards 'on-the-job' training. This was all very well when the industry did take on some training responsibility. The problem is now that the old informal training structure has gone and anyone wanting to enter the industry who expects effective on-the-job training is likely to be disappointed. Neither the BBC nor ITV can afford to train on a large scale, and because there are fewer permanent posts in these institutions, fewer people are being trained by them. If it used to be difficult in the past to get a staff job in the BBC or ITV, it will be even more of a problem in the future. Training will still be offered to core staff, but an increasingly large percentage of workers will be freelances who generally will be expected to have received their training elsewhere.

The crucial question, however, is where? The answer is that it will probably be through privately run, industry-sponsored schemes. However, these are unlikely to offer the broad systematic training which the BBC offered or anything approaching the rigorous apprenticeships that the craft unions sponsored. Private training schemes will pop up all over the place to meet demand, but most of them will be short-term and of varying quality and the users will have to pay. Inevitably, therefore, given this situation, more weight in the future will be placed on the courses offered by colleges and universities. Those who intend to go into the media industry should take account of this. The collapse of training provision in the industry has necessarily shifted the balance further towards the media courses provided by higher and further education, which are moving in to plug the gap.

University Media Courses

Higher education in Britain has traditionally been devoted to the pursuit of knowledge for its own sake. There was always a sort of snobbery about technical courses which dirtied the hands. Anything which smacked of vocationalism in higher education was regarded as illegitimate. Even within media studies courses the technical/vocational aspects of the curriculum were generally underplayed. Critical awareness was stressed above practical knowledge. Courses which took students into a studio and exposed them to the actual equipment were not highly regarded; too much (or even any!) emphasis on technical knowledge was considered intellectually limiting.

85

This attitude is finally beginning, slowly and painfully, to change. In the last ten years there has been a shake-up in higher education, thanks, in part, to the government's emphasis on the market-place and its determination to increase the numbers of students. The end result has been the erosion of academic elitism. The conversion of polytechnics into universities and increasing student numbers are two aspects of this trend.

More and more higher education is consumer-led; institutions of higher learning are no longer able to afford to ignore 'popular' courses in a world where they have to 'bid' for students. The government has used the funding weapon as a means of implementing change: the more students a university takes on, the more money it gets. While the educational reforms have their critics, what it means in practice is that the universities (including the former polytechnics) are having to offer courses which will attract 'the customers', that is, students.

What many customers want are media studies. Media studies is the fastest-growing university course in the country. Applications were up by 54 per cent for 1994-5 with 38,863 students attempting to gain a place on a media course (compared to 26,416 applications for maths and 21,442 for physics). Eighty universities now offer varying types of degrees which fall under the broad title of media studies (*Observer,* 21 January 1996). Communications and media studies courses everywhere are oversubscribed and are flooded with applicants. Since the entertainment industry is apparently going to be one of the powerhouses of the next century it appears inevitable that media courses of all sorts will burgeon. As higher education responds to the market-place, and to the impact of high technology on employment, it will have to accept that young people want knowledge and jobs in an expanding area.

Be warned, however: many media studies courses contain no element of practice or work experience and are in no way related to working in the industry concentrating instead on analysing and examining the 'texts' that film and television produce. They make no claims about preparing students for employment. Yet students who apply to academic university courses are frequently unaware of this. Many applicants for media studies degrees labour under a delusion that somehow, like a medical, engineering or accountancy degree, a media degree is a professional qualification and will provide an 'open sesame' into the audio-visual industry. It won't! Such a misapprehension is a recipe for disaster. Many media studies courses are very academic in their orientation and are a branch of cultural studies. Their lecturers are interested in media theory, and students who embark on such degrees can often be surprised to find themselves exploring the ideas of Foucault and Baudrillard and the more exotic realms of semiotics and gender studies. Media

86

degree courses which do have a technical and business component may put students in a more powerful position in entering a competitive audio-visual labour-market but again there is no guarantee.[2]

The Media Degree: Its Market Worthiness

School-leavers who want to enter the audio-visual industry (which is what this book is about) but who want to do a degree first are likely to find that in future a 'relevant' degree will have the edge over a degree in a more academic area. This is especially the case for courses that include a practical component. With BBC and ITV training cut back, and union power in retreat, would-be employers will be looking for students who already know something about the practical side of the industry. In market terms, over the next few years anyone who wants a job in the industry will find that the stock value of a degree in film, television, media or communications studies will increase vis-à-vis other degrees, particularly if it includes an element of practice perhaps combined with a work placement as part of the course.

At the present time the British Film Institute is carrying out a tracking study of people employed in the British television industry: 88 per cent in the 21-30 age group have received higher education and just under a quarter of them have done media studies, film and television studies or communication studies as a degree course. As this group moves into the higher echelons of the industry (as one presumes they will) the traditional bias against media degrees is likely to ease. Managers tend to employ people in their own image and likeness. The problem in the old days was that few managers had any experience of media degrees and were, consequently, prejudiced against them. This is set to change.

Practical Advice on the Media Degree

Just as the audio-visual industry was in the vanguard of change in employment, so the evolution of media degrees in universities and polytechnics heralds a shift in approach in higher education. Most degree courses will probably ignore the vocational element for some time to come (for as long as they can, if some academics have their way), but media degrees will not be able to do so. They are being driven towards a more vocational bias by the crisis in training in the industry at large. Indeed, as higher education and industry move closer together, the impact of one on the other will be an increasingly significant phenomenon in other industries and other degree courses as well. In the marketplace money speaks: if students demand to study film, video and television then universities, if they want to stay in 'business', will provide them with the chance. This means a major change in the ethos that has governed higher education in Britain since universities began.

However, a word of caution is in order: the change in higher education is not all positive; there are pitfalls to avoid. As higher education moves into the market-place, the onus is on the prospective student to be consumer-conscious and well-informed. One of the great strengths of higher education in Britain has been a rigorous control of standards: Britain's universities were notably uncorrupted. When only a very small percentage of people went on to university, and when the staff-to-student ratio was small, standards were very high. The awarding of degrees was very carefully supervised and there was a consistency about the courses offered and the levels which had to be reached. A degree from any institution of higher learning in Britain had a universal value.

The significance of this can be understood by looking at the United States, where there was little overall supervision. In some notorious cases small American colleges (usually in the South, it is said) would award degrees and doctorates to candidates regardless of their ability. Since the courses were not cheap, there was more than a whiff of 'buying a degree' about them. It was always necessary to know where an American degree came from: a doctorate in science from the Charismatic Christian College of Nowhere, Tennessee was obviously not to be compared with one from Harvard or the Massachusetts Institute of Technology. In the future, no matter what politicians and academics say, as student numbers increase in British universities, there will be an inevitable slippage in standards and supervision. In the race to grab students some institutions and departments will offer courses which may be inferior in quality, there will be more 'cowboy' or 'mickey mouse' courses around.

Some canny students ('customers') will see an advantage in this if some degrees offer an easy option. However, be warned: the industry is already favouring those with high standards. In a world where degrees have a vocational component, employers will quickly suss out the courses that produce well-qualified students. It is perhaps overstating the case to suggest that some media courses will be rip-offs, but students will have to be increasingly discriminating about the degree courses they choose to embark upon. There will be a much greater variation in what is on offer and there will be some poorly financed and under-resourced courses. Despite the ballyhoo about the free market, it is as well to note that shabby goods are one of the less attractive features of the increase in consumer choice.

Practical Advice

What practical advice, then, can be offered to the school-leaver who wants to study for a degree with the aim of ending up with a job in the industry? First and foremost, degrees that actually study film, television or modern communications will be increasingly valuable if the courses have a practical component, work placements, high standards and are close to the industry. This is part of the fall-out of the crisis in training and the shift to a more vocational element in higher education.

Secondly, school-leavers will have to become knowledgeable about the courses they wish to embark upon. In a tough, economically competitive climate where training may be difficult or very expensive to find after graduation, students should not start a three-year undergraduate course with the vague hope of getting into the industry. Some of the courses may qualify them for nothing. They should go to the college and university open-days, see what is available in terms of equipment, talk to the staff (and the students, if possible) and be prepared to ask pointed questions about the course-work, equipment and tutors. They should not trust the increasingly PR-type descriptions in the handbooks or the prospectuses.

Many people employed in higher education, even in media departments, have no first-hand knowledge of the film and television industry. They know the theory but have not practised the art of film- or programme-making. This is perfectly acceptable in a theoretical course, and higher education must never be solely about fitting people into the labour market. However, if a course has a practical component and the vocational element is what is attractive to the student, then the people who teach it should know that they are talking about. A lecturer who teaches students to write scripts for television, but who has never managed to sell one himself, should be treated with caution.

So what type of questions should prospective students ask? Some of the following may provide an idea:

How many students are there on the course?
What is the staff to student ratio?
Is there any hands-on training?
Are there work placements, and if so where are they?
Have the staff who teach practical components first-hand knowledge of the industry?
Have previous students found jobs?
Has the Department built up any close links with regional or national broadcasting or media companies?
Does the Department welcome guest lecturers from the industry?
Is the equipment in the department reasonably modern?

The last question is important because film and video equipment is very expensive and higher education is not wealthy: this is especially the case in the art colleges and arts faculties where most media studies are based. Higher education institutions are unlikely to be able to afford the equipment of a really up-to-date television station, but they should have access to technical information about the newest technology and the existing equipment should not be ancient. There has been some research on interactive video systems as a means of retraining people in television: similar software packages may be a viable option for colleges and universities in the future. CD-I holds out particular promise in this area. In addition, if the government's educational reforms are successful, there should be more employer-led industry involvement in college-based courses, particularly in terms of money and personnel, and this also should help.

Quality Control
The Broadcasting, Entertainment, Cinematograph and Theatre Union (BECTU) used to provide creditation of a few courses at certain institutions, colleges and universities. Central to the union's criteria was that the course should be as relevant as possible to the demands and requirements of the industry. In addition, however, they also wanted a theoretical component that included an understanding of technological development, industry trends and current and future practices, as well as an appreciation of the social, cultural and political context within which the media function. BECTU courses also had to incorporate 'a critical understanding of the influence the media have on public attitudes to issues of race, gender, sexuality, class disability and political beliefs'.

BECTU now liaises closely with Skillset, the industry training organisation (see Chapter 8 for more detail), and the whole system of course creditation is under review. At the time of writing the situation is fairly fluid as Skillset itself comes to grips with the vocational element in higher education. Higher education is changing so rapidly (as the colleges and universities adjust to the changes in the industry and in the way they themselves are funded) that it is extremely difficult to develop a system that monitors the courses on offer.

The significance of union accreditation in the past was that qualifications from certain colleges and universities entitled the holders to an automatic union ticket with their first job. Since the unions are not as powerful as they once were, this is no longer so vital. However, union accreditation did recognise high standards and was only ever awarded to those institutions that had excellent reputations for their combined theoretical and vocational provisions. Nowadays it is far more difficult to assess the value of what is on offer and it will take time for Skillset to evolve suitable criteria.

Factory Fodder for the Future

More than most, academics teaching media studies are involved in the central task of creating a new higher education system for the next century. However they are having to do it on a piecemeal, *ad hoc* basis, weighed down by an administrative and teaching burden that has increased enormously over the last few years and which leaves them with less and less time to create and sustain those values which traditionalists believe a university is all about. Many academics feel that presently there is a vacuum in educational philosophy, a lack of an overall synthesis. The government seems to believe that the emphasis on education and training is enough, that these are two halves of one whole. Many university teachers see this as inadequate to the task in hand and are wary of the idea that such a simple approach can be the solution to such complex problems.

Academics who are critical of the government's reforms in higher education argue that the emphasis on training springs, not from a concern about developing human potential but rather from a materialistic view of the workforce – as human fodder to stoke the industries of the future. In the next century employers will need skilled workers to slot into jobs to keep their industries profitable: the Conservative Party, as the party of employers, is prepared to provide this – or so the argument goes. Traditionally, British higher education has produced critical, analytical minds which have irritated politicians by questioning society and government. As universities and colleges move closer to the job market, and numbers expand, some observers believe that the critical, intellectual elite that has always dominated the universities will be reduced to an impotent rump. This is what some academics believe the government wants and the potential loss of this critical ideal is mourned in many quarters.

The claims for vocational-type training in many modern media courses aggravate these fears. Some academics believe that media degrees are moving away from the coherent critiques and analyses of the media in society that used to characterise the discipline and towards 'how to' courses in film and television production techniques and to an obsession with the wizardry of high technology. In other words, they believe that media studies in higher education are losing whatever intellectual content they had and are in the process of being redefined.

Other college and university staff welcome the new practical element because it means that students who wished for a practically oriented rather than a theoretical course can now be catered for. Previously such students followed theoretical courses half-heartedly: higher education which is now broader in its appeal is developing more targeted courses tailored to the particular wishes and desires of the more practical and technologically oriented students. Many lecturers also believe that one of the major effects of the reforms in higher education is that student opinion is now being taken into account more than it has ever been. Most lecturers accept and welcome this, while recognising that it could provoke some tension and strain in the short run.

On Your Guard!
In the 90s the word 'media' seems to have an incredible resonance for students. With university finances closely tied to the number of student who walk through the door, many departments feel themselves pressured to increase their student numbers by establishing degree courses with popular appeal. Courses and universities are now in the cut-throat business of attracting customers into their 'shop' and beating off their rivals, and there have been sinister rumours that, in some cases, existing courses are simply being renamed, incorporating the attractive and fashionable word media to create an up-to-date image. (Overseas students who pay higher fees are a particular quarry.)

At the present time the student consumer has little understanding of or protection from all this, a situation that worries many responsible lecturers and teachers. In the future there may have to be an equivalent to the Advertising Standards Council to monitor higher education and a *Which* magazine to test out and inform students about the best courses on offer. There is a strongly expressed unease on the academic shop-floor that some courses make extravagant claims they can not deliver and that students should be aware of the danger.

Media students must also be aware of the persistent hostility in some areas of the industry towards media degrees. Many of the people working in the industry have little understanding of the shift in philosophy in higher education, many of them went to university before the reforms or never went to university at all. Consequently they nurture dark thoughts about incompetent lecturers, new and fashionable courses and 'trumped up' graduates waving their useless degrees around. Again, this suspicion and down-grading of other professions is a peculiar British trait and is especially disturbing when it is combined with a rampant anti-intellectualism which can still be found in many areas of the industry. In part, however, it is fed by the naivety of some students who believe that a media degree is a professional qualification which will guarantee entrance at the highest levels. It must be emphasised over and over again that a media degree is only a beginning, that there is no substitute for experience, and that working in the industry is no longer about being employed on a staff job by the BBC, ITV or Channel Four. Today the entertainment industry is a broad church and runs the gamut from the corporate video world to the computer games sector. New graduates who can do the job and know that they are good must simply grit their teeth and prove their critics wrong.

Summing Up

Media studies that *combine* the theoretical and the practical, technical and academic knowledge, are tailor-made for the educational and training climate of the future. Their time has come; purely academic degrees will be of less significance except in terms of university research. The point of the government's reforms in higher education is to increase the practical work and industry-related component (which is part of the reason why the formerly separate government ministries of Education and Employment are now combined into a single Department of Education and Employment). In future one cannot simply have a good degree and expect that training will be tacked on for free in the workplace: it won't be. Proven skills in technical and practical matters will be more highly valued as the inequality between vocational and academic training diminishes. However, the new system has not yet settled down and it will take time for the new approach to education to be accepted and understood.

In any case, neither academic or vocational qualifications will be of any use at all if not backed by enthusiasm and hard work. This is an industry which values commitment more than most. Georgina Henry, deputy editor and former media editor of the *Guardian*, says that in her experience, 'It matters not a whit if an applicant has a BA in media studies. What counts is their experience, talent and determination' (*Observer*, 21 January 1996). We will discuss the character side of the issue later in this book but, in the meantime, take note!

Other Degrees

This chapter has concentrated on the shift in the perception of media degrees and on their increasing significance (and on the persisting hostility in many quarters towards them). There are, however, other areas of study which will be of value and importance to the industry. As we have seen, communications are an increasingly significant asset in a country's viability in the globalised information economy. Policy issues will therefore play a large political role. In the 21st century those who have studied communications policy will have an advantage. Law degrees that consider transfrontier and copyright issues will be useful, as will degrees in politics, if they encompass media policy. Degrees in drama or art and design have always been valuable in the industry. Drama training can be useful for film directors and, of course, for performers. Art and design degrees, especially when they have a work-related component, will help people find employment in areas such as

93

costume, make-up, graphics and scenic design. In the digitised world there is the need for computer experts, right across the board from animation to management. In fact, the best media studies degrees, from the industry viewpoint, are those responding quickly to the information revolution and incorporating courses associated with the electronic media.

However, it is students with degrees in financial services such as accountancy who may be in particularly short supply. As we noted above, in the past television was partially sheltered from the marketplace. This is no longer the case. Finding the money, securing the loans, persuading the backers to release more funds, have all become part and parcel of the making of programmes for television, just as they have always been for the making of feature films. While making money might not seem as obviously exciting and creative as making films, it will become of major importance to creative survival. There will be no shortage of jobs for those with the right financial qualifications. Of course, a narrow accountant mentality at the top can be a disaster in a creative industry – a matter for heated debate at the present time.

Further Education and Training
There are all sorts of further education colleges offering courses in media crafts leading to qualifications varying from a BTEC to Royal Society of Arts or City and Guilds awards. The principle that applies to degrees affects these qualifications also: the crisis in training will increase their usefulness in securing a job. After all, if the industry is not training people as it used to do, it has to look elsewhere. When employers want a new recruit they will want someone who has received some form of training; if this has been acquired in further education, then so be it. Again, just as in degree courses, financial skills are very much in demand. The industry needs people who know about VAT and how the Inland Revenue functions. Knowledge of contract administration, performing rights and payments are also much in demand.

At the present time there is a revolution going on with the introduction of a new system of vocational qualifications that puts a premium value on on-the-job competence (rather as the unions used to do). This will affect the courses offered in further education and the whole education, training and employment picture. Anyone leaving school, college or university and wishing to enter an industry must understand the implications of what could be a massive sea change in the British attitude to vocational training. Employers need to understand it too. The next chapter will examine the new vocational qualifications in detail.

94

Notes

1. In the end, it may be decided that the British managed the conflict between deregulation and public service television better than other countries, but it was touch-and-go all the way and the unforeseen fall of Margaret Thatcher in 1990 probably contributed most to the survival of a modified public service ethos.
2. Details about the increasing range of choices offered by colleges and universities in the fields of film, television and video can by found in *Media Courses UK*, an annual guide edited by Lavinia Orton and published by the British Film Institute. For more detailed information see the section on BFI publications at the back of this book.

7

THE BRAVE NEW WORLD
OF VOCATIONAL TRAINING

Except for the favoured few who inherit fortunes or win the lottery, most people have to earn a living. For all of us the cherished dream is to work at a job we thoroughly enjoy so that there is scarcely a barrier between the workplace and our leisure activities. For our work to be play, and our play to earn money, is probably one of the most deeply held desires of contemporary life. Perhaps it is for this reason that so many young people today are attracted by the idea of working in the entertainment industry.

The *Concise Oxford Dictionary* defines vocation as a 'divine' call to, or 'sense of fitness' for, a career or occupation. While the divine element in career choices is perhaps not exactly compatible with modern ideas, the sense of fitness is very important. When jobs fit people and people fit jobs the sum total is an increase in human happiness.

Unfortunately, the sharp division between the academic and the non-academic in British society (often class-based) has had over the years a negative influence on British economic success and productivity. A largely apathetic, unqualified, untrained workforce has been economically uncompetitive and Britain has slipped behind Western Europe, Japan and the United States in economic strength. In the last decade, however, we have begun to wake up to the deficiencies which our education system has fostered and the debilitating effect this has had on economic prosperity. As a result, there is a new emphasis on the idea of continuous training, initiated at school and continued later in the workplace.

Since 1986 an ambitious system of vocational training has been gradually introduced into Britain which, it is hoped, will no longer carry an implication of intellectual inferiority: people who missed out on education after the age of sixteen will now have opportunities to seek qualifications later in life. It has finally been recognised that British education was in many ways more suitable for the 19th than the 21st century, and steps have been taken to remedy the situation.

Chapter 6 touched briefly on the 'inequality of esteem' between education and training and the injurious effect this has had on British economic success. The cornerstone of the Conservative government's attack on the problem has been the introduction of a post-sixteen training qualification system, the GNVQ (General National Vocational Qualification) for those in full-time education and the National Vocational Qualification (NVQ; in Scotland, the Scottish Vocational Qualification – SVQ) for those at work. If GNVQs and N/SVQs succeed, they could be the most important reform of the British education system since the 1944 Butler Act.

The development of the GNVQs and the N/SVQs is the culmination of the government's efforts to bring education, training and employment closer together. This was the central aim of the government papers *Working Together: Education and Training* (London: HMSO, Cmnd 9832, July 1986), the *Review of Educational Qualification in England and Wales* (London: The Manpower Services Commission and the Department of Education and Science, 1986) and the 1994 White Paper *Competitiveness: Helping Business to Win*.

The 1994 White Paper expressed the underlying philosophy of the reforms: 'The most successful nations in the future will be those which develop high quality, skilled and motivated workforces, and make good use of them'. On the whole, both the political Left and Right approve of the new emphasis on training, although the government has been criticised for not providing sufficient funds for the job to be done properly. Whatever the deficiencies, training is now a major priority on the political agenda and anyone currently entering the job market must understand what is happening and come to grips with the changes because they are going to have a major impact on employees in the workplace of the future.

If all goes according to plan, the traditional gap between the graduate and 'the rest' will no longer exist. Practical work and on-the-job training will garner as much respect as the theoretical, academic education that used to be the prerogative of the small elite. The result ought to be a highly skilled workforce, trained to do jobs they enjoy. This has enormous implications for all sides of British industry: perhaps the audio-visual industry more than most.

The route into higher education in Britain has always been very clear, straightforward and well-understood (at least by teachers, academics and the middle classes). Most people recognised that 'a degree means something', even if they were not sure exactly what. In contrast, the provision of further education and training were always something of a muddle – even chaotic, confusing and complicated. It is doubtful whether the vast majority of people in Britain has ever really understood how the training system worked. The routes towards vocational qualifications have been incomprehensible to many young people at school and also to those who, having found higher education closed to them, wished later to train or retrain but were utterly confused by the alternatives on offer.

The accrediting bodies in further education were, and are, various and include: BTEC (the Business and Technology Education Council), the RSA (Royal Society of Arts) Examination Board, and the City and Guilds of London Institute. While these were absolutely excellent, considerable incoherence in the pattern of courses and the qualifications they offered did create problems. The diversity of provision discouraged many young people. 'Where is it all going to lead?' was the usual question, and when there was no obvious link-up between the qualifications and the working world there has been no truly satisfactory answer. As a result, in the past many young people in Britain simply left school at sixteen because there seemed no point in staying on. Had the vocational courses on offer seemed straightforward (in the manner of a degree course route), or had they in some way qualified students directly for employment, or even set them on an alternative route to higher education, this would have been a different matter. The system, however, never functioned in a clear-cut way.

Over the past decade the government has tried to tidy up the whole area and create order and simplicity out of the chaos. Unfortunately, because so much has to be sorted out, there has been a proliferation of initiatives, only contributing to further confusion. We are assured that in the end all will be well and training will be sorted out, but it has meant that the pace and scale of change has produced its own problems. One needs almost an official qualification in 'new training initiatives' to understand the twists and turns in Government policy on education and training and employment.

Employer Involvement

One of the major principles to keep in mind is that a fundamental part of government dogma is that education and training are no longer the sole prerogative of educators, and that continuous retraining must be a fact of working life. Employers are increasingly involved in 'education', and educational institutions and the workplace are moving closer together. This is the pivot of government policy and, as has been mentioned earlier, an important symbolic transition occurred when the formerly separate government departments of employment and education were merged into one – the Department of Education and Employment. In schools, the introduction of the National Curriculum, with its emphasis on science and technology, was also part of the whole reforming thrust, and in higher education the provision for widening access (although without a pro-rata increase in resources) was another piece in the jigsaw of educational reform.

The Forerunner – The Technical and Vocational Education Initiative (TVEI)
A word of caution is in order: one of the major obstacles to an understanding of what has happened, and what is happening, in education and training is the bureaucratic delight in acronyms. Since policy changes all the time, organisations come and go with astonishing rapidity. Some bodies remain basically the same but alter their names (and acronyms) with changes in policy emphasis. Those 'in the know' fling the jargon freely around to the immense bewilderment of everyone else.

TVEI was one of the first training/educational reforms introduced by the Conservative government in 1983. Although the reform has now been concluded, in a sense it paved the way at school level for what has happened elsewhere and is worth mentioning because of this. TVEI was not actually a course but represented a philosophy of education, the aim of which was to orient schoolchildren to the world of work and provide them with information about where they were going in the future. Schools, the argument ran, had existed in a vacuum for far too long: they had been quarantined from the real world. This isolated children who had no conception of what would happen once their schooldays were over. Suddenly at the age of fourteen they were faced with the crunch: what were they going to do when they left school? TVEI aimed to orient the 14-19 age group towards their future in the workplace. It is also attempted to reshape the educational curriculum to include vocational elements with a technical bias so that education would be more relevant to employment. TVEI tried to enhance students' technological awareness and knowledge. (A large proportion of TVEI schemes included media studies because media studies fitted in well with the philosophical concept.) Training and Enterprise Councils (TECs) have eventually taken over TVEI-type responsibilities.

Training and Enterprise Councils (TECs) – What Are They?
The Training and Enterprise Councils (TECs) were set up in 1989. They are 81 independent companies which have multimillion-pound contracts with the government. Their purpose is to forge a partnership for business information and training and they have gradually taken over the local work of the government's Training Enterprise and Education Directorate (TEED) which is the central government body. An important part of the TEC remit is the development of

links between education and industry. (Some suspicious people see the TECs as Trojan horses paving the way for the government to snatch education and training funds from the hands of local authorities.) TECs have varied in quality and success across the country. Some TECs, especially in Scotland, have worked splendidly because their directors have forged strong links between school, colleges and local industries.

COMPACT – Closer to the Classroom

COMPACT is a scheme that forges actual links and exchanges between industries/employers and schools. Employers guarantee jobs with training to young people who reach an agreed standard of education. Students at school go on work placements and employers are given the opportunity to provide input into the educational curriculum. The overall aim is to strengthen employment opportunities for school-leavers by allowing them to gain direct knowledge of working environments and of the skills associated with particular jobs.

Other Training/Education Initiatives

Other initiatives have included the Certificate of Pre-Vocational Education (CPVE; now obsolete) the Professional Industrial and Commercial Updating (PICKUP), and Enterprise in Higher Education (EHE). EHE is a national programme helping higher educational institutions to develop in an enterprising and business-conscious way. During their studies, university students are brought into closer contact with the world of business, often through work placements (this is part of the trend discussed in Chapter 6).

In 1996 Education and Employment Secretary, Gillian Shephard, stressed her own 'big idea', a scheme called 'Closer to the Workplace' which is another refinement of all these schemes. Shephard proposes giving 14-16 years olds more experience of actual employment. When the notion was first mooted in 1995 there was some outrage expressed at the idea of work placements for 14-year-olds. The Minister, however, is persisting and working with employers to increase their links with schools.

National Vocational Qualifications

The jewel in the government's crown, however, is the post-sixteen provision of the General National Certificate in Vocation Education (GNVQ)and the National (and Scottish) Vocational Qualification system. These are the most significant breakthroughs and have momentous implications for those proposing to enter the workforce now and in the future. The basic aim of the GNVQ/NVQ/SVQs is to change the whole of the British qualification system from school through to further and higher education and right into the workplace. It proposes to weave education and training into a coherent and rational pattern.

How the Vocational System Works
In 1986 the government set up the National Council for Vocational Qualification (the Scottish equivalent is SCOTVEC, which was established somewhat earlier) to oversee the new system. The Council's mandate is to establish the NVQs in a coherent national framework that facilitates open access (meaning that anyone can try for an NVQ) and progression (people can move up the various levels). The Council accredits awarding bodies but it does not award NVQs itself. It also has to ensure that the NVQ qualification will be relevant to the needs of industry. As we have seen, the involvement of the employer is an important axiom of government policy and employers are a key element in the new structure. They are actively encouraged to invest in the training of their workforces.

The Council's major responsibility is to secure standards of occupational competence and to ensure that the new vocational qualifications are based on these standards. It is upon this idea of competence that the N/SVQs rest. At the present time a complete framework of vocational qualifications for all occupational sectors, 'from pest control to ballet dancing', is being designed and set up. (This includes the film, television and video industry, but more of that later.) Each industry has to set up an Industry Training Organisation (ITO) which agrees on the job descriptions and national standards required for their workforce. The ITOs scrutinise what their particular industry does and arranges for analyses and breakdowns of the jobs and tasks which workers carry out and which could qualify them for an N/SVQ at a particular level. Each N/SVQ is developed by the people who know the industry. Candidates achieve an N/SVQ by demonstrating competence in a given role against the standards set by the industry.

The ITO for the audio-visual industry is called Skillset and the one for performers generally is The Arts and Entertainment Training Council. ITOs have to take proper account of future needs in the industry, especially with regard to technology, markets and employment patterns (this is of particular significance to the media industry).

It is worth repeating that *competence* is the key word. NVQs are about employees having the skills, knowledge and understanding to do their jobs well in the real world. It is not about written tests. It is about practice not theory. It means the ability to perform a whole job to the performance level expected in the actual employment situation. A competence statement is not about a narrow skill and knowledge

101

specification: it matches the job performed in reality and includes the ability to adapt to new situations. N/SVQs encompass not just technical ability but the capacity to organise, plan, innovate (if required) and to respond to non-routine events. They may also include, if these are part of the job, interpersonal skills, that is, dealing with people such as colleagues, clients, customers, subordinates and superiors.

The revolutionary aspect of the N/SVQs is the proposal to recognise learning acquired through experience at work. *N/SVQs are not a training system*; nor are they about courses or curricula, they are about *qualifications*. They have a strategic significance in that it is expected that they will encourage employees to seek further training and employers to provide training as they identify their industry needs. The criteria for the award of an N/SVQ have nothing to do with the manner in which the person achieved the required level of competence. This does not mean, however, that people arrive at the standards required without undertaking training. As N/SVQs become more universal they are already leading to a growth in the demand for post-sixteen education and training and also for adult learning opportunities provided by colleges. N/SVQs are also now offering an alternative route into higher education.

The besetting sin of the British educational system used to be that most people had their last contact with any form of training, learning and qualification by the age of sixteen. People had their one shot at being 'educated' at school and, if they missed the boat for further training, they missed out for ever (with the praiseworthy exception of the Open University). Thanks to N/SVQs, people will be encouraged to seek education and training throughout their lives.

It is important to realise that plans for N/SVQs run parallel with the government's plans to expand university places (discussed in the previous chapter). The hope is that Britain will truly become a 'learning society'. The logic is: educated societies are more successful; educated people are better off; technologically skilled societies do well. N/SVQs are designed to develop a flexible, multi-skilled, adaptable workforce that is better able to cope with the continuously changing demands of businesses in the future.

Upholders of the British class system have often put forward the idea that the so-called working class did not really want to be educated. Evidence suggests that the demand for post-compulsory education and training is on the contrary a function of supply. The experience of the Open University, and the expansion of polytechnics and colleges of higher education during the 80s, suggest that British people actually do wish to learn if they are provided with opportunities, if the entry route is clear and comprehensible, and if they are not humiliated in the process (here A levels are a stumbling-block).

Some people still fail to see the necessity for work-based qualifications, and particularly for a system which is as all-embracing as the N/SVQs propose to be. Qualifications, however, are psychologically important because they give people a sense of self-respect and make them more ambitious. Many people in Britain feel they 'failed' at school and this puts them off education and training for life. With N/SVQs, if someone is already doing a job to the right standard, as set down by a particular industry, then he or she can immediately get the credit towards an N/SVQ. NVQs have now been developed in many industries from engineering to health care. At the beginning of 1996 there were around 800 N/SVQs in place and more than a million had been awarded

N/SVQs now recognise five levels of achievement, with Level One the basic and Level Five the most complex:

Level One shows competence in the performance of a range of work activities. These are mainly routine and predictable or are tasks that provide a broad foundation primarily as a basis for progression;

Level Two means an individual can do a range of work activities and some of these are complicated and non-routine. People can take responsibility for working on their own and may also work with others as part of a team;

Level Three again involves complicated non-routine tasks and there is also a responsibility to guide and control the work of other people. The job involves a great deal of responsibility and the necessity of working on one's own;

Level Four shows competence in the performance of complex, technical specialised and professional work activities including those associated with design, planning and problem solving. At Level Four the individual takes a great deal of responsibility for his or her work and it may be necessary to show competence in supervision or management at this level;

Level Five means doing a range of complicated activities in a wide variety of working conditions. The individual carries a great deal of responsibility and often allocates resources. He or she also designs, plans, carries out, and checks on other people's work as well as their own.

The great attraction of N/SVQs is their portability. They will, in fact, represent a logbook of work experience.

GNVQs

The government has also introduced a new qualification system called the General National Vocational Qualifications mainly directed at 16 to 19-year-old students in schools and colleges. The GNVQ is an alternative to the academic routes offered by GCSEs and A Levels. GNVQs began with phased introduction in one hundred educational institutions in the autumn of 1992 and covered five areas: Art and Design; Business; Health and Social Care; Leisure and Tourism; and Manufacturing. The system proved to have some problems and changes were made before it came into general use in 1993. In September 1994 three new GNVQs were added; Construction and the Built Environment; Hospitality and Catering; and Science.

GNVQ students must gain three core skills units in communication, mathematical calculation and information technology. GNVQs are available at three levels: a *Foundation* GNVQ which is equivalent to four GCSEs at grades D and below and is usually a one-year full-time course; an *Intermediate* GNVQ which is equivalent to four or five GCSEs at grades A to C and again is usually a one-year full-time course; and an *Advanced* GNVQ which usually takes two years and is equivalent to about two or more GCE A levels (see below).

The key fact about GNVQs is that students take more responsibility for their own learning, they develop skills in real areas of work such as doing projects, planning and organising events, designing products and services, and they also usually have the opportunity for work experience. The most relevant existing GNVQs for the Film and Television Industry will probably be in the areas of Art and Design and Construction and Built Environment.

The Dearing Report which came out in March 1996 and reviewed qualifications for 16 to 19 year-olds made certain recommendations about GNVQs. As pointed out in Chapter 5 the basic principle now is to bring A levels and GNVQs into close alignment, enabling students to build up portfolios in A levels and GNVQs. The proposal is to rename the Advanced GNVQ and call it the 'Applied A level'.[1]

Benefits

Only time will tell if the GNVQ and N/SVQ system will be successful, but research does support the view that a workforce that has qualified in some way is more efficient because it is more self-confident and motivated than one that is not qualified.[2] In addition, the system has a built-in flexibility: employers will be able to update skill requirements as jobs come and go (the average British company only lasts five years), while employees will go on earning qualifications to adapt to new circumstances. Everyone agrees that there will be a sea change in the way training will be carried out. Murray Butcher, a divisional manager at City and Guilds, has described it as a new culture, where 'training should become an integrated aspect of every workplace, as common as the telephone and as frequent as the weekly pay cheque' (quoted in *Arts and Entertainment Training Council: Training Matters*, No. 3 December 1991). Research indicates that over 90 per cent of adults in a survey had heard of the NVQs and almost three-quarters of them knew that they were competence-based.[3]

Critics

On paper the whole National Vocational Qualification initiative looks good but there have been criticisms of the way it has worked in practice. The 1995 Beaumont Report highlighted a number of problems to do with too much bureaucracy and the assessment criteria and some offending NVQs had to be redesigned. There were worries also about the government, the National Council for Vocational Qualification and the TECs doing too little to ensure a uniform standard in training and assessment. Older established training qualifications which were directly linked to qualifications (and which NVQs are supposed to replace) are still better known. In addition, despite the government 'hype', many employers, especially small companies, have shown a marked reluctance to invest in the training of their workforce. Since research indicates that the most common single form of motivation for individuals to achieve an NVQ comes through the encouragement and support of employers, their contribution is crucial.

It is also apparent that some people still find it hard to understand qualifications which are not course-related. Some critics think that the new Vocational Qualification system will never work in Britain because, despite the rhetoric, skills will never acquire 'parity of esteem' with academic knowledge. If this is true, then the future looks ominous for the British economy. The fact is that we have to have a better-trained workforce or our competitors will outstrip us. Academic qualifications are extremely valuable, but in Britain they have led to the denigration of practical skills. If N/SVQs, GNVQs and the proposed 'Applied A level' help to counteract this, they will serve their purpose.

However, it is certainly the case that some educators are disturbed by the GNVQ and the NVQ approach. They dislike the speed with which the whole system has been introduced and point out that, since standards are industry-initiated, there is a tendency to lose sight of any notion of broad educational values. Inevitably, employers take a utilitarian and somewhat mechanistic approach to their workforce and skills are emphasised to the exclusion of everything else. Any underlying theory and philosophy of education is missing: in other words too much training and too little education. There has been criticism that an approach to training that consists of working backwards from an industry's perceived need is flawed. The accusation that the system treats young people as the fodder for the businesses of the future may have some truth in it and there is a sense that GNVQ students, despite all the talk of flexibility, are being directed into fixed areas too early. In addition, while in theory it is wonderful to allow students at the GNVQ level to work at their own pace, in practice there have been financial constraints and most experienced educators do not really understand the concept of students negotiating their own learning.

Degrees versus GNVQ and N/SVQs?
What about degrees versus N/SVQs? will it be worth going straight into higher education or will it be better to go into further education via the N/SVQ route? The question cannot really be put like that. Degrees will always be valuable to the individual, and, if they have a technical component, increasingly valuable for the employer. They also indicate a certain intellectual competence and development. What the N/SVQ system should mean, however, is that the vocational and technical route will no longer be looked down upon and the overwhelming prestige of the degree could very well diminish vis-à-vis a more practical training. Also, since N/SVQs now provide an alternative routes into higher education for those who want it, this will mean the end of the one-shot chance at higher education and a lowering of the frontiers between higher and further education and training. There should be no need to compare other qualifications to the degree: they will all be part and parcel of the education and training provision. The particular benefit of the N/SVQs is that people who have missed out on education and training and who previously have never been able to qualify in anything (even though they were highly competent) may now have their abilities recognised and will then be encouraged to go on to seek out further training to gain higher levels of qualifications.

Industries that are strongly skill-based have always valued standards of competence. In the audio-visual industries, and especially in film, union recognition of skills and practice has always been more important than any theoretical knowledge because it was being able 'to do the job' which mattered. The question to ask then is: What impact is the new system of vocational qualifications making on the film, television and video industry? The next chapter will consider in more detail the effect of the N/SVQs on the film, television and video industry.

Summing Up
In the past, many young people failed to finish the punishing horserace which the British called an education system. Failure at school sapped confidence and interest and for most people there was an apathetic drift into jobs that were rarely enjoyed. The idea of choosing what we wanted to do was an unrealistic dream. The world of work was often dull

and boring. Jobs were endured: real life began at the end of the day or week. With little education, and virtually no training, most people could find no way into interesting jobs in industries that were, and could afford to be, highly selective in their intake.

However, for the few who passed the finishing-post and went on to college or university, the situation was not so dire. They were part of an educated elite who were somehow entitled to 'an interesting career' as a reward for jumping the academic hurdles. Graduates were rare and favoured souls who usually got the plum positions, often enjoyed their jobs and, moreover, were well-paid for doing so. Even among the favoured few, however, jobs in the media were thin on the ground. Only 'the brightest and the best' were selected, especially for the rarefied world of broadcasting.

In the last decade, however, we have begun to wake up to the deficiencies of our education system and the debilitating effect this has had on economic prosperity. As a result, there is a new emphasis on vocational training and, perhaps more importantly, on 'retraining'. 'Training' will no longer carry an implication of intellectual inferiority, and people who missed out on education after the age of sixteen will now have opportunities to seek qualifications later in life. In future the gap between the graduate and 'the rest' will no longer be so vast. If all goes to plan, practical work and on-the-job training will finally be given 'parity of esteem' with the theoretical, academic education of the graduate elite. Indeed, the lines between education and training will have dissolved. The result could be a highly skilled workforce, trained to do jobs they enjoy. This has enormous implications for all sides of British industry: perhaps the audio-visual industry more than most.

Notes

1. Ron Dearing, *Review of Qualifications for 16-19 Year Olds* (Hayes, Middlesex: SCAA Publications, March 1996).
2. *See* Geoff Mason, S. J. Prais and Bart van Ark, *Vocational Education and Productivity in The Netherlands and Britain* (London: National Institute of Economic and Social Research, November 1990). This compared biscuit factories in The Netherlands and in Britain and showed that the British often had the more expensive and modern equipment but were less efficient and productive than the Dutch. In Britain the workforce was untrained, while the Dutch workers were trained and committed to the job. On the whole this meant that the Dutch factory functioned efficiently and that the Dutch could handle problems well, for example when the equipment broke down.
3. Research conducted by Jonathan and Ruth Winterton of the Work Organisation Research Unit and reported in *Implementing NVQs: Barriers to Individuals* available from the Department for Education and Employment, Moorfoot, Sheffield, S1 4PQ.

8

TRAINING OPTIONS IN THE
BROADCAST, FILM AND VIDEO INDUSTRY:
Getting In and Other Problems

The ongoing revolution in training is having a major impact on the film, television and video industry. This chapter will examine the training system presently being developed under the direction of the Industry Training Organisation – Skillset – and, against the background of Skillset's broader activities, will also examine the opportunities for what is generally referred to as 'new-entrant training', in other words, the very few, small-scale highly competitive schemes that help people 'get in' to the industry.

Any careers book that portrays the 'getting in' process as simple is simply not worth the paper it is written on. Although today the media industry is more permeable, less cliquish and less elitist than ever before, it is still difficult for newcomers without contacts to breach the barriers in any sector. People in this industry like people they know, and feel they can rely on, so new entrants find it especially difficult. Recent research carried out by the British Film Institute indicated that 38 per cent of 21–30-years-olds obtained their first job though personal contacts.[1]

Getting in requires perseverance and dedication. It also requires knowledge and understanding (which is why Part One of this book was written). As we have seen in Chapter 6 a media degree is no job guarantee. The training route is equally problematic, partly because an efficient universal system is still not in place in the United Kingdom, although Skillset is making a huge difference.

The Training Crisis
Chapter 5 showed how, at the beginning of the 90s, training was in crisis. The industry, which relied on 'on-the-job' training, suddenly found that the system was falling apart. There were many contributory factors including: the recession, which made many employees in the film and broadcasting industries redundant; the tightening of financial belts at the BBC and ITV; the decline of union power; and

the effect of the franchise auction, which had led to redundancies and unemployment in ITV. Some of the new franchise holders for Channel Three were not producer/broadcasters in the old ITV mode, they were publisher/broadcasters on the lines of Channel Four. Thames Television, a producer/broadcaster company, had slimmed down its workforce from 1,400 to 1,200 for its franchise bid but still lost out to Carlton Communications. When Carlton, a publisher/broadcaster, took over from Thames in 1993, it was very lightly staffed with a permanent employee-base of around 400.[2]

The Contract Culture

All this meant changes in the workplace, especially in television. The days of a 'career' in broadcasting, in the sense of a lifetime job, have gone forever for most people. By the mid 90s working in broadcasting was showing a marked similarity to working in film, where freelancing has always been much more common and where people are always hired on contract for specific short-term periods. Even if, for some employees, short term contracts were renewed continuously, the contract culture created a nervous and uncertain working climate. Instead of a few, large seemingly permanent units of production there were now numerous, smaller, unstable and volatile companies, all of them exposed to the bracing climate of the market-place. Small production companies struggled from commission to commission and, to survive, their owners-cum-producers worked their employees, and themselves, harder and harder. With the recession the number of jobs decreased overall and large numbers of unemployed and semi-employed television workers began to compete for each job. According to one expert 'the centre of gravity of the industry [was] shifting towards a casualised labour force of the kind which characterised manual jobs in the 19th century'.[3]

About 60 per cent of workers in the British audio-visual industry today are freelances. Many of these were trained 'yesterday' under the old BBC/ITV systems. It is perfectly clear that rapid changes in technology will mean that workers will have to train and retrain as often as the demands of the industry require, but the problem in the new era is where can they find any retraining and, perhaps more crucially, who is going to pay! In the old public service days the BBC and ITV would have automatically updated the skills of their largely permanent workforce.

Employers also have problems, especially in the smaller companies. Functioning in a cut-throat, competitive market with low profit margins, they cannot afford to train new staff and yet the pool of highly trained workers is diminishing. In addition, how do they evaluate a prospective employee's competence? One of the exquisite ironies in the early 90s was that employers, who formerly detested and resented union power, often had to ask prospective film employees if they held a union card because it was a guarantee of competence. In the new open market many employers have had their fingers burned through allowing inexperienced and inadequately trained (but cheap) staff to touch expensive equipment. Even its critics began grudgingly to acknowledge that the union system, while it was cumbersome, unfair and restrictive, had trained people very well.

The Training Levy

In 1993 problems associated with the increasing casualisation of the workforce, especially in the independent sector, prompted employers, working through PACT (Producers' Alliance for Cinema and Television), to establish an independent production training levy. At the time of writing the levy is 0.25 per cent of total overheads and budgeted costs and is debited against the production fee to a maximum of £6,250. Most of this money goes into Skillset's Freelance Training Fund. Skillset, the Industry Training Organisation for the Broadcast, Film and Video Industry, has emerged as the prime mover in the industry's overall training strategy.

Skillset – Industry Training Organisation

Skillset is the industry body which, in the 90s, stepped into the breach and has since brokered the huge organisational and financial arrangements associated with training. Skillset is the official name of the Industry Training Organisation (ITO) and Industry Lead Body (ILO) for the Broadcast, Film and Video industry (see Chapter 7) and since 1993 it has had the difficult task of laying the foundations of the NVQ infrastructure. The groups originally involved in Skillset's foundation were the Advertising Film and Video Producers' Association (AFVPA), the BBC, Channel Four, the Federation of Entertainment Unions (FEU), ITV, the International Visual Communication Association (IVCA) and the Producers' Alliance for Cinema and Television (PACT): in other words, a powerhouse of industry employers and unions.

Skillset was formally launched in January 1993 and since then has achieved much. On-the-job competence, which played such a great part in the old film union training system is, of course, a central plank of the NVQ philosophy and it is Skillset which has the responsibility for getting the whole vocational scheme up and running. It has set a pace for action and efficiency that is the envy of other Industry Training Organisations and, in its second year of operation, won the Good Practice

110

Award of the National Council of Industry Training Organisations (the ITO 'BAFTA'). Skillset's stated mission is 'to encourage the delivery of informed training provision so the British Broadcast Film and Video industry's technical, creative and economic achievements are maintained and improved [and] to respond effectively to structural, technical and market changes in the UK and abroad in order to enhance the industry's national and international reputation for quality'. A key role for Skillset, as one would expect given the philosophy and rhetoric of government reforms, is to assist employers with decisions connected with the resourcing of training. Skillset's work falls into three main areas: *informing and influencing; producing standards and qualifications*; and *investment*. [4]

Informing and Influencing

In 1988 a number of interested parties, troubled by the training crisis, commissioned a report called 'Skill Search' which analysed employment patterns, training provision and skill shortages throughout the industry.[5] The report, which was published in January 1990, surveyed about 8,000 broadcasters and freelances and was an important stage in the 'mapping' of the industry. With the N/SVQs in view, 'Skill Search' set out to identify the broad functional groups, the existing occupational standards and current qualifications appropriate to each sector of the industry. Trade unions and professional associations were asked to submit a complete list of job titles, staffing structures and membership grades. The result was a list of over 800 different job titles! This process was the beginning of a systematic analysis of industry jobs.

Obviously, rationalisation was necessary and a working party was set up to review jobs and designate common functions based on knowledge of job content. The exercise showed that the various sectors of the industry were converging and that it made sense to integrate both job titles and the terms used in production.

The eventual establishment of Skillset was part of the industry's response to the original 'Skill Search' report. Skillset has continued to do research and has produced its own high-quality surveys which have examined employment trends and training needs. These have included an analysis of technical grades and set crafts, and freelance workers in features. There have also been media surveys of employment trends in Wales, the Midlands and Scotland and of women freelances. At the time of writing, Skillset is examining the patterns and training needs of Broadcast Journalists and Broadcast Engineers. For young people Skillset has produced an excellent *Careers Information* booklet and, working with the BFI, it is developing a data-base (updated on a yearly basis) with information about college and university courses.

111

Producing Standards and Qualifications: Skillset and the NVQs – A Brief background

In 1991 hundreds of technical, production, craft and design professionals met together to draft standards for what had been identified as the fifteen main occupations in the industry (following on from the 'mapping of the industry' exercise originally carried out by 'Skill Search'). In 1992 the draft standards were distributed for consultation with the industry and other interested agencies. Consultation meetings were held throughout the UK and there were also briefing sessions at twenty regional meetings. Circulated widely, the standards were discussed by key organisations including those representing broadcasters, independent producers, trade unions, associations, guilds and freelances. The Department of Employment then selected Skillset to develop an implementation plan as part of a pilot NVQ programme.

In 1993 Camera, Lighting, Sound Production, Research and Journalism were chosen as priority areas and working groups of industry professionals began to design qualification structures and assessment guidelines for the first thirteen N/SVQs. The Open University agreed to work in partnership with Skillset to set up quality-control and jointly award the new qualifications. The thirteen qualifications were piloted by a wide range of companies including the BBC, Granada, Samuelson Lighting, Mentron Films, Mersey Television, LWT, Yorkshire TV, Grampian and Radio Trent.

By 1994 the awarding arrangements with the Open University were finalised and it was agreed that the guardians of industry standards had to be practitioners with experience at the highest levels in the relevant craft, production or design field. The first thirteen NVQs in Camera, Lighting, Sound, Production, Research and Journalism, at levels 2, 3, and 4 were then accredited by the National Council for Vocational Qualification and SCOTVEC (the Scottish equivalent of the NCVQ). External verifiers were appointed and trained by Skillset and the Open University to approve centres and to ensure that standards and criteria were maintained at a national level. The BBC and CYFLE (see below) led the way in setting up assessment systems for employers/trainers and freelances. Development work is continuing at the present time on standards and qualifications for all other occupational areas including Make-up, Costume, Editing, Animation, Projection and Film Processing.

In January 1995 Skillset launched the first industry N/SVQs at BAFTA (British Academy of Film and Television Arts) and the first NVQ certificates were awarded to candidates. The launch was attended by senior industry figures who thereby acknowledged the three years of hard (but very productive and successful) grind which Skillset had spent developing industry standards.

112

The N/SVQ system now means that 'for the very first time' the broadcast, film and video industry has a training framework which can guarantee competence across the board. New entrants, who perhaps secure a job through a small video company can, if they do a particular job well, be assessed for an N/SVQ (or a credit towards an N/SVQ). Again it must emphasised that NVQs are not a training system but their very existence encourages people to seek out training and also provides a way of acknowledging on-the-job competence (which has always been a central plank of the film and newspaper industry's approach).

Investment
One of the most important of Skillset's responsibilities is the management of the Freelance Training Fund which was originally established in October 1991 by ITV and Channel Four. The fund then consisted of £300,000 and was used to subsidise the cost of training courses for freelances. At the time the BBC did not put money into the scheme because it was putting millions of pounds into its own training schemes. By 1996, however, thanks in part to the independent production levy, the fund stood at over £1 million and was supported by a range of employers, including the BBC. The Freelance Training Fund gives money to training organisations to help subsidise high quality courses. More than five hundred, mainly short courses (including retraining courses), have been supported by the fund and they run the gamut from training on the new non-linear editing equipment to courses in special effects make-up. There are also courses being developed for new entrants in areas such as production and technical skills, set crafts and art department, writing, directing and animation. Skillset and the Freelance Training Fund support guarantees quality.

At the present time Skillset is working to develop regional/national training consortia which are independent bodies, industry-led and managed by employers and unions in the regions. They are in regular communication with key trainers and educators in their areas and have a close relationship with Skillset.

Skillset – Converting the Doubters
Anyone wishing to enter the industry should be aware of the ongoing debate about education and training. As we saw in Chapter 7 the government's training philosophy tends towards the mechanistic and utilitarian which some people in the industry find distasteful. Training today is task-oriented and industry-led. In no way is it geared to cater to any idealistic notions about choosing an area of work out of a need for creative self-expression. There is much valid criticism of this from traditional media practitioners and educators, but at the present time

the dominant principles are that the 'market rules', and 'employers know best'. New entrants will simply have to accommodate to this.

There is also some scepticism around about the effectiveness of the N/SVQs. Some people still simply do not believe it is possible to structure a universal qualification system that is recognised across the whole industrial sector. They point out the film industry survived very well for years without paper qualifications (although the union card was crucial).

Critics also insist that the audio-visual industry is not an industry like any other because it deals with cultural and intellectual matters. They point out that N/SVQs were first developed for industrial sectors such as construction, engineering, hotel management and catering. The creative work of programme-making is different altogether. While many talented people (and old-timers) accept that it may be possible to set standards of competence for technical skills, they are almost in-sulted by the idea that it is possible to dissect any of the artistic, creative jobs in the industry and establish standards that will lead on to an assessment of competence. Creating a feature film or video or television programme, they say, is not a measurable activity. There is some truth in this, but Skillset's measured and sensible approach has gone a long way towards convincing the doubters and creating a climate of under-standing about what N/SVQs are about.

In any case we should be wary of the word 'creativity', since it can be used in many senses. When creativity means producing something that is clearly new and unique, that does not fit within the bounds of what society expects and is used to, then vocational training has no place. Pure creativity, in the sense of a totally new way of looking at the world, is not open to assessment. However, the production of a film, video or television programme, while it is a creative activity, is not totally new and unique every time: much of the production process is routine. Yet there is certainly a creative aspect to most of the routine jobs because they can be done badly or well and this will affect the final product and its novelty and originality. Although it may be difficult to specify the criteria to make a judgement of good or bad quality in production, it is nonetheless possible. Some of these criteria can be set down and regard-ed as preconditions of competence.

Other criticism of NVQs has centred on the fact that possession of the necessary skills to do a job will not necessarily guarantee employ-ment in the industry, that there are other intangibles which people in the industry value. It is argued that working on a film is not at all like a routine factory job: the hours of work are irregular and circumstances are often uncomfortable, so qualities of character are important. Qualities mentioned include persistence, a capacity for hard work, calmness under stress, the ability to ride the ups and downs of unemployment, imagination, the ability to take rejection. How, it is asked, can the N/SVQs possibly take account of this and other abstract qualities such as flair?

The answer is of course that they can't. But, leaving aside the rather patronising assumption that factory workers need no special qualities, not everyone in film, television and video is exceptional (even if some think so). For the vast majority of employees, qualifications can provide self-esteem, confidence and recognition, all of which redound to the benefit of the industry. In addition, in a market economy with a casualised workforce, the inadequate, the lazy and the uncooperative will be quickly weeded out: they will not secure the necessary contracts in a world where a reputation for doing a job well is the main guarantee of employment. N/SVQs won't solve every problem in any industry, but they will solve some. Possession of N/SVQs will not ensure another job: that depends on all sorts of factors (personality, the general employment picture, luck). It was ever so, but at least would-be employers will have industry standards for assessing the abilities of prospective candidates for jobs.

From another point of view, assessing competence in the workplace is probably less radical in the audio-visual industry than anywhere else, since it has been always been an aspect of the way the industry functions. Film certainly only ever cared about performance (and union membership) and the performance side of the job has always been very exposed to public assessment. While N/SVQs might not be perfectly attuned to certain characteristics of the entertainment industry, they can provide a qualification framework which is all they claim to do. For an industry with a training vacuum and piecemeal provision, sometimes of a very inferior kind, the strategic implications of an emphasis on industry-wide qualifications is important.

In any case, as Skillset has consolidated its work, the cynicism appears to be fading. The 'grumps' are getting old and retiring from the industry and the general attitude towards Skillset has improved immeasurably as its work has become more appreciated and understood.

New Entrant Industry-Based Training Schemes
New entrant training is perhaps one of the hardest problems for the industry to solve. There are a number of new-entrant training schemes available but they are usually linked directly to operational need. The BBC, which used to train most of the people in the industry, now trains very few, but both the BBC and ITV have positive recruitment and training policies for people who are under-represented in some sectors – such as women (especially in the technical and craft areas) and black

115

and disabled people. The BBC also publishes a booklet called *The Way In* which offers advice for new-entrants and includes some brief information on the Corporation's Television Production Training Scheme, Regional News Trainee Scheme, Local Radio Trainee Journalist Scheme and Network Radio Production Scheme. These opportunities are also advertised in the national press at certain times of the year.

The two-year BBC Television Production Training Scheme is highly sought after and, as the advertisements themselves say, competition for places is 'tough'. Trainees are paid a good salary and learn a range of skills from researching, script reading and writing to the direction of short items.

Some ITV companies recruit and train small numbers of multi-skilled operators and occasionally they do advertise trainee positions. ITN runs a News Trainee scheme which is advertised in the national press. This is an eighteen-month programme which provides a thorough grounding in News Journalism and Production. The scheme is opened to new graduates and of course, once again, is extremely competitive.

Channel Four funds two production training schemes every two years. These schemes are targeted at people with disabilities and people from ethnic backgrounds. Unusually today the training is broad based and consists of both formal college training and placements with independent production companies. Again these are advertised in the national press and are closely associated with ft2 (see below).

Ft2 (Film and Television Freelance Training)
This scheme used to be known as Jobfit – the Joint Board for Film Industry training. Now known as ft2 this is a new-entrant training scheme for technical assistant grades in the film and television industry. Originally supported by Channel Four, Thames Television and the unions, Jobfit was founded in 1985 and was initially concerned only with film. However, the demand in the industry for technicians skilled in both film and videotape led to the establishment of a pilot scheme in videotape training which was supported by independent companies and IVCA (the professional association for visual communication users). Today ft2 is managed by representatives from PACT, AFVPA (The Advertising Film and Video Producers' Association), BECTU (Broadcast, Entertainment, Cinematograph and Theatre Union), ITVA (Independent Television Association) and Channel Four.

Since 1985 ft2 (and Jobfit) have trained some 150 people for film and television of which over 120 presently work as freelances and many of these have now progressed to the senior technical grades of the industry. At the present time ft2 trains new-entrants on its New-entrant Technical Training Programme to become freelance technical assistants in

116

the grades of Camera Assistant/Clapper Loader, Assistant Editor, Sound Assistant, Art Department Assistant, Grips, Make-up /Hair and Production Assistant. In 1996 ft2 embarked on a new initiative, the Setcrafts Apprenticeship Scheme, which will cover training in fibrous plastering, scenic painting and carpentry.

Ft2 provides an industry-managed, two year, full-time training programme. It follows an apprenticeship-style model with trainees spending 80 per cent of their time attached to a range of professional productions. The remainder of the programme is taken up with specially designed short, off-the-job courses delivered by recognised industry training providers. While on the scheme trainees receive a weekly allowance which makes it especially attractive. Consequently, competition for ft2 is fierce and the scheme attracts about 300 applicants for each available space. Ft2 advertises annually in the national press and about 10 per cent of applicants are invited to interview. It only selects people with evident commitment and talent. The age range in 1995 was between 18 and 30. Some people come in from the workshop production sector, others have experience in production and some come in directly from education. According to David Martin, ft2's director, trainees all have one thing in common, 'a deep commitment to the business and the right attitude towards training'.

One of the great strengths of ft2, unlike many schemes, is that it provides trainees with a broad understanding of the industry (the principle which the BBC training always stressed). Moreover, it has also carried out a vigorous equal opportunities policy which has meant that it has trained a large number of women and people from ethnic minorities. Ft2 also manages Channel Four's positive action scheme for people from ethnic minorities – 4FIT. Recruitment is co-ordinated by Channel Four and four trainees are selected at intake. Ft2 organises and monitors 4FIT's training and production attachments in parallel to its main new-entrant scheme.

The design of ft2's training has been informed by the national standards of competence developed by Skillset and it has been approved as an assessment centre for the NVQs in Camera, Sound and Production. In this way ft2 not only provides access for new-entrants but the opportunity for assessment and certification for freelances already working in the industry. At the time of writing, for example, it is running a three-week training programme for production assistants based on the NVQs.

Cyfle

Cyfle is a Welsh word which means opportunity. The organisation was set up in 1986 to meet the needs for Welsh-speaking technicians in the freelance film and television sector in Wales. Cyfle run a two-year full-time, new-entrant course, a one-year 'in-service' training for production company employees, and a number of short courses. Trainees are trained in all grades within the industry – camera, sound, make-up, animation, scriptwriting, research, costume, editing, lighting and so on. Of those trained by the organisation 95 per cent now work regularly in the industry and many of the credit lists on programmes transmitted by S4C contain ex-Cyfle trainees.

Scottish Broadcast and Film Training: Freelance New-Entrants Training Scheme
A Scottish Film Technicians Training Scheme was originally organised by the Scottish Film Training Trust, which was launched in 1982. At that time the Trust was the only registered charity in the UK devoted solely to training people in the professional skills of film and video production. Today an organisation called Scottish Broadcast and Film Training is in partnership with BBC Scotland, Scottish Television, Grampian Television, Border Television, the Gaelic Television Committee, PACT, the Scottish Film Council, the Scottish Film Training Trust and the Federation of Entertainment Unions and it provides an eighteen month new-entrants scheme which provides trainees with the skills, contacts, training, knowledge and experience needed to work as freelance assistants in Scotland. Up to eight trainees are recruited at a time in craft, technical and production specialisms. In addition to production placements, trainees receive intensive short course training. The scheme is funded by Skillset's Freelance Training Fund and by the European Social Fund co-ordinated through Skillset.

Gaelic Television Training Trust
This Trust, which is part of the Gaelic Television Committee, has developed an advanced two-year course in production and craft skills, one year of college-based activities centred on a television training studio in a further education college is followed by one year devoted to industry-based training. The course is validated by SCOTVEC and eight full-time trainees were recruited in 1994-5. In addition the Trust has provided for nine-month placements within the industry for six trainees. The Gaelic Television Committee also funds twenty-three individuals on placements and short courses to advance skills already developed by working in the industry.

The National Film and Television School (NFTS)
The NFTS is the Rolls Royce school for those wishing to train in the industry. Founded in 1971 the NFTS is funded by the government

118

and by the industry and is increasingly developing a flexible range of courses to meet contemporary conditions. It is not an easy institution to describe. As its prospectus says, it is not a production house, a technical or training college, a university or a conservatoire but its full-time programme is designed to educate and train students to the highest professional standard in craft skills and in the development and creative realisation of original and ambitious ideas and productions. The full-time courses which last three years (except for the scriptwriting course which lasts for two years) incorporates elements of theoretical based study as well as practice. One of the great appeals of the NFTS is that distinguished guests from the industry are invited to the school to contribute to the teaching. Entry requirements vary depending on the area of study but there is no qualification or achievement that provides automatic access. Candidates need to demonstrate basic practical skills (usually by a 'portfolio' of completed work or a demonstration tape) and knowledge of the theory within their chosen specialised area. The average age of students is twenty-five and to gain entry on the courses they have to go through a rigorous selection process. After being short-listed, this process involves interviews and induction workshops which usually take from two to five weeks to complete and allows tutors to assess potential participants .

Retraining: Short Courses for Established Freelances
This book is intended for newcomers to the industry so that, strictly speaking, courses oriented towards updating or retraining people already working in the industry are somewhat outside its mandate. However, today people enter the industry without training and have to seek training and retraining once they can do the job. Young freelances who have landed themselves a job should be aware of the existence of some excellent short training courses. One example is the National Short Course Training Programme (NSCTP) of the National Film and Television School. The NSCTP was founded in 1982. At the time of writing the NSCTP is chief co-ordinator for the Skillset initiative to train freelances up and down the country in non-linear editing techniques and has provided over fifty three-day courses for people wishing to learn Avid non-linear editing. At the end of 1995 the NSCTP provided over ninety courses in camera, sound, lighting, writing, art, editing, production, direction and music composition.

Ravensbourne College of Design and Communication also has a short course unit with an excellent reputation (Ravensbourne has always worked closely with ITV in training). Scottish Broadcast Film and Training provides short courses and has an innovative scheme called 'Changing Places' which is directed at women freelances in the

Scottish industry who wish to move into direction and into other grades and areas where women are under-represented.

Trade organisations, such as The Moving Image Society (formerly the British Kinematograph Sound and Television Society – BKSTS), also offer technical courses and the International Visual Communications Association (IVCA) runs *ad hoc* professional evenings. The Royal Television Society organises a wide range of courses and conferences in London and in the regions. Students and young people can learn a great deal by attending these and meeting working practitioners. The Directors Guild of Great Britain also has an associate and student membership category.

Training for Women
Networking is a membership organisation for all women working, or seeking work, in any grade or capacity in film, video and television. It is concerned to cover worldwide and European media events. Since 1989 the organisation has been run by Vera Productions, an all-women production and training partnership. The newsletter contains information about training and other events, production awards and reports on national and international conferences.

Training in Europe
In January 1993 the European Film College (EFC) opened its doors in Ebeltoft in Denmark to 101 students from 25 countries. The College offers a four-month course in film combining theory and practice. The basic idea is that students will find out from the course whether they wish to be directors or make costumes or write scripts. Once they find out what suits them best they can then go on to further more specialised training. The EFC is supported by the Danish government and is also under the patronage of nineteen leading lights of the European film industry. Recently it received support from Hollywood film-makers.

For more information, addresses and telephone numbers of all these organisations consult the listings at the back of this book. Other useful sources are *A Listing of Short Courses in Film, Television, Video and Radio,* compiled by Lavinia Orton, and *Schedules and Assignments,* edited by Christine James. These are both published by the British Film Institute.

Work as 'Vocation': Summing Up
Learning through playing has been one of the axioms of modern educational thought. Alas, in practice, the idea has been concentrated in primary schools so that for most people the transfer to secondary schools has been traumatic. Suddenly notes had to be made, facts had to be

learned, exams had to be passed and the golden age of playing, experimenting, enjoying *and* learning all at the same time faded into oblivion.

No wonder then that many people, when they finally kicked the dust of school off their shoes, longed to pursue the ideal of work as play in their adult lives. Since television and film have provided the main source of entertainment for adults in the second half of the 20th century, it has been equally unsurprising that many school-leavers and college and university graduates have dreamed and fantasised about working in the media. As a result, entry has always been fiercely competitive and the vast majority have longed in vain.

In the future, however, more people could have the skills to work in film and television and therefore have the capacity to make their dream a reality. The communications industry is a growth area. Instead of the restricted entry of the past, which frustrated all but the extraordinarily able, the lucky, or those with 'good contacts', in the future there will be a variety of routes 'in'. In a multi-channel environment there should be no reason why anyone who is really drawn to the industry, who feels that it fits them and they fit it, and who is prepared to work hard, should be prevented from 'getting in' for at least a part of their working life. This is the plus side.

But since life is not a fairy tale there is also a negative aspect. The well-paid, protected and glamorous jobs of the past, the careers that usually lasted for life, are giving way to something new and different, tougher, more temporary, constantly shifting, with periods of unemployment as a fact of life.

Chapters 5, 6, 7 and 8 have looked at the way education and training are changing in Britain. Traditionally, academic qualifications have had great kudos in our society. In the year 2000, in a world saturated by information and entertainment, a purely academic qualification may be less valuable. There will be more emphasis on understanding technology and on an ability to do a specific job – and most jobs will require skill and technical competence. If the new vocational qualification system works, the British will no longer finish their education at sixteen or twenty-one, but will be part of a society which is continuously learning. Retraining will become a constant fact of life – that, at least, is the goal.

The GNVQ and the N/SVQ system is designed to help all this along. Most experts say the learning society is not an option but a necessity: when the workplace and the technology are changing constantly a person who can not adapt will certainly come to grief.

A Word of Advice
As we have seen, the traditional academic route, the degree course, is changing to meet this situation. Higher education is incorporating

training and expanding its numbers. 'Enterprise in Higher Education' is providing students with a taste of work experience. Further education is being simplified and vocational qualifications are being awarded for competence in the workplace.

At the present time, all would-be candidates for employment in every profession (graduates, those with practical qualification and those with no training at all) face a difficult situation. The best course of action for the media industry, if you really have talent, is to use it and show it. Get hold of a video camera and make your own tape, or join a community video workshop which can provide you with hands-on experience while you are looking for work. There are independent workshops which provide training and experience.[6] The great advantage that media graduates have over other applicants for jobs is that, on practice-based courses, they learn how to make programmes or mini-films which they can then hawk around to possible employers. This is still one of the best methods of getting into the industry.

Camp on the doorstep, put your foot in the door, do anything to get someone to look at your work. If you are talented and prepared to work hard, someone in the smaller independent companies may take you on. Don't expect to be made a director straightaway or to be paid well: many companies are run on a shoestring and there is some evidence that salaries are dropping. If you say you'll do anything you must mean it otherwise you will be out on your ear.

If you have the right temperament, a freelance career in film, video and television can be engrossing and exciting. However, if you are someone who wants to know exactly what you will be doing in the next ten years, then this is not the right industry for you – but then few other industries will suit you either. Change is the one certainty of contemporary employment. With little union protection we are all entrepreneurs now. We will all have to 're-invent' and 're-market' our careers constantly. The Learning Society is here to stay and NVQs are part of that revolution.

Notes

1. British Film Institute, *Television Industry Tracking Study, 1994-1997* (An Interim Report published in October 1995) p. 14.
2. At its peak in the mid 1980s, the BBC employed more than 28,000 full-time staff of which more than 17,000 worked in television (*BBC Annual Report, 1986*, London: BBC, p. 26). ITV employed around 18,000 most of whom were also full-time (see note 3). Today the BBC employs about 24,000 people but about 75 per cent of these are contract staff and there are very few part-timers except in the clerical or secretarial grades: the core permanent staff is around 6,000.

3. Colin Sparks, 'Unions and Casualisation', Stuart Hood (ed.)*Behind the Screens: the Structure of British Television in the Nineties* (London: Lawrence and Wishart, 1994).

4. For much of this information see *Skillset: A Report from the Industry Training Organisation for Broadcast Film and Video, 1992-1995.*

5. Final report by Carol Varlaam, Patricia Leighton, Richard Pearson and Scott Blum *'Skill Search': Television Film and Video Industry Employment Patterns and Training Needs,* (Brighton: Institute of Manpower Studies, Sussex University, January 1990).

6. See the British Film Institute's annually published authoritative and widely consulted *Handbook.*

PART THREE
PRODUCTION: WHAT IT'S ALL ABOUT

9

SO YOU WANT TO BE IN FILM OR TELEVISION?

I've been really serious about this as a career since I was twelve years old.
(Steven Spielberg)

The most important question of all is: Why do you want to enter the industry? You should try to answer it as a very first priority. If you wanted to be a doctor, you would probably be able to explain yourself easily, perhaps something along the lines of wanting to help suffering humanity. Wanting to be in film or television is altogether different. Some of the reasons you may be ashamed of: they may seem trivial. You want to enter the industry because it looks glamorous or fun and you get to meet famous people? Perhaps it's the excitement: you see yourself as a television journalist reporting from a war front? Or you want to earn lots of money and have heard what newsreaders and Anthea Turner earn? Perhaps you think it looks easy to appear on camera – after all you only have to look good and read the Autocue. You may like the idea of being recognised: if you do, then obviously you want to work in front of the camera, because no one recognises producers, directors or editors on the street (even though they are the most important people of all).

It is important to come to an understanding of yourself and your motivation. Film and television are entertainment media. Our most delightful fantasies are wrapped up in the images they convey. Imagination is an essential part of human life and is probably the most vital element in all film- and programme-making so you have one appropriate talent. But, as you spin your dreams about your future, try to separate reality from fantasy. There is no shame in wanting to be a star – stars have usually wanted to be stars – but the odds on success are poor. Be realistic about the chance of success. It's easier for a man than a woman. (How many women over sixty read the news? Equal opportunities have still to hit the screen.) We all build castles in the air and many of us nurture the old Hollywood dream of 'being discovered'. In the meantime, build yourself something on solid ground to be going on with while you wait. If you want to be a star you are not being realistic, but then the stars were not realistic either.

Character

Success in the entertainment industry is as much to do with temperament and character as talent and good looks. Everyone will tell you this and what they tell you is absolutely true. If you want to work in film or television you are entering a dynamic, high-pressure, roller-coaster world. When you *are* working, the hours could be long, the circumstances uncomfortable, job security minimal and the pay, at the lower levels, abysmal. This is increasingly the industry of the freelance and you will need patience, persistence and, most important of all, a very thick skin.

As profit margins get lower and financial risks greater, employers are increasingly hard-nosed. If you are not up to scratch, little mercy will be shown. You will need to be able to take humiliation and criticism and to bounce back. Some directors can be very bad-tempered when something goes wrong at an expensive location or on the studio floor. Big money is involved, which puts everyone on edge. This is a temperamental industry and the emotional temperature in a television control room can get very high indeed. Can you stand being yelled at – totally unjustifiably? Directors don't want explanations: they want results. Resilience is essential for survival.

Do you enjoy working with a team or are you a loner? Producing a film or a television programme is a group activity. This does not mean that there is no place for the individualist and the introvert in the industry, but you have to know your own character to know where you are best suited. It is easy to recognise our strengths, to know in what ways we are talented or gifted; it is more difficult to know our weaknesses and faults, yet these can be just as crucial.

Creativity

Perhaps you are not quite sure why you want to be involved in the industry. Perhaps you can't really say what it is that attracts you, but you know it is there and it drives you on. It may be that it is almost too profound for you to acknowledge. You may have a view of society that you want to convey, and feel that you could express it best through the medium of film, video or television. Somewhere inside you is a gut feeling that you have your own particular voice which seeks expression and that the visual image rather than writing is a more natural medium for you. You feel that working in the industry will provide you with the opportunity to express what you have to say. This desire to communicate one's own particular

128

vision is an essential ingredient of all creativity. Make its acquaintance. Try to find out, and articulate, why working with film or video attracts you. Try to write it down on paper. (This exercise will stand you in good stead when you go for an interview.)

There is a multiplicity of reasons why people want to enter this industry. Probably the only inappropriate reason is looking for a secure job with a pension. If that attracts you, look elsewhere. There was only ever limited room for that in the past and now there is no room at all. This is an extremely high-risk industry and it is likely to become more so. Unions warn of the dangers inherent in what they call the 'casualisation' of the industry, both in terms of employee safeguards and in work quality, and they are right. Be warned, but, if you want to accept the risks, press on.

Preparation

You want to enter a workforce where the competition is especially fierce and where your fellow employees are often very talented, highly ambitious and driven. It is no use vaguely thinking it would be nice to do 'something interesting' in films and hope that this will see you through. Competition even for courses to begin to learn about the industry is intense. Academic and technical courses at every college and every university receive a deluge of applicants every year. If you get as far as an interview you've overcome the first hurdle, but you will never get any further unless you are well briefed. Before you even step into the interview room, be sure you know how films and programmes are made. You can be certain your fellow interviewees will know.

People who work in film are especially passionate about their work: not to say obsessive and fanatical. They live, breathe and eat the world of the cinema. Most of them have been like that since they were young. Would-be film-makers today are mad about film or video, both watching it and making it. They watch films all the time and most of them already know about camera angles and technique. Outsiders often say the film people are 'different': they say it because it's true. Don't for a moment hope that you can turn up for an interview for a course or a job relating to film airily expecting the interviewer to tell you what the industry is about. You will be expected to know. Not everything, but something.

If you want to get into any British film school you should know about the work of American, European and British directors, both past and present. You should be reading film journals such as *Sight and Sound* at least occasionally and you should be going to films regularly and thinking about techniques and scripts. The same applies to television. This bring us to the second major question in this chapter.

129

What Do You Know about the Industry and How it Functions?
The first part of this book presented an analysis of the present state of film, television and video. Many school and college leavers will try to skip this as the hard bit. In fact, if you want to get anywhere today, you would be well-advised to become acquainted with the major issues. The first piece of advice is to read the section on the industry trends and then get hold of the media pages in certain newspapers and copies of the trade journals listed in the back of this book. Keep up to date. Know what is going on.

After that, get down to practical details. Television especially is all-pervasive in this society, but do you know anything about how a programme is made? Do you know how a film is made? Do you ever imagine what is going on behind the camera? Do you ever think about the preparation that making a film or television programme entails? When you are sitting in the cinema engrossed by a film, or are watching a television programme at home, do you understand how they have been put together? How much do you know about cuts and editing? Do you, in fact, know what an editor actually does? Do you appreciate the difference between film and video? The following chapters will tell you something about all these matters. Use it as a starting-point and then seek out more information.

Of course, the home video camera market has had an impact. Video magazines have begun to urge buyers to involve themselves in post-production and there are cheap post-production devices available which allow the do-it-yourself video owner to edit, produce titles and graphics and mix sound. The results can be seen on programmes such as *Take Over TV* on Channel Four and *Beadle's Hotshots* on ITV. This is part of whole multiskilling phenomenon which is currently disturbing many in the industry who fear that it could de-professionalise programme-making.

The Constructed World of Film, Television and Video
Films, commercials, television programmes, pop videos, whether fictional or factual, are all 'constructed'. There are very few occasions where a camera records a variety of scenes and the pictures are then transmitted or projected without any change.

To understand the significance of construction in the moving picture industry, consider for a moment the 'unconstructed' family video. This has a very limited audience because it is invariably numbingly boring, except of course to the participants. The audience of a home-made video are usually the people recorded by the camera. They are waiting to see themselves: not a vision with universal appeal. The home video rarely has a theme, there is no storyline and no argument. No one has planned the shots or organised the participants. If feature films, television programmes or commercial videos were made on the same principle there would be no industry since no one would ever watch them. Off-the-cuff shooting rarely produces a watchable result: it is in the 'crafting' of a film or programme that the art of picture-making resides. It is the combination of many highly talented (and well-trained) people working together to construct a production that makes it 'professional'. A multiplicity of finely honed techniques and skills in numerous craft and design areas lies behind the professional entertainment which films, programmes and videos provide.

It is this ability to communicate effectively, so that the audience is seduced into continuing to watch of their own free will, which is what the communication industry is all about. The audience wants to watch a feature film because the director has orchestrated a group of people doing many different jobs to produce images and dialogue which engage its interest. The simple images are the result of a complex process called production.

The way a film or a television programme is constructed depends on the people involved making certain choices. They are guided by what they believe makes a good film or programme; this belief is based on their own ideas and perceptions and on experience, since they are inevitably influenced by the knowledge of what has worked well before.

People working in the various production areas have an individual viewpoint arising from their personal expertise. The camera operator, in a film or on a news shoot, may choose to take certain pictures rather than others (in television studios, however, camera operators are strictly controlled by directors); the scriptwriter selects specific words to describe a situation; the editor has arranged the pictures in a certain order and has thrown away those frames which do not accord with his or her idea of 'good' editing. Other camera operators, scriptwriters or editors would have made other choices and the end result would consequently have been very different. If the funds were available, it would be an interesting experiment to provide two experienced directors and crews with the same story-line and then given them a free hand. Two very different films or programmes would probably result. In short, choice and decision-making by a wide range of professionals lie behind the creative process of film and programme production.

In the following chapters we will look at the various jobs in the industry and see what the people in them actually do. You can then decide where your own interests and talents lie. In the past the boundaries between job areas in the industry were clearly defined because the technology was unwieldy and complex. Each element in the production process was the responsibility of one person or a team of people who were experts in those particular jobs. Union power ensured that no one who was unskilled or inexperienced ever put their hands on the equipment.

Today many jobs in the industry are still very highly skilled (some of the new computerised equipment needs special technical staff who require constant retraining as the equipment becomes more sophisticated). But the widespread use of video and the introduction of digital technology are changing the working practices of the industry. Video, for example, in comparison to film is cheap to use and in some ways simpler to handle. This, together with the reduction of union power, has led, as explained earlier, to 'multi-skilling' (referred to more pejoratively as 'de-skilling' or 'casualisation').

Multi-skilling simply means that the same person can do several different jobs. This has revolutionised the way the industry works, especially in video production companies. Huge crews are a thing of the past, except in big-budget feature films and some very expensive television dramas. The boundaries between jobs have become blurred, as have the divisions between the various sectors of the industry, because video now produces a high-quality image.

Ten years ago any analysis of the production process would be dealt with under two separate headings 'film' and 'television' (the independent video industry being hardly mentioned since it scarcely existed). That division accurately reflected reality because the two sectors were very different, both in their working practices and in their culture. This is no longer the case and people now work in all sectors and even sometimes in different job areas.

For these reasons it is simpler (and more relevant) to view film, television and video production together as variations of essentially one overall process. Differences in methods that still exist between the various sectors are often the result of the dictates of the recording medium, whether film or electronic video. There are, however, specific traditions and practices (especially in the film sector), and these will be noted as we go along.

Historically, films used to be made in big studios and each studio possessed its own 'stable' of actors, directors, scriptwriters and camera-operators. Studios tended to be big, sprawling, untidy, messy places with a high level of excitement and a great deal of glamour. Today the managers have taken over and digital technology is altering the craft and atmosphere of movie-making and programme creation. According to one film-maker the new executives 'find the computer realm extremely attractive because it looks like what they're used to! It looks like accountants working together in these tiny controlled environments – its clean, fast and logical! It's not that down and dirty carnival atmosphere. It's clean rooms, clean clothes, well-shaven, well-kept people.'[1]

Producing the entertainment product today is about slickness, speed, big business and profits. The industry is preoccupied with cutting costs and controlling budgets. According to many old-timers the fun has gone out of it. That is for you to decide for yourself and most young trainees, despite low pay and long hours, still believe that 'its better than working for a living'. It all depends, of course, on your expectations. However, do take heed of the warnings. The industry is not what it was and its allure and mythic status, even for its own employees, has evaporated in recent years.

Case Histories

RICHARD HOLMES

Richard Holmes is 33 and a film producer. With his friend, the director Stefan Schwartz, he runs a company called The Gruber Brothers. According to Variety: *'Holmes and Schwartz ... are the leading lights of the so-called multiplex generation of British film-makers, a new wave of twenty-something talent brought up on Hollywood movies, whose ambition lies in popular entertainment rather than art-house fare.' Richard and Stefan have worked together for more than a decade. Richard is also a founder member of the New Producers' Alliance.*

I went to York University and read philosophy which was not very practical from the career point of view but I really enjoyed it. While I was there I met Stefan who was doing Electronic Engineering. I'll embarrass him by saying that he was the best looking electronic engineer of his year. We really got on extremely well and in 1984 when we graduated we formed a comedy double act called the Gruber Brothers. We did the usual things – toured Northern England Clubs, appeared at the Edinburgh Festival Fringe – and eventually we took the act down to London and, of course, performed at the Comedy Store.

For the first year after graduation we got by – doing a bit of acting and writing and performing our Gruber Brothers act. What was significant though was that our humour was film-based; films provided us with ideas so we would write, for example, a sketch from *Star Wars* in two minutes – that sort of thing. Writing comedy sketches can be pretty painful and eventually we began to think that for the same effort we might as well write a proper film script so that's what we did. We wrote a short sci-fi film called *Bonded*. Then we decided we might as well go ahead and make it! So off we went and made a film. We tried to make it as grandly as possible – given our financial resources. We did it on 35mm.

Looking back, its success in artistic terms is a moot point but it certainly made a huge difference to our lives because Roland Joffe (the director) saw it and liked it and, together with the First Film Foundation, commissioned us to write the script for a feature based on *Bonded*. That was all tremendously exciting. Then nothing happened. We wrote the script but nothing came of it. It was quite a shock. When we had been writing and performing our own material we were in complete control. Now suddenly we were in other people's control and we were not used to it.

Anyway, in the end, while we were still hanging around waiting for the project to come off (it never did) we decided to write and produce another film called *The Lake*, a half-hour thriller starring Frances Barber, David Threfall, Jane Lapotaire and Peter Capaldi. *The Lake* was another 35mm and it won a special commendation at the Melbourne Film Festival and attracted the attention of a very rich sponsor who said that he would like to fund a feature film. This was incredibly lucky. We had this absolutely dream meeting with the sponsor and the end result was a proper feature – *Soft Top, Hard Shoulder* – written by Peter Capaldi and produced and directed by us. It was still very, very, very low budget. Stefan pushed to the limit what we could do for the money. Technically, the film was very ambitious.

Soft Top, Hard Shoulder turned out to be very successful. It won the 1992 London International Film Festival and two Scottish BAFTAs – for best film and best actor. The reviews were good, it got world-wide distribution and was shown at film festivals in Palm Springs, Vancouver and New York.

For a while there it was a really golden period with everyone ringing up and saying, 'What are you going to do next?'. We didn't know. In the end Stefan worked as director on Screen 2 and I co-produced a film called *Solitaire for 2*, a feature written and directed by Gary Sinyor who had made *Leon the Pig Farmer*.

What the sudden success meant was that we had to become more realistic about what we were doing and what we were going to do. We had to be more grown-up about money for one thing and we had to have industry credibility. It was no use relying on one hit. I was married by this time and, although I'd been film-making throughout my twenties, I had never really made any money. My father was beginning to wonder whether I'd ever earn a proper wage.

Then Gruber Brothers got into a sort of house keeping deal with Chrysalis which gave us financial support. This was wonderful – but it all fell apart after about six months. It was really frustrating, although the whole experience was a real education and I am still grateful to the people involved.

After the Chrysalis deal fell apart we had to force ourselves to say, 'This is what we own, this is what we've got in the bank, what are we going to do?' We had to do something. Desperation got us going again.

Again, luck was a factor. Glynis Murray who runs *Tomboy* films stepped in. Everyone should have a patron like Glynis. She is a very successful businesswoman and she offered us office space and assistance to keep us going because she believed in us. She has a very good business head and the connection with *Tomboy* has provided stability. We have really gained from the connection. It has worked out very well.

In the meantime, while all this was going on, we decided to re-develop *Lake* as a full feature and started to write another film called *Entrepreneurs*. The European Script Fund provided money for *Lake* which has been written by Stefan and myself and it will be made with a German producer. *Entrepreneurs* has been funded by the National Lottery as well as Entertainment Film Distributors. It begins shooting in August [1996].

If you ask me why I have kept going through the ups and downs I would have to say that my professional partnership with Stefan has been absolutely essential. You need someone to help you through the bad times when the s--- really hits the fan and also for the good times when you are euphoric and need some realism. You need someone to bounce your ideas against. Stefan is diametrically opposed to me in personality which is why the partnership works.

I know it seems boring to say so but so much is down to luck and timing. Also you have to keep going. I cycle into work everyday and it's the same thing. Success is 90 per cent stamina and 10 per cent talent. I'm no golfer but my father is and he quotes, I think, Tony Jacklin who said something like, 'It's strange – the harder I practise the luckier I get.' I think that says everything. When the Chrysalis deal fell apart it was a really bad time but it forced me to get down to knowing about the whole film business. I decided I had to know who everyone is, how the whole industry works and everything about the whole film-making process – right down to the smallest detail. Consciously, emotionally and technically, I gave myself a complete make-over. I used to be embarrassed to tell my neighbours, or someone who knew nothing about the business, that I was a producer. During the tough period I felt I had to turn myself into 'a real film producer'. I worked at it.

135

I now really believe in planning ahead. I have a five-year plan. There are three kinds of movies I want to make – the low budget small ones which are great fun and which I've done, the independent, modestly budgeted British films which I am making now, but I also want to make a big studio-based picture. As a producer what I want to do is make unashamedly commercial films which are popular and make lots of money!

CHRISTIAN CANTON

Christian Canton is 25 and is Interactive Designer Project Manager working for a company called EMG (Epic Multimedia Group) which is based in Brighton. EMG, which is Europe's largest multimedia agency and production studio, is typical of the increasingly important interactive multimedia sector of the entertainment industry. The Company markets very sophisticated productions in both education and entertainment and illustrates the developing interface between the film and computing industries. Christian's career to date reveals the growing significance of computing and mathematical skills on the production side of the entertainment industry.

I read Maths and Management Science at King's College London and while I was there became interested in the psychological and philosophical side of mathematics and especially in artificial intelligence. Then, typical of the usual angst-ridden student, I did not really know what to do for a career so I decide to travel for a while. I had some distant relatives in Jamaica and I made contact with them and worked in Jamaica for ten months, partly as an accountant.

I travelled round and saved a little and went on to California where I also had some relatives. While I was there I met someone who really enthused me about pediatric dentistry and I thought I'd like to try and train as a dentist and live in America! However, the whole cost of studying there was too expensive so I came back to Britain and decided to do a Masters in Knowledge Based Systems at the University of Sussex. This reflected my earlier interest in Artificial Intelligence.

While studying at Sussex, I got involved with Apple Computers Interface Design Competition. This is a forum for leading research institutions around the world to provide innovative solutions to communication and design problems posed by Apple. My first real work project was with Penguin Books who were producing their first book in electronic form. This was called *Host* and was a sci-fi fantasy novel by Peter James. From Penguin I moved here to Epic and got involved with converting some of the huge mass of Japanese Manga animation and comics into an interactive format for CD-ROM.

Now I'm into designing games and presently working on a game based on a feature film called *SpaceTruckers* starring Dennis Hopper. The film is being shot in Ireland under the direction of Stuart Gordon (who directed *Fortress, Honey I Shrank the Kids* and *Honey I Blew Up the Kids*) and has a big budget for an independent. It's set in 2094 when the Earth is overpopulated and resources are all depleted so people are moving into space to inhabit new worlds. Rocket-powered rigs have replaced trucks to haul cargo to colonists through out the solar system. With the 'world' so much bigger truckers are in big demand.

The hero is a loner played by Dennis Hopper who refuses to play by other people's rules. The film's theme offers all sorts of possibilities for a game and we are working closely with the film-makers, the special effects team, the model makers and the make-up and design people. We go to Ireland and shoot the footage for the game mainly using the same storyboards as the film, so the relationship between the two is close.

People have said to me that the games industry is very like the animation industry, that the structure of organisation is very similar to that of the animation studio. There is a producer at the top and then various team leaders deal with the design, or the programming, or the audio-visual aspects. All the teams have to collaborate and communicate with each other or it could go horribly wrong. Talking to each other is really important and so is trying to keep close to the film's 'feel' and atmosphere.

Usually when film companies and game companies work together the film company has a very large say in what goes on because they have often put a large amount of money into the games project. We have been pretty lucky because the company producing *StarTruckers* trusts our professional judgement and competence. Often when the games industry and the film industry get together there can be difficulties because films and games have different sets of priorities and problems and too much unthinking interference from the film people can stop our creative juices flowing!

The trend for major studios, such as Universal and Warner Bros., to invest in games has had a dramatic impact on the games industry. Only a few years ago games design and production was very much a cottage industry, with enthusiasts constructing games almost in their own bedrooms. Then, virtually overnight, you got the power and might of the major studios taking an interest and making a tremendous impression on what was really a very small community. The marrying of games and films brought in huge amounts of money to the games industry which was obviously important; the programming budgets were vast – millions of dollars for the *Phantasmagoria* game and a similar sum of money for *Wing Commander IV*. What the studios did was bring film production values to games so there was much more emphasis on, for example, the quality of the picture – on stunning graphics.

All this created a problem though, because the really good people got sucked into the major film projects and the rest of the games industry tended to be left in the hands of some newcomers and anyway the games industry on its own could never recoup such a high level of investment. From the Hollywood viewpoint, of course, a game all helped to support the film and raise the profile.

The impact was not all positive because film people have a long history of entertainment and they tend to think they know everything about what is going on and, in fact, often they don't really know much about games and computing. Film and game cultures can be in conflict because film narrative is linear while the player of a game has a degree of free will. In a way there is much more that you can do with a game – games provide a means for expression of free will, and often film people don't understand that. They also sometimes don't grasp what can, and what cannot be done, by the technology. In fact, there is a big issue to be resolved about whether film and game approaches to multimedia products can really be compatible. Film-makers have had a lot to offer the games industry in terms of creative and aesthetic values and especially their emphasis on the way a production looks.

The games industry originally was focused on the activity itself and on the player's reaction to the experience of game, the 'buzz' did not come from the quality of the picture. The collaboration with film-makers has really revolutionised production values.

I think the games world is undergoing a shift. There is less emphasis on the isolated, boring 'nerd' playing at his computer all on his own; people are becoming more interested in the social side of 'virtual reality' with scenarios where people meet each other inside the game: game-playing can bring people together. The isolating element of games has probably been overemphasised. There are now interactive social games on the net such as *Command and Conquer* (Westwood Studios) and *Civilisation* (Microprose). In *Command and Conquer*, the players are mining for resources, financing their own factories and silos and commanding a real force, while simultaneously battling against other human players over a network. Increasingly games are taking place in real time with things happening simultaneously. Already the technological possibilities available have opened a multitude of cross-genre games, such as *Dungeon Keeper* (Bullfrog), a combination of God-game and Doom-style 3D beat'em-up, or *Rebel Assault 2* (Lucas Arts) which combines filmic video sequences with action sequences.

Electronic technology is becoming incredibly flexible. I have been working with rotascoping which is when a real person is recorded jumping or running or whatever. This is then digitised, outlined and traced and then recoloured and retraced so that it capture the lifelike spirit of the original footage on the computer screen. Again, in this way computer on-screen production levels are going up dramatically all the time. This is already yesterday's technology. 3D motion capture and control has stepped into the picture with increasingly realistic human and animal movements controlling photorealistic game characters. *Toy Story* (Pixar) showed that 3D computer-generated 'characters' can have real personality, but the hardware, cost and time to reproduce images of this quality are a little way off yet for the average project. With its flexibility and adaptability 3D is rapidly progressing towards being able to create styles ranging from manga to the photorealism of *Toy Story*. Expense is still a major consideration, as is the difficulty of bringing 3D characters convincingly 'to life'.

There is a great issue surrounding the question of interactivity and the media. Some people on the games side think that film is no longer the way forward and interactivity is the thing that matters, but there is a big question over the issue of passivity versus activity. Do people really want interactive news?

Note

1. Phil Tippett in an interview with Iain Boal in *Resisting the Virtual Life: The Culture and Politics of Information,* ed. by James Brook and Iain Boal (San Francisco: City Lights, 1995) p. 259. Tippett is the Oscar-winning animator who created the tyrannosaurs and velociraptors of *Jurassic Park*.

10

THE STAGES OF PRODUCTION

You have to reconcile what you think is good with what you think is profitable. (Tom Pollock, President of Universal Pictures in 1989)

Producing a film, television programme or video involves several distinct stages, usually referred to as pre-production, production and post-production.

Pre-production
Pre-production basically means planning. It is the stage when all the components are organised and assembled in preparation for the actual filming or recording. The starting point in any production is the idea. A feature film may start with a producer's idea for a story. The producer may have purchased the rights to a novel or a play (which in the film world is called 'the property'). The idea for a television commercial may be thrashed out in the advertising agency after it has received the commission to publicise a product. In television, a scriptwriter might come up with a 'situation' for a situation comedy.

Once the idea has been thought of, however, it must have some physical reality: this usually means it has to be committed to paper. The film producer might ask a scriptwriter to come up with a 'treatment', or outline, of how the idea might be made into a movie, and from which a script may be developed. In television, a 'commissioning' editor might like the scriptwriter's comedy idea and commission a script, or it may be that the editor has come up with the original idea and then commissioned a writer to script it.

Raising the Money
Wherever an idea comes from, what it needs to be realised is money. After the brainwave must come the finance. Getting backing has always been a nightmare for British film-makers. Often the only available backing is American, which leads to the question of how British a

140

British film made with American money actually is. 'He who pays the piper calls the tune' has been too often the unfortunate experience of many British film producers – a situation that has also disheartened many young idealistic film-makers. Very few British investors have been prepared to back the home-grown feature film, which has always been thought as a high-risk area. Neither has the government ever offered much support. As a result, British cinema has always faced an uphill battle, which explains why the support of Channel Four for the feature film industry was such a surprising and encouraging initiative (see Chapter 2). However, one positive development in recent years, which has offered hope to European film-makers, is the increasing interest in 'co-production', where the money is raised in several countries to spread the risk and gain European financial support. As a result the film is given a more international flavour. Co-production, however, is also criticised in some quarters because the products of such co-operation have tended to be rather bland and 'unlocated' in a region or country.

In contrast to film producers, television producers used to be a protected species. In the old days, producers in the BBC and ITV who had a brainwave for a programme only needed to secure managerial support. They did not have to hustle for money in the market-place. If a programme idea was 'accepted', producers were given a budget and their principal obligation was to produce the best programme they could. If behind the scenes, in managers' offices up and down the country, there were rows about budgetary shortfalls, television producers, on the whole, did not have to dirty their hands by grubbing for money in the outside world: finance was a managerial responsibility. The 80s changed all that and today BBC producers are now exposed to the calculations of the market-place. Even in television those who have business acumen and a nose for money, in addition to creative talent, are the ones who are most likely to succeed. Chapter 6 pointed out the importance of financial training: accountants and business graduates interested in media production will find no shortage of jobs in the industry.

In theory, the film industry, because of its own historical experience, has not had to make the same adjustment. It is extremely unlikely that the cultural arm of the government will do much (in terms of grants etc.) to encourage a more positive climate of growth in British film, although the industry will benefit from money from the National Lottery. Cynical observers, in fact, doubt the government's long-term commitment to a serious cultural policy on film at all. If you want to work as a producer in this industry, therefore, be it in film or television, the best advice is first to make sure you know about money, how to get hold of it, how to earn it, how to look after it and how to increase it.

The British and American film industries have always worked on the money principle. However, British film, and to a lesser extent television, are massively disadvantaged by the overwhelming odds in favour of the American product. In practical terms, people who want to make films or good television programmes have to learn how to talk to investors, bankers and accountants as a first priority – and this sometimes means playing their game. It may mean wearing a suit rather than dungarees for a finance interview (most bankers are highly conservative people and alternative styles of dress can frighten them off).

Organisation

Once the money for production is secured, the people – 'the talent' – can be assembled and hired. The size of the crew will depend on the type of production. A feature film usually means many people and so does a television drama production, whether it is shot on film or tape. Most television programmes, however, as well as pop videos, corporate and training videos, will need far less. Many independent production companies will try to get by on as little as possible. Most of the people working on a production will be freelance, hired on short-term contracts for as long as the production lasts. During pre-production, once the crew is hired, locations (real places for outdoor and indoor scenes) are arranged and a budget and shooting schedule prepared.

On feature films the people hired will include directors, casting directors, performers, scenic and graphic designers, camera operators, make-up artists, production managers, directors of photography, property buyers, location managers, property masters, gaffers, the first, second and third assistant directors, script supervisors, boom operators, art directors, set directors and so on. All these jobs, with the exception of performers, are behind-the-camera jobs, and setting the standards of competence for these parts of the industry is the responsibility of Skillset (see Chapter 8). Over the next few years it is expected that every one of these jobs will have N/SVQ qualifications attached to them.

Some of the jobs listed above are only found in the film world, or they are called something different in television. It was part of the task of people participating in the NVQ workshops of Skillset to bring some order into job descriptions. When the film and television industries were more separated, as they were until the late 80s, the fact that similar jobs had different titles was acceptable. As the industries have drawn closer together this could no longer be maintained, especially since, as we have seen, many freelances work across all three sectors. It is simply too confusing to change job titles for what is essentially the same work.

142

Traditionalists hate to see some of the old job titles go, especially in the film industry, but the establishment of the NVQs have inevitably encouraged the streamlining process since qualifications are awarded by job function. It is sad to see old titles wither away as the NVQ nomenclature becomes accepted, but it is the inevitable result of change and casualisation. The tight *esprit de corps* of the traditional film crew is being eroded and, although this is to be regretted, it is unlikely that it will ever return.

In television, as far as the BBC and some of the ITV companies (such as Granada and Yorkshire) are concerned, pre-production still involves a fairly high (but steadily decreasing) proportion of core staff. However, Channel Four and some of the new franchise holders (such as Carlton) function as publisher/broadcasters. In other words, they do not themselves make programmes, but instead order (commission) them from independent film and video companies. These independent production companies function rather like the feature film companies in that they employ only a handful of permanent staff members and hire in extra freelances when the need arises, for production time only.

Semi-permanent Staff
Although the BBC and those commercial companies that still function as producer/broadcasters have to allot 25 per cent of their programming to the independents, their regular programmes, such as the evening news on the BBC, will probably still be produced, directed and organised by staff personnel. Increasingly, however, many of these people will be contract rather than permanent employees, although their contracts are likely to run for three- or five-year periods rather than for the few months characteristic of the film and independent video sector. Make-up artists, graphic designers and behind-the-scenes journalists associated with the pre-production of these regular programmes will be what could be called 'semi-permanent' staff.

Production
Production is the actual recording or filming. For a feature film this can take months or even years; for a television programme it might be an hour of high-pressure studio time (with or without an audience). Some behind-the-camera jobs, such as that of the casting director for a big feature film or a commercial or television drama, may have moved on at the end of pre-production. Production involves performers of all sorts: actors, stunt artists, presenters, journalists, news reporters, news readers and so on. This is the high-profile, glamorous aspect where well-known stars and entertainers work for the high salaries so often highlighted by the tabloid press.

143

Most of the equipment used in the film industry is still very traditional, although it has become more compact and lighter and there have been impressive advances in sound using Dolby noise-reduction systems. The size and format of the film varies according to what it is being used for. Feature films can be made on 16mm or 35mm film and some more recent productions have used 70mm for better resolution and clarity. Film is increasingly being used in drama for television, in part because of the increasing convergence of the two industries. Television dramas are now, in some cases, distributed for cinema exhibition.

In pre-production the script has already been broken down into 'scenes' and a shooting schedule prepared that lays down which scenes will be shot on which days. For economy's sake all the scenes on one set or location will be filmed at the same time, regardless of the order of events in the story-line. If a film begins and ends in Paris, but takes place mainly in London, the Paris scenes will be shot together. A continuity person keeps careful notes to see that the actors' costumes and hairstyles look the same in scenes which are supposed to be close together in the story, although they may be shot weeks apart. Continuity also takes notes on the timings of every take. In television, this work is usually done by the production assistant.

Scenes are dealt with as 'shots' and 'set-ups' when the camera is moved to a new position and the lighting is changed to accommodate this. Each shot may take several 'takes'. For actors and actresses film work can be very technical, because they have to walk to exact marks on the floor and turn and gesture at the correct moment to suit the camera and the lighting. They also have to keep in character and maintain the appropriate emotional attitude in scenes that are shot out of sequence and may, from day to day, bear no relation to each other.

Electronic technology, which has had an enormous impact in recent years on television production, is increasingly having an effect on film, especially because of its increasing use in post production. This will only increase with the introduction of digital systems. Today it is possible to remove mistakes during the editing process and some commentators suggest that this is destroying some of the old movie-making skills: 'Digital technology has allowed film-making to get sloppier: if there's a problem with a setup you can fix it digitally. In *Jurassic Park* a scene accidentally included one of the grips ... standing in the shot, smoking a cigarette. This kind of mistake can be digitally removed.'[1]

Most day-to-day television programmes are recorded in a studio by as many as six electronic cameras operated by cameramen or women. These cameras are usually rather large and are supported on a pedestal on mobile mountings. The images are recorded directly on to videotape which is then taken to the editing suite to be crafted into a programme.

Today, all television equipment is in the process of major transition as the digital revolution sweeps all before it. One of the major areas which will be revolutionised by digital technology is news gathering. Today camera crews shoot video footage on Betacam tape which is viewed by a journalist and is cut by an editor. Tomorrow's TV journalists, using digital cameras and digital equipment, will shoot, edit and transmit their own stories (for a further discussion of this see Chapter 12).

Some television programmes go out 'live'. They are not pre-recorded and then edited, but are transmitted directly without editing. These are mainly news and current affairs programmes and chat shows. Many live programmes also include pre-recorded and edited inserts which are sometimes referred to as 'films' though nowadays they are almost always shot on video (so-called 'film inserts' have usually been recorded electronically). Coverage of a by-election result, for example, will often include a live studio discussion and live reports from the constituency but will also feature short 'films' describing the campaign and the constituency during the weeks leading up to the election.

Live shows are the high-risk area of television because so much can go wrong: a guest can be drunk or swear or slander someone; or the newsreader can give an introduction to an insert about cot deaths only for pre-recorded pictures of animals in a zoo to appear in a box in the corner of the screen. This type of juxtaposition can jar the audience and deeply wound and offend many viewers. It requires a certain amount of coolness and nerve to cope with this type of problem and similarly with an Autocue malfunction, and those who can do so on camera deserve their high salaries.

In the early days of television everything was live and many of the traditional procedures in television date back to that period. Live television means that the staff are usually on a knife edge and have to be extremely efficient and alert. Pre-recording of programmes has meant a considerable relaxation of the emotional tension in television, to the chagrin of many of the people who now fondly remember the old days when television was 'real'.

In addition to the heavy cameras used 'in-house', outside the studios much use is now made of small video cameras which are hand-held and supported on the shoulder. Single video camera production (Portable Single Camera or PSC), sometimes referred to as ENG (Electronic News-Gathering) or EFP (Electronic Field Production), has revolutionised news-gathering because of its ease of use and speed of editing. The ENG operator sums up the *as it happens* public image which television likes to present to the world. ENG operators from all the broadcasting companies of the world, with cameras on their shoulders at the ready, squinting through the eyepieces, crowd together on the tarmac to record President Clinton as he flies into Ireland on a peace mission. This is the all-pervasive image of television news recording today.

Some dramas are also now recorded on small hand-held cameras, especially plays which aim at a gritty realism. The single-camera recording has the flavour of a news report about it because the audience has become so attuned to the technique via television news. *The Bill* uses this technique: policemen rush up and down corridors and in and out of offices with the camera operator following close behind. There are very few cuts and edits, which increases the *actualite* atmosphere. A great advantage of this is that, besides being effective, it is also relatively cheap!

The most elaborate of all recordings in television is the Outside Broadcast (OB). The OB unit is essentially a mobile studio control room built into a van with a number of cameras linked to it. The OB is mainly used for state occasions, political conferences or sporting events. There are, however, an increasing number of smaller mobile units that use portable single cameras (PSCs).

Again, however, all aspects of the industry are changing with the introduction of digital equipment. Computer giants like Sony, Avid, Quantel, Tektronix, BTS and Panasonic are all fighting to develop a complete computer system for the newsroom of the future where everything a journalist could need to put together and transmit a story could be located in a single desktop computer linked to a central storage system called a 'server'. Again, this reflects the move towards multi-skilling and raises concerns about the survival of traditional craft jobs.

Non-broadcast sector
Work in the industry is now no longer restricted to feature films, commercials and television. All types of independent companies are now producing programmes for television, but there are also companies producing videos for the corporate sector, for education and training and for the pop industry. These companies produce videos which are tailor-made for a particular audience and their distribution is therefore limited. They are not broadcast and the companies producing them are sometimes linked together and referred to as the *non-broadcast sector*.

On the whole companies that are part of the independent non-broadcast sector use less sophisticated equipment than those independents involved in broadcasting. Broadcast standards require highly sophisticated and extremely expensive hardware, and it would make no economic sense for a small company with a limited market to spend astronomical sums on such equipment. The quality of the hardware, however, does make a difference to the finished product.

146

Non-broadcast production sometimes lacks the finished polish of broadcast television and feature films. Sensing this, many would-be newcomers sometimes turn up their noses at joining small video companies as a way into the industry. This is a mistake, because the technical and creative skills required in this sector are similar to those of broadcasting. It is a good place to learn about production and gain experience in a variety of jobs in order to see where your particular interests and talents lie. Multi-skilling is endemic in this sector and so it is the place to experience the whole production process, from beginning to end.

A Word of Comment
In Britain we have become used to extremely high standards in our films and on our television screens. This is because we have a long tradition of sophisticated and well-trained craftspeople using first-class equipment. As television becomes more fragmented, individual companies will have less money available for broadcast purposes. Although with digital technology the quality of the image will improve, it is still the case that, unless people have been properly trained, professional standards (in terms of the manner in which a story is told) could fall.

In the United States, while high technical standards and professional skills have been maintained on the large screen, some commentators suggest that there has been a deterioration in production values on the small screen. This may also partly be because of the widespread presence in the United States of community television on cable. While community television is an extremely positive development in that it allows public access, it may have 'softened up' American audiences for less polished presentation in mainline television.

In Britain, when people talk about 'quality television' they are usually talking about the content of the programme and this is often linked with the idea of public service broadcasting. Note, however that 'quality television' is also used to refer to the quality of the image presented. A multitude of different aspects – good design, sophisticated camera technique, clever editing – have accustomed the British audience to very high standards overall. Lack of training, combined with fragmentation of the industry, could lead, as in the United States, to a decline in production standards in Britain. It is a matter of conjecture as to how British audiences will react to this.

Post-Production
For both film and video the main task of the post-production period is editing. The completed production is then marketed and distributed. While pre-production and production are often the work of the same

company, post-production is often done by a separate company which offers specialised editing facilities. Companies offering editing equipment and skills are sometimes referred to as 'facilities houses'. By the post-production stage most of the people involved in pre-production and production have moved on and a group of new employees with new tasks takes over. Producers and directors remain throughout all three phases, but post-production involves the hiring of editors, dubbing engineers, composers, special effects engineers and graphic artists (to work on the titles and the credits). The post-production stage can be quite straightforward and quick for most television programmes, but it can take longer than the actual filming/recording on feature films, pop videos and commercials, especially those with dramatic special effects. Pop videos have made a virtual cult out of the editing stage and most of the budget can be spent on this phase.

Most post-production jobs are now freelance (even in television) and qualified people move between all three sectors of the industry. This flexibility has been one of the notable benefits of technological advance. Computer technology has brought great changes to post-production and this is having a knock-on effect on working practices, business operations and the way film and television programmes are put together. In the 50s the craft of editing bifurcated with the development of video, and from then on, until about 1993, there were two completely separate forms – film editing and videotape editing. This separatism is now collapsing. New techniques in post-production are making an impact in both film and television production and will be discussed in more detail in Chapter 15.

Traditional post-production of film involves the processing of the exposed film by a laboratory and the transfer of the sound recording to a magnetic tape. This is then followed by editing and completion. Soundtrack, opticals, titles and special effects are added once the film has been cut. A sound editor or dubbing editor puts together several different tracks, which are mixed at a dubbing session in a sound studio to make the final soundtrack. The tracks include the actors' dialogue, sound effects (sometimes created, but often borrowed from the sound effect libraries) and recorded music to match the timing and mood of the edited film (see Chapter 12).

The fundamental difference between film and videotape is that film is physically cut in the editing process and videotape is not. The film editor's hands actually touch the film which he or she cuts while viewing the film frame by frame on a Steenbeck (a film editing table). Many films have been recovered from disaster in the cutting room by able editors who necessarily possess a highly developed physical dexterity which has to be exercised on a daily basis if the skill is to be maintained.

All editors remove errors and tighten the overall structure but, in contrast to film editors cutting films in cutting rooms, video editors pushed buttons in editing suites. Videotape editing requires sophisticated electronic editing machines, but these were, and are, relatively easy to operate from the physical point of view. The editor of a videotaped programme views the original tape with the producer or the director and then the scenes that are to be retained for broadcast are selected. These are then copied on to another tape while the first tape remained untouched. Sound effects and music are added and the finished programme is ready for transmission.

With the introduction of non-linear editing in the last three years, editing rooms have been changing. Broadcasting, which for seventy years has functioned with one technology – analogue – is about 'to go digital' and provoke a post-production revolution. As explained in Chapter 4, in the past fifteen to twenty years, computers have made an enormous impact on business, commerce, record keeping and scientific research. Suddenly, in what really seems to be a space of two or three years, sound, music, video, sophisticated graphics, as well as text and data, can also all be expressed in binary digits and re-assembled for computer speakers and screens. Inevitably, this has had an impact on the entertainment industry and especially on post-production. As the technology decreases in price and increases in power, not only will non-linear editing become more common but the whole of post-production will be transformed.

Exhibition, Transmission and Sales

For film, once the editing is completed, the finished picture and sound go back to the laboratories for 'combined prints' to be made for distribution to cinemas, where they will be exhibited. In television, once the video editor is finished, the programme is stored away for future use in the appropriate slot in the schedule. The actual showing of a programme is known as transmission. Transmission control is part of the technical side of television and it is concerned almost exclusively with the day-to-day scheduling of programmes. Transmission controllers make sure that programmes go out on time and in sequence. The public image of a television station depends on this job being done well. If a television company puts out a programme at a time which is different from that listed, it irritates the viewer. Viewers are also used to a seamless sequence of pictures: blank screens can be very disconcerting and will alienate an audience. When a mistake occurs that the audience sees, it is usually the transmission controller's fault.

Once a television company has transmitted the programme it may then seek to sell it in the increasingly globalised marketplace on terrestrial,

149

cable or satellite television, which is one of the reasons that sales jobs in the entertainment industry are increasing relatively rapidly.

Both film distribution and programme transmission will inevitably change as the Internet and the information superhighway pipe films and programmes down telephone lines and highband cable systems (see Chapter 4).

A Word of Advice

These then are the various stages of production. Books that describe the production process in more detail are listed in the back of this book. In many schools media studies are part of the curriculum and more young people are following such courses at GCSE level. The information in this chapter is therefore familiar to them. Others, however, are at schools where media studies are not part of the curriculum. Such students are increasingly at a disadvantage when it comes to applying to study film or television at higher or further education level.

Another option is to buy tapes and teaching aids designed for teachers of the media from the British Film Institute. Recently the BBC published a book about the making of the series *Pride and Prejudice* which describes its production process. Focal Press, which is an imprint of Butterworth-Heinemann Ltd., publishes specialised technical books about particular production tasks and techniques.

Useful addresses and information are given at the end of the book and the bibliography also contains some recommended books for more extensive reading. Finally, anyone wanting to understand the production process should try to visit one or more of the following: the Museum of the Moving Image, South Bank, London; Granada Studios Tour, Water Street, Manchester; the National Museum of Photography, Film and Television, Bradford.

Case History

SIMON PRICE

Simon is 24 and he did a BA in Film and Television at Surrey Institute of Art and Design, Farnham, which is a BECTU accredited course. He is currently working as a Development Producer for Carlton UK.

I started by doing a two-year B/TECH in Performing Arts in Ipswich (near where I grew up) concentrating on acting and directing. After finishing the course the students started their own theatre company called *Just Add Water* and I directed their first play but I left after six months to go to the States to Richmond, Virginia, where I directed children's plays for a Camp America summer camp. I specialised in drama direction. The day before I was due to go to Richmond though I heard that I had been accepted by the film school at Farnham so I stayed in the States for four months and then came back and went straight into a three year BA Hons in Film and Video.

One of the strengths of the Farnham course is it provides a very free atmosphere. We did a lot of group work on video and film and we did get experience using 16mm film which is a lot more difficult these days because it is so expensive. Colleges can't afford to do much of that anymore. We did a lot of film theory which I had never done before and which was really fascinating. I learnt a lot. It taught me how to look at things in new ways.

We had to make a film a year 'off our own bat' as part of the course. My first year effort was a black-and-white drama shot on video. In the second year I did a standard love story but used loads of different forms, such as pop video or documentary, to tell the story in different scenes. At the end of the third year I made my graduation film on 16mm. It was a thirty minute drama about three girls. The film was called *Rage* and it was about a violent incident and its repercussions. It cost about £3,500 to make which was a lot of money for a student film. We had a large crew on location and it all took about seventeen days. *Rage* got into the local cinemas in East Anglia.

I was then unemployed for about four months and I wrote to about one or two hundred production companies. I did not ask for a job but just asked if I could come and meet people working in the companies. It did not actually result in work but it kept my enthusiasm up. You have to keep motivated and you must have a foot in the door in some way. Anyway, while still unemployed, I decided with a friend of mine to make a documentary about British politics. We called it: *But What Can I Do?* and, although it was fundamentally about British politics and the failure of British democracy it looked at other issues, such as the Criminal Justice Bill. I was the lead character in the film and the camera followed me around as I tried to find out what, if any, political change could be brought about through visits to my MP and so on. Really I was keeping my hand in at film-making.

Then a lecturer at Farnham phoned to tell me about a new training programme at Carlton UK called *SHIFT*. I applied and got in. *SHIFT* is a late-night/early-morning strand — it goes out at 1 am and a group of six of us work together as a team doing everything for each other. I suppose you would call it multi-skilling, we act as each other's editors, camera operators, scriptwriters, etc. as necessary. The *SHIFT* programme can be anything — drama or comedy or documentary.

I have made a number of pieces ranging from simple interviews with celebrities thought documentary items and dramas of various lengths and subject matter. *SHIFT* is a Carlton training initiative that seeks to employ eight new trainees every year to make hour-long programmes transmitted every week.

I've just had my contract renewed as a Development Producer for the *SHIFT* programme which means I am working at producing ideas for documentaries.

Note
1. Phil Tippett in an interview with Iain Boal in *Resisting the Virtual Life, The Culture and Politics of Information*, ed. by James Brook and Iain Boal (San Francisco: City Lights, 1995), p. 260.

PART FOUR
THE JOBS

THE PRODUCTION TEAM

Film, video and broadcasting encompass many different jobs. In the previous chapter we looked at the way films or programmes are constructed through the creative and technical expertise of a production team drawn together to 'craft' the final result. In this section we will look at the individual jobs more closely and examine the various options open to those who wish to work in specific areas.

Most career books start with a discussion of entry grades because they are obviously of great significance for new recruits. However, despite the elements of normal industrial production in film and television (which it is correct to stress), the world of moving pictures is not, and never will be, an industry exactly like any other. There is a special quality associated with the production of entertainment which makes the work more a way of life than a job. This is true for all aspects: technical/ craft, artistic/creative and even administrative/management. In virtually all areas people can become hooked on the industry in a way which is quite unusual and rare in other jobs. They all share a sense of working towards the final result. In film and television it is virtually impossible to dig oneself into a bunker and take a blinkered approach towards one's own specific task area. A sense of camaraderie and a commitment to team effort is an absolute rule if a production is to be successful.

For these reasons it is unwise to view the job market only within the context of those areas which are of particular concern to you. As we have seen in the previous chapter, you ought to have an overview of the whole production process. This was the strength of the BBC training system and its eclipse is almost universally regretted. Understanding the top jobs in the industry is vital: the men and women in those jobs put their stamp on the whole production. Even the humblest runner, hired for the summer by a film company to make the tea, should be aware of this.

The movie and television industry is always more than the sum of its parts. In addition, this is an industry at the cutting edge of massive

155

change in employment patterns and technology. As we have seen, this had produced a shake-out in the old rigid job structure. While there can be no doubt that the industry is in a state of flux and that the employment market is not especially buoyant, there are clear opportunities for young entrepreneurs who want to make their own programmes and have the business skills to finance them.

Reference has been made at several points in this book to campaigns in the 70s for 'more access' and the emergence of the 25 per cent quota. Make no mistake, despite the recession, these development have widened opportunities for the individual within the entertainment business. Consequently, a few (a very few) young people of exceptional talent and ambition have managed in a very short time, and with great good luck, to go all the way to the top. Many producers in the pop video sector are very young and other young people are running independent film companies, and therefore getting their own programmes on television. Although many young people complain about the present situation, these successes would have been unthinkable a decade ago.

We will look first at some of the most important jobs in the industry. It is important to remember, however, that multi-skilling is now endemic and strict craft and professional divisions are no longer as rigorously observed as they used to be. This is especially the case in small video companies.

Starting from the top:

THE PRODUCER (creative/management/financial)

Film

Once I became interested in stories and getting stories told, I realised I had to be a producer to get them told in the right way. (Warren Beatty)

Producing is the key job in film or television. *Producers* deal with ideas, money and organisation, three vital ingredients. Many young people who do not understand the industry confuse producers and directors. The producer usually has the original idea, commissions the script, secures the finances, hires the director and is involved in casting, finding locations and hiring the crew. Producers animate everything else. (For a description for the director's role, see below.)

Producers are often also closely associated with the marketing of films. He or (increasingly) she is the organising supremo, the presiding genius. Producers need to be multi-tasking types; they need to have a finger in every pie and must be highly disciplined and organised, because everything depends on them.

156

The best producers are highly intuitive. They must have a nose for a good idea and be able to sense the way the wind of public taste is blowing. They often take great financial risks and the best are prepared to back their hunches against the criticism of the cautious. They need to have either great personal charisma to win over the doubters, or an extremely good track record. Investing in a film is a risky venture and bankers are never over-enthusiastic about putting their money into what, in financial terms, is a long shot.

Increasingly in the feature film sector, the dominance of the big companies has meant the production of formula films made according to a set pattern based on market research. The research indicates what audiences want to see on the screens (boy gets girl, sexy love scenes, no sad deaths, car chases, special effects, violence, exotic locations, good punch-ups). The producers of the calculated blockbuster are often held captive by the accountants and have to produce films that abide by a formula. The films are designed to make a great deal of money – and most of them do – but their organisers are sometimes rather alien to the film-making tradition. They are more like hard-headed accountants and grey-suited businessmen so that many people regret the disappearance of the colourful buccaneer entrepreneurs of the past. One film maker has commented:

> Digital technology gives a great deal more participation to the business community, the managers. Everything in the studios right now is very heavily managed – there's not a filmmaker among them: they're all MBAs, lawyers and agents. That's who runs the motion-picture racket. There are no directors, producers, or actors in management.[1]

Fortunately, there are still film-makers around who follow their own hunches and produce movies which might not have 'marketable' themes. Every now and again they confound the market researchers by producing a film (sometimes referred to as a 'sleeper') that everyone wants to see. The best producers combine financial wizardry with artistic horse sense (a rare combination).

To bring a story to the screen, producers surround themselves with the best talent the budget can afford. They have to keep a tight hold on the purse-strings while allowing talent to flourish. This can be very difficult in a world of competing temperaments and supercharged egos. The final film will depend on the quality of the people the producer employs, and he or she must ensure that the performers and crew function efficiently as a team and without too much aggravation and conflict. The result can be an artistic masterpiece – or a flop!

Television and Video

In television drama, the producer's job is similar to that of a producer in features. He or she is the main organiser and, nowadays, can also bear the major burden of raising the money (this is always the case in independent production companies). However, on the whole, the production team in television is smaller than in feature films, even if the drama is actually filmed (as opposed to recorded on tape). Once again the producer may have the original idea and assemble the production team, and it is his or her responsibility to ensure that a high-quality programme is produced on time and within budget.

Most television programmes are not dramas, however, and require nowhere near the same degree of complex organisation or financial commitment. Today many film producers start in television or in video companies or in companies making commercials. Producers of television programmes tend to be interest-oriented rather than business types (although this is changing), because different kinds of programmes call for different kinds of abilities. Thus: producers of documentary programmes often have a background in journalism; producers of quiz programmes must have an instinct for light entertainment; producers of pop programmes must know about contemporary music and also about lighting and sound effects; sports producers have a fascination with sports and are sometimes themselves ex-athletes or ex-footballers.

It is very easy to confuse the functions of producer and director in television and in small video companies, because people in these sectors of the industry do take on both roles especially with the increasing reliance on multi-skilling: producer/directors are very common in the independent sector. In television, much more than in film, the producer is part of the creative team. Television producers can have a hands-on role in the studio and on location, particularly if they are also trained directors.

So how do you get to be a producer?

By working your way up and showing a flair for the job! There is no cast-iron qualification for production except proving that you can do it. (Some colleges, however, are now modelling their training on the BBC approach and providing students with the chance to work on all the various elements of the production process. Courses in 'production' are now offered as an option by some universities, especially at the postgraduate level but you are unlikely to be appointed to a producer position after qualifying.) In film, some producers have a background in business, accountancy or law, because knowing about money has always been essential. Some film producers were originally agents and came to know the business that way.

In television some producers come up via the technical route, as camera operators or directors. This is particularly true for light entertainment; documentary and news producers are more commonly graduates who have previously been employed as researchers to gain experience. In the past it was very unusual for anyone with a business background to end up in television production, but the move towards independent companies has changed this. In fact, in the independent sector people with entrepreneurial talent form their own companies and produce programmes for the market-place. In that sense, the independent production companies have a similar 'culture', though on a smaller scale, to the feature film industry.

DIRECTORS

Film
Concentrate on the story, leave the details to others – and sit whenever you can. (John Huston)

In feature films, as the name suggests, *directors* direct the performances of the actors and dictate the camera shots. Directors have the key creative hands-on role. They are responsible for deploying the technical and artistic resources in the best possible way so that the picture ends up in the can for developing and editing. The director's main concern is with production and post-production, although he or she usually has a hand in such pre-production tasks as location selection.

What the director does is to take a script provided by the producer (and the writer) and guide the actors through it in rehearsal. He or she must then draw good on-screen performances from the actors, so many directors have some knowledge of acting techniques. They must also have technical knowledge of cameras, lighting and the eventual editing process, because they have to communicate clearly the pictures they want the technical crew to provide. Directors have to possess a good visual sense: they have to be able to read a script and see in their mind's eye the end result in pictorial terms. They discuss the set and wardrobe with the respective designers. Not surprisingly, many film directors come from a theatrical or visual arts background.

On the set or on location the director is there, on the spot, talking to the actors, instructing the camera operators, debating changes in the script. The producer can be thousands of miles away negotiating with the backers for money as the film goes over budget. The classic image of the director in the old Hollywood films is a temperamental individual with a megaphone, shouting instructions here, there and everywhere.

At the end of a day's shoot film directors view the 'rushes' in a preview theatre to ensure that the required image has been shot. If things are not quite right they can retake scenes the next day, although this is expensive. A director's hours are long and the emotional tension and stress levels are very high, but it is also possibly the most creatively satisfying job in film. Really talented directors are always in demand and salaries can be very high indeed. However, it takes a great deal of skill to be a director and there is no substitute for experience.

On feature films, directors are assisted by first, second and third *assistant directors*. In a sense the word director in these cases is a misnomer because they are in no way trainee or deputy directors (there is usually only one director on a film set and he or she is *God*). Assistant directors have responsibilities more analogous to producing than directing. In fact, the career route for assistant directors may be towards production management rather than towards direction (see below for a description of the duties of a production manager).

Assistant directors are part of the organisational and administrative side of film-making, rather than the cinematic and creative side. The first assistant director carries out the director's practical requirements, such as supervising the discipline and general organisation of the daily shoot. In the pre-production period the 'first' will work with the production manager to 'break down' the shooting script and examine likely requirements and responsibilities. The first assistant will also work with the director to find out how the film is visualised.

The first assistant director usually hires a second and third and their responsibilities too are organisational. They keep the production running smoothly with the second assistant working closely with the production office, and the third assistant working on the set making sure that artists receive the calls and appear on time (minutes must not be lost in such an expensive activity as film-making).

In television, the equivalent of a first assistant director's job is that of studio/floor manager (see below). In fact, when a television team goes out on location, studio managers can be renamed first assistants.

Television and Video
In television the *programme director*, like the film director, converts the script into the images and sound that eventually appear on the screen. In television drama they must have an excellent visual sense and sound technical knowledge. It is directors who coax good

160

performances from the actors and performers in drama and light entertainment. Directors in television are assisted by production assistants (PAs, see below).

Producer/directors who combine both roles are often found in television and can be very powerful.

How do you get to be a director? – 'Let me count the ways'.
Most directors today work in all three sectors. They are mainly freelance, although there are staff directors in the BBC and ITV. The cutbacks in television have undoubtedly affected the training of directors and the Skill Search report identified this as an area where a shortage exists. The problem for the newcomer is that the shortage is mainly one of experienced directors. Many film and television directors come up through the ranks. They can be former camera operators or (especially in television) studio floor managers or editors.

Major drama schools, film schools and vocationally oriented colleges and universities that offer media degrees provide courses in direction, and some fortunate graduates with good track records and glowing references may get jobs immediately in the non-broadcast and pop video sector. However, no one should go to college or university expecting a job to fall into their lap: it won't. The industry does not work like that, you need contacts and a reputation for being reliable and that only comes with experience.

Increasingly in the new freelance world there are many privately funded short-term courses in direction available to those prepared to pay. The well-respected ones are nearly always for people who already have some experience or a job in the industry.

The National Film and Television School provides a National Short Course Training Programme (NSCTP) in all aspects of film and video, but this is mainly designed for experienced freelances already working in the industry who wish to retrain or update their skills. For the experienced camera operator who wishes to move into direction the NSCTP will probably have a suitable course for him or her. Anyone working in the industry who is interested in retraining should be aware of these courses. But beware! More and more short-term courses are springing up in response to the crisis in training. Check them out first for quality and industry acceptance (see Chapter 8).

PRODUCTION MANAGER (administrative/managerial)

Film
Some of the guys were bitching about their hotel rooms. When I started in the business, we used to sleep in tents. (John Wayne)

Production manager is a job category mainly found in the film sector, and less commonly in television and video. The production manager is the producer's deputy and is actively involved in the day-to-day problems of filming. He or she prepares a detailed budget for shooting and a shooting schedule, arranges the hire of equipment and obtains permission to film in certain locations. On a large production the job can be divided into two: a line producer in charge of administrative tasks such as budgeting, crew hire and contracts; and a location manager responsible for finding locations.

Location managers are sometimes found in television. This is because major television dramas can be as complicated to make as feature films and require outside locations. The location manager, in film and television, discusses the script in detail with the producer and the director and then tries to find places that will match what he or she believes the producer and director want. Location managers need imaginative gifts, as well as common sense and organisational skills. In choosing suitable places a variety of factors have to be considered, such as noise, aeroplanes passing overhead, and so on. It can be very difficult to find locations for a pre-twentieth-century drama: one episode of a drama about Renaissance Italy was reported to have aircraft trails in the sky! Viewers love to spot such errors and write in if an accidental anachronism occurs. However, as we have seen, digital technology is solving the problem and putting an end to sharp-eyed viewers' fun.

On their initial visits, location managers will take photographs of the possible locations and bring these back to the production office for discussion. If a location seems suitable, then the production team will visit it to see if it lives up to the location manager's promises. If everything is fine, location managers will arrange for terms and the drawing-up of contracts. The public can be paid if their houses are used (though this is not as much as the uninitiated expect!). Location managers have many liaison jobs to do in the course of filming. If a large-scale shoot is going to take place, both the police and the local authorities have to be notified in advance. They must also ensure that everything is left as it was before the film crew arrived.

How do people become production managers?
Generally this is not a job for new entrants. Production managers on large-scale projects have to know the business very well indeed. They sometimes have a legal or financial background, but mostly they have worked in television or film for years and have developed a 'feel' for the job. In small independent companies production manager functions will often be carried out by the producer or director – another example of the trend towards multi-skilling.

FLOOR MANAGER (organisational)

Television

The *floor manager*'s job is mainly found in television and it is focused on the day of the recording. Before the recording date, however, the floor manager usually receives a copy of the script and he or she must then consider any problems that could come up. Floor managers usually attend the last planning meeting of the production team so that they know exactly what is going to happen on the day. They make notes about any changes and bring up potential problems.

Floor managers have two main areas of responsibility on the day of recording: they liaise with the programme director; and they manage what happens on the studio floor. Since the TV director sits in the control room above the studio floor, separated from the studio by a glass screen, he or she needs someone to handle events down below and this is where the floor manager comes in. The director has to concentrate on the viewing monitors and which pictures he or she wants to go out to the viewers, so he or she needs a subordinate to communicate to the floor. This is done through a 'talkback' system with the floor manager.

If you visit a television studio as part of the audience, the floor manager is probably the person who 'warms you up'. He or she will talk to you before the recording and tell you what to do: for example, 'When Chris Evans appears, please clap when I give this signal.'

It is the floor manager who gives the director's instructions to performers and who also gives cues and prompts. Floor managers co-ordinate and manage everything that happens on the set on the day of recording. They make sure performers know where to stand, and what to do, that props and microphones are in place, that booms and cameras are in their proper positions.

How do you get to be a floor manager?

In the past, floor managers started their careers as floor assistants, which were the equivalent of gophers and runners in the film industry. Now floor assistants hardly exist (because of job cutbacks) and floor managers are recruited from a wide variety of jobs within television. They are rarely recruited from outside unless they have similar experience in the theatre. There are no formal qualifications for a floor manager except knowledge of the job and the right temperament combined with organisational ability. The writer certainly knows of one case where a security guard at the BBC eventually ended up as a floor manager. Floor managers have to be very cool and calm since the job can involve a great deal of aggravation: there are

163

frequent last-minute crises which might cause panic in normal people. Floor managers must never panic!

PRODUCTION ASSISTANT (Administrative/Organisational)

Television

Despite their name, *production assistants* (PAs) assist the television or video director as much as the producer. For many years the job was almost exclusively done by women with expert secretarial skills, who acted as the director's personal assistants. This description, however, does not do justice to the scope of the job. PAs, more than anyone else in television, need to have an all-round knowledge of the way it works – technically, administratively and financially. Anyone who knows television will acknowledge that the PA is often the key element in the success of a production. Feminists within television used to argue that had the job been traditionally done by men rather than women it would have had much higher pay and status. PAs bear a great weight of responsibility and are with a programme from beginning to end. Recently the job of production assistant has begun to change and it does vary from company to company. Today, with the increasing emphasis on 'costings', financial, computing and accountancy skills are as important as secretarial training.

Production assistants are assigned to a particular programme from the very beginning; they help to keep control of the budget and do most of the organisation. The PA is the main point of contact for all members of the crew and production team. They accompany directors to production team meetings, which involve the lighting supervisor, sound supervisor, graphics, wardrobe, make-up, studio managers and others, and they keep records of these meetings. They also do the routine office work such as booking rehearsal rooms, technical equipment, hotels for performers, dressing-rooms, catering facilities, and so on.

Sometimes the PA job is divided into location PAs, who assist the director on location, and studio PAs, who organise recording sessions in the studio, but most PAs combine both roles. It really depends on the size of the production. Drama, for example, could have two PAs if it involves a great deal of location work. When television uses film on location, location PAs may keep the 'shot list', which means making a record of each shot, noting the number of the camera roll, the sound roll, the length of the shot and the general description. The purpose of the shot list is to provide the editors with a written record of the film when it reaches the cutting room. This process is simpler for video, but location PAs still keep very accurate notes of what is going on. This aspect of the work is similar to the role of continuity people in feature films.

On location on a large production PAs look after transport, lodging and food and ensure that everyone gets to the location on time. PAs must be able to absorb grouses from the crew about hotel accommodation, food and daily rates, as well as cope with temperamental directors. For example, if the weather misbehaves everything may have to be reorganised efficiently at a moment's notice. Woe betide the PA who fails to cope.

The rise and rise of non-linear editing has tended to reduce the location aspect of the PA's work on smaller shoots. In addition, many new young directors who have come into broadcast television from the independent video sector may never have worked with a PA and have little understanding of the experience and knowledge that characterise the PA. They ignore this resource because they do not understand it. Some PAs complain that the job has, therefore, become increasingly office-bound and consequently much less interesting. It has also meant that many young, inexperienced directors have made more mistakes than they need to!

The studio side of the PA's job involves many tasks: booking the studio for recording; outlining which studio facilities will be required; specifying the number of cameras; reserving the dressing-room for performers and so on. PAs set up a final planning meeting about ten days before a studio date, and the lighting supervisor, sound supervisor, floor manager, set designer, make-up artist, wardrobe designer, vision mixer, graphic designer and director all get together for a final 'talk through' of the script. Scripts are changed all the time during pre-production and the PA has to note the changes and type and retype the script to take account of the alterations. Often changes are made at the very last minute, almost at the point of transmission, so they have to be fast and accurate typists.

On the day of a studio recording PAs sit in the control room (or, as it is sometimes called, the gallery), at a long desk facing a bank of TV monitors labelled Camera One, Camera Two, VT, and so on. The PA always sits at one end, opposite the time monitor and next to the director; on the other side of the director sits the vision mixer. PAs time the individual elements within the programme as well as the whole programme, so they have to be able to use a stopwatch – in fact two stopwatches. PAs remind the producer if the recording is running fast or slow; they count in the VT inserts ('Run VT'); and they also have to answer the phone in the gallery and pass on any of the director's final orders. The PA gives instructions to the camera operators via the talkback system, reminding them when they will be 'on air'. In a live programme timing is particularly crucial. PAs have to remain calm under pressure and be able to do several things at once. As there is no daylight in the control room, the atmosphere can be claustrophobic and tense. After the recording PAs used to attend VT editing sessions and ensure that the programme was edited to time. This aspect of PA work has changed as post-production has changed with new technology. For the PA today post-production mostly involves paperwork, including paying performers.

The job of PA requires stamina. It is rarely nine-till-five and it can involve a great deal of time spent away from home. On the other hand, PAs meet interesting people and are at the heart of programme-making.

How do you become a PA?
Again, PAs usually need to have experience in the industry. Most PAs start as secretaries in the television companies and then compete for traineeships. Competition for these traineeships in the BBC or any of the ITV companies is very intense. However, it is likely that television companies will continue to train PAs because the job is so vital and because PAs really have to be familiar with all aspects of production. A broad general education and secretarial skills are essential; often the ability to read music is required since there can be a great deal of work in light entertainment and PAs have to count the beat in the gallery (although computers can now do this!). Character and temperament are important elements in the successful PA. The highly strung are not suitable for the job. Very rarely, small video companies will allow a secretary to carry out the functions of the PA. This is truly on-the-spot training!

This chapter has looked at the jobs which form the kernel of the programme-making process. Directors, production managers and PAs, however, could not do their jobs without the support of the technical/creative staff.

Case Histories

FIONA WINNING

Fiona Winning is 24 and has just finished her training as an Assistant Director with Scottish Broadcasting and Film Training.

I've always been interested in photography because I worked with my father who is a professional photographer and was brought up to be very easy around cameras. When I first went to college I was going to train as a photographer but when I wanted to do an HND in Photography at the College of Building and Printing in Glasgow they more or less felt that I had had a lot of training already from my father and that the place should go to someone who needed the course more. So I shifted direction and went to North Glasgow College instead and did a Scottish National Certificate in television and sound production. That got me interested in film. It was a studio-based course and was a good introduction to programme-making.

After that I went off to Cardonald College and did a year's HND in television production and I began to get really enthused. I had access to video cameras and I was experimenting all the time. I was always asking my friends who were writing scripts if we could do some work together. At the end of the course you were supposed to make a three-minute commercial but I did a fifteen-minute documentary about my cousin who has a small record label for dance music.

After that I applied to the Scottish Broadcast and Film Training. I hoped for the best. At the interview I said I was trying to get into the industry and that I would do anything! At the time I was trying every angle I could think of, trying to make promos for small bands and so on. Anyway, I got a place on the assistant director/'locations' course at the SBFT and have been training as an assistant director/and locations assistant for the past eighteen months. It was absolutely the best thing that could ever happen to anyone. They have really channelled me into jobs and it has been hands-on all the time.

As part of the training I have been working on features and dramas and on documentaries. I worked as Third Assistant Director for a week on the BBC drama *Nervous Energy*. At the present time the BBC is moving towards the American approach to film-making – a more freelance mode. What you are getting is the film industry traditions being grafted onto the BBC and the BBC is having to get used to the freelance culture. The BBC's terminology for their jobs was different. The work done by Third Assistant Directors in the film industry roughly used to be done by Assistant Floor Managers at the BBC. The BBC's old training system were very good but there are now fewer permanent positions so it is having to change.

The Third Assistant Director looks after the cast and works with the First and Second Assistant Directors. The First Assistant is in charge of organisation and matters like Health and Safety and making sure the film runs to schedule. If the First Assistant decides that lunch is to be ten minutes early then the Third has to make sure that everyone knows: she's like the First Assistant's tannoy! Second Assistants work mainly in the office and arrange the call sheet for the following days. Seconds make sure that everything is set up for the next day, that the supporting cast is all arranged, the transport call times and 'pick-ups', and so on. Second Assistants are there from early in the morning to last thing at night. I would quite like to go on to be a Second Assistant. I'd like to have a go at the job and see. That would be quite unusual because most Thirds want to go on to be Firsts.

Since *Nervous Energy* I have also worked on documentaries at the BBC and I learned a lot there through observation and about location work – part of my job as a trainee was to be a location assistant. On the documentaries I realised how much I'd learned from being on a feature film.

In August [1995] I worked on a Ken Loach film called *Carla's Song*.[2] It was a lovely experience from start to finish. Loach is really a great guy to work for. Tommy Gormley, who was the First and works on a lot of Loach films, really helped me a lot. Loach's way of working is quite different. Sometime he does not give the script to the cast until the night before and they have to learn their lines for the next day. There is a lot of improvisation and he sometimes also uses people who are not professional actors. He likes to use people off the street at extras so it was great fun going up to people in the street and saying, 'Would you like to be in a film?' They usually enjoy it so much that they get such a surprise when you come to pay them. They don't expect it. They are so excited. Different from the normal extras who have to do a lot of hanging about for long days. Loach is a humanitarian to work for. He treats his staff decently and doesn't make them work overly long hours.

I've also worked on a Gillies MacKinnon film called *Small Faces* and a David Hayman film called *The Near Room* but now I'm off to India to take a break. I finished my training a month ago. When I come back I will look for work as a Third Assistant Director or a locations assistant.

It's funny when you are working on film. You go through a set pattern. For the first few week you love everybody and then the hours are so long you begin to think, 'Why the hell I am doing this?' Then it gets towards the end of the film and you think 'I love all these people and I won't see them again and I'll miss them and its awful!'.

I have to emphasise that it is really exhausting working on a film – the hours are crazy, you have no social life, you have to be really close to your boyfriend because it is hard for them to put up with it. It is so hardgoing, you work such long hours but it is all worth it. In the end when you see the film and you know you have been part of that, helping to create it and your own name is up there on screen – it's marvellous.

RACHEL WRIGHT

Rachel Wright is 22. She graduated with a first class honours degree in Media with Business Management and Information Technology from

University College, Warrington (which awards Manchester University degrees) and then went to Middlesex University to do an MA in Video Production

I've always been interested in film and television. I joined the Royal Television Society in the North East when I was about 14. My parents had to drive me to the meetings. I was the RTS's youngest member and the only female but they were all so interested in helping me. They supported me from the beginning. In fact, in the end my parents joined the RTS and they have become interested too! I did various work placements at BBC North in Newcastle and at Tyne Tees. In fact I did a lot of work experience in the Newcastle area. I joined the Darlington Video Workshop and I was always making my own videos. I was really interested in working in the industry and when I went to university I was determined to go on a degree course that involved practice where I could get my hands on the equipment. At Warrington I was able to specialise in video production and I really enjoyed the course because there were so many opportunities and I did a work placement.

I finished my MA in September 1995 and then I saw an advert for a trainee programme called Project Oak at the National Film and Television School. It's funded by the European Social Fund through Skillset. They were advertising a programme of training and work experience in conjunction with the NFTS full-time programme and one of the traineeships was for Production Management which has always interested me. I thought that you would have to have a lot of experience before you could be a production manager – and you do – but I did not know there were any training programmes anywhere. I didn't think I would get on the course because the NFTS is so competitive but anyway I did and we began with a two-week intensive training. There were workshops and guest speakers who were experienced production managers. We had to get to know everything about the whole production process in film, breaking down scripts, location work, and so on. We were given all the paper work to do and shown how to fill it in – everything. I learned more in that two weeks than I have ever learned in my life before. It was all so focused and so structured and so hard – by the end I was suffering from brain overload!

This has been my first real introduction to film before that I really concentrated on video. Feature films are much more complicated, there are a lot more levels of staffing which the production manager has to control. There are eight production managers on the course with me and I am working on a documentary film called *Red Rose* about Rose Kerrigan who was a Communist activist. We are given a budget which we have to manage completely and we have to organise the schedule:

pre-production, shooting and post production – right the way through. It is really exhausting.

You've really got to keep at it to get on in this business because there are so many obstacles. I think it is really important to remain flexible because you have to be ready to take any opportunities that come along and then they might take you off in a direction which you hadn't thought of. It's not possible to get a job as a production manager straight away so, when I finish this traineeship, my plan is to get a job as a location or assistant location manager on a feature film, get more experience and then go on from there. I just love every aspect of the industry – film, television, video. It is hard work but it is worth all the effort and time and concentration.

Notes

1. Phil Tippett in an interview with Iain Boal in *Resisting the Virtual Life, The Culture and Politics of Information,* ed. by James Brook and Iain Boal (San Francisco: City Lights, 1995), p. 259.
2. *Carla's Song* premiered at the Venice Film Festival in September 1996.

12

THE TECHNICAL TEAM

In the previous chapter we looked at jobs most of which are closed to new entrants. This chapter deals with the technical areas of television and film, which have a major creative element but which, at least in principle, are available to school and college leavers at the entry/trainee/assistant grades. In the absence of any widespread pattern or logic to industry training, educational degrees and diplomas with a vocational component are now more helpful to new entrants and job seekers than they used to be. At the top levels, of course – such as cinematographer on a film – recruitment is still confined to those with extensive experience and proven talent.

In television, many of the categories described below used to be permanent staff positions. Young people accepted by the BBC or ITV, for example as trainee camera operators, were given on-the-job instruction. This still goes on, but cutbacks have affected employment opportunities by reducing total numbers within these companies. This is especially the case for ITV, where the move towards the publisher/broadcaster model, as opposed to that of producer/broadcaster, has meant, and will mean, that far fewer permanent jobs are available. Consequently, camera operators, vision mixers, lighting technicians and other technical (and craft) people increasingly work as freelances, many of them receiving their start in the non-broadcast sector. In the independent video sector new entrants often find themselves doing jobs for which they have not been specifically trained and it is here that the National Vocational Qualifications will make a significant impact.

National and Scottish Vocational Qualifications in various technical areas (such as in Camera, Lighting and Sound) and at different levels have been established and more are coming on board all the time. Once the NVQs become standard, they will stimulate people to train and retrain in several job categories, as industry needs ebb and flow and shortages and surfeits become apparent. Remember, however, that it is increasingly clear that people will have to do so at their own expense. The government is proposing to encourage an atmosphere that promotes training, but it expects employers and employees to pay for it.

The technical/creative sector of the industry was (and, to a degree, still is) unionised and many job titles and job categories were associated with union traditions in specific areas. In the multi-skilled, cross-sector freelance environment of today, some of these titles are becoming redundant. In addition, some of the more gender-specific film terms are being replaced with more neutral descriptions, such as technician or operator. As this book goes to press the introduction of new technology is also beginning to make an impact as new digitised equipment changes working practices.

CAMERA CREW (technical/creative)

CINEMATOGRAPHER/LIGHTING CAMERA OPERATOR/
  DIRECTOR OF PHOTOGRAPHY
LIGHTING DIRECTOR
EXTERIOR CAMERA OPERATORS
CAMERA OPERATOR
CAMERA ASSISTANTS
ROSTRUM CAMERA OPERATOR

The most beautiful woman in the world can look like dog shit on camera. Fortunately for me, it also works the other way around. (Mel Gibson)

The camera crew is at the very heart of film-making and there are many traditions in the working practices which impart a particular flavour to their activities. *Camera operator* is the job which people immediately associate with working in the industry, and for many little, and not so little, boys and girls it has been a dream occupation (rather like engine-driving used to be fifty years ago). In the past the crew were all union-ised and almost invariably male. Some camera crews worked together over many years, moving from film to film, with the union providing a bond of brotherhood (although there was always a strict hierarchy in the jobs). There is a mystique about a film crew which, despite the vast social and economic changes of the past few years, still lingers on. It is closely associated with the almost legendary reputation which British film crews earned for themselves.

The basic function of a camera crew is to produce, on the director's instructions, the best possible images in terms of artistic interpretation and technical quality. The most senior job in a film crew is that of cinematographer/lighting camera operator.

172

Cinematographer/Lighting Camera Operator/Director of Photography

Cinematographer (sometimes called the director of photography) is a title usually associated with very distinguished lighting camera operators on high-budget feature films. Cinematographers can be as famous as the director – indeed some of them are also directors. Nicholas Roeg is one example.

The basic responsibility of the cinematographer/lighting camera operator is the supervision of lighting and camera angles in order to provide the film's visual 'mood'. He or she chooses the appropriate lens and filters to create this. The cinematographer discusses with the director the way the cameras are to be positioned, the composition of the shots and how the scenes are to be lit for the best possible result. After consultation with the director, he or she draws up a pre-arranged camera script which gives the order of the camera shots and also sets out lighting details. Cinematographers rarely handle the cameras on a day-to-day basis, but they always have camera operation experience so that they know how to instruct their subordinates to produce the right shots.

Lighting Director

Lighting director is the job in television that corresponds roughly to lighting camera operator in the film sector. Lighting directors work closely with electrical technicians, but basically, as in film, most of them begin as members of the camera crew. Sometimes, however, they may have come in from the theatre, or have a background as an engineer or electrician, or they may have moved across from film.

Lighting directors use light to capture the atmosphere of a programme. If a drama is supposed to be set in evening light the lighting director arranges this. Lighting directors decide the position and strengths of the lights and the colours (Redheads and Blondes) in order to enhance the mood of the production.

Lighting directors must work closely with the camera crew, the sound department, make-up and the set designers as well as the directors. They also need to understand and direct the work of the lighting electricians. In preparation for a programme, lighting directors design the chart indicating the lighting rig, that is, decide which studio lights should be situated where. Electricians use this chart to change the lights.

Trainee lighting directors are sometimes called lighting assistants. They begin on fairly straightforward programmes and their work is supervised by a lighting director.

Exterior Camera Operator

Exterior camera operators do more or less the same work as the lighting camera operators but on smaller productions. This level in the hierarchy is now rapidly disappearing.[1]

Camera Operators

Camera operators actually operate the camera under the lighting camera operator's overall direction. In film especially they can have considerable artistic input because they know how to secure the best shots and angles. Camera operators produce the pictures, the basic raw material of a film, which means that their talent and ability is at the core of a high-quality production. They are helped by camera assistants. In television, camera operators probably have less creative input since directors tend to determine camera angles and shots in pre-production time (see below).

Camera operators in television mainly work with electronic rather than film cameras. However, as mentioned earlier, people often refer to events being 'filmed' when they actually mean they are being recorded on tape.

Studio cameras are fairly large and are positioned on pedestals supported on mobile mountings which allow them to glide smoothly over the floor. Studios can have several cameras in operation at one time and usually each one is operated by one person. Some studio cameras are mounted at the end of a jib on a motorised crane. The crane is used for very high and very low shots (within a few inches of the floor). It has to be driven and swung by camera crew members.

In a studio the cameras have long cables which attach them to sockets and, via the sockets, to the control equipment. The cables have to be constantly moved to allow the camera freedom. This is known as 'cable bashing': the cable bashers, who move and untangle cables, are usually very junior trainee camera operators. Studio equipment and procedures will change, however, as digital equipment becomes widespread.

Camera operators in television have less control over the shots than film camera operators: the artistic/creative component of the job is perhaps less dominant. In television the shots are usually decided by the director after discussion with a senior member of the camera crew at a planning meeting. The director provides the camera crew with a pre-arranged camera script giving the order of shots. During rehearsals for recorded programmes, camera operators practice the positions. At the recording proper, directors cue the shots from the gallery: 'Camera two', 'close-up', 'two-shot', 'zoom' and so on. In some very static programmes, such as news, the cameras are operated and positioned by remote control and there is no camera operator in the studio.

In Outside Broadcasts (OBs) the camera operator functions in the same way as a camera operator in the studio. The classic outside broadcast is a great state occasion, such as a royal wedding. This would be handled by an OB unit (indeed several OB units), basically a mobile studio control room in a large van to which the outside broadcast cameras are linked. The grey outside broadcast vans of the BBC are well-known and are likely to set off a flurry of interest whenever they take up residence in a street prior to a recording. In 1995 the BBC introduced its Central Mobile Colour Control Room. It has a forty-channel vision mixer and a sixty-channel stereo sound desk and is the flagship of the OB fleet. According to vision engineer, Jeff White: 'It has made a huge difference to how we work. Effects and procedures that were difficult to achieve before like digital visual effects are now a standard feature' (*Ariel*, 5 December 1995).

Outside broadcasts on a smaller scale are recorded by portable single cameras. These are used by the camera operators rather like film cameras. The great advantage is that on most modern electronic cameras the operator can immediately review the shots on a tiny screen, a practice now familiar to thousands of amateurs with domestic video recorders. The increasing sophistication of all professional and domestic camera equipment is, however, going to make for even more multi-skilling. Camera operators in the future will be editing as well as shooting and reviewing (see below).

On the whole television camera operators lead a more prosaic life than film camera operators because there is probably less location work. The one great exception is the *news camera operator*, one of the hardest, most prestigious and most glamorous jobs in television. International news cameramen lead exciting lives; they have to be quick-witted people with a strong individualistic streak who know how to look after their own skins: they can, after all, find themselves on the front line covering wars and more than a few camera operators have died on duty. Typical of the breed is Mohammed Amin, African Bureau Chief for Visnews, who lost his left forearm in an ammunition dump explosion when Ethiopian rebels seized control of Addis Ababa. This left him unable to focus the lens, but a special camera was developed so that his right thumb can operate the focus. 'I want to be a cameraman again,' he says, 'and filming where there is danger is the only life I know.' *(FTT and BETA News*, October 1991).

Increasingly, news camera operators work on their own and without directors. This is a big change from the old days when news crews could consist of several people. If in addition to pictures a report is required, the news team will consist of two people – the camera operator and the reporter. Independent news camera operators have to carry out a complex range of jobs: sound, lighting, simple editing and maintenance. They also relay their recordings through telephone modems and satellite links back to base.

In the future the distinctions between the camera operator, the journalist and the editor are likely to dissolve completely. Multi-skilled television journalists will shoot and 'cut' (edit) their own stories completely. At present two cable news operations in London and New York employ multi-skilled video journalists. The journalist Sue Lloyd Roberts, working on her own, travelled around China (with the dissident Harry Wu) to record forced work camps. Although this was dictated by the secret nature of the assignment, this mode of work will soon be commonplace.

Understandably, the trend towards multi-skilled journalists is not greeted with enthusiasm either by camera operators or journalists and many experts believe that it will lead to a deterioration in craft skills – the 'eye' of the camera operator seeks out the quality pictures while the journalist concentrates on 'writing' the story. However, managers and accountants, who increasingly today have the power in broadcasting, are likely to favour multi-skilling since it looks better on the bottom line.

Camera Assistants (Grip/Clapper-loader/Loader/Focus-puller)

The position of *camera assistant* is mostly associated with film. The camera assistant's job has been aptly described as 'baby-sitting the camera'. The assistant does all the housekeeping tasks: watches the level of the stock; keeps the production team informed about the amount of film stock being used (so more can be ordered if necessary); does basic maintenance of the equipment; and is also responsible for the safety of the camera during shooting (any piece of technical equipment which is moved is liable to accidental damage and film sets are loaded with potential dangers). Assistants may also drive the camera car on location. If the film team goes abroad they are usually responsible for making sure the equipment goes through customs safely.

Newcomers to the industry probably do not take account of the basic administrative work which film crews crossing boundaries have to negotiate. Countries governed by dictators are often not too keen on having their inadequacies revealed and they sometimes use customs procedures as a means of slowing everything down and of just being plain awkward. Camera crews usually have a fund of stories about the delays they have encountered dealing with obstreperous customs officials, especially those who want to strip down the equipment to search for drugs!

Assistants set up the camera on location, load up the magazine with film, make sure that the lens is clean and check the focus. They prepare the clapperboard, which should bear the name of the film, the director, the date, and they also operate the clapper, usually at the beginning, but sometimes at the end, of each shot. In addition, they make a written record of all 'takes'. After filming has finished assistants unload the magazines and check that they are accurately labelled. They prepare camera reports which should include special instructions about processing and also provide details of the lighting and filters which have been used. These go first to the laboratories and then to the editors along with the film.

All these assistant jobs can be painstaking and boring, but they are a vital training-ground and can provide evidence of suitability for the job. Although the industry is less hierarchical than in the past, junior technicians in all jobs in film or television are expected to 'put up or shut up'. It is an exaggeration to compare it to the army, but, although the situation is changing, juniors are still expected to have respect for senior members of staff. This can be quite a shock to people who have not worked in the industry before. It creates a curiously old-fashioned ambience but is a direct result of the discipline and teamwork which were required in the past.

On small shoots one camera assistant will do all these jobs, but on a big shoot assistants are divided into jobs with strange and evocative names such as *focus-puller, clapper-loader* or *grip*. The focus-puller ensures that the correct lens is on the camera and that the distance between the subject and the camera is correct to get a shot in focus. The focus-puller needs considerable technical knowledge and must work smoothly with the camera operator. If the camera operator alters a shot while filming, it is the focus-puller who operates the focus ring on the lens. Sometimes the director wants the foreground high-lighted and the background misty: this is where the focus-puller comes in. Lenses are expensive and must be carefully handled.

The grip's duties are moving the camera and operating dollies and cranes (the mounts for particular camera shots). Grips sometimes even design special rigs and they build and lay tracks for tracking shots. They are responsible for the camera's safety; grips also drive the camera car on location.

The loader or clapper-loader loads the clapper and loads and empties film. He or she also notes equipment details so that the laboratory and the production office can be informed.

Rostrum Camera Operator

In film, television and video anything which cannot be done by live action can usually be achieved by a fixed rostrum camera, which is used for superimposing animations, titles or effects. The most famous operator of all is Ken Morse, whose name must have been included in more credits than anyone else in television

How do you become a camera operator?
You have to look out for various traineeships and courses. The main qualification, however, is familiarity with a camera. You should have a good general education with GCSE or A levels, perhaps in maths or physics, and have the right personality to cope with a non-routine job. Knowing about different types of cameras is important; a flair for, or interest in, photography is an asset and will help you to secure an interview. The interview will be quite technical, in that it will explore your knowledge of cameras, so be well-prepared. Make sure that you can actually describe, for example, the function of the lens. You may know what it does, but make sure you can explain it clearly. Practise by saying it out loud to yourself. We often think we know something in our heads and then fumble and hesitate when asked for a precise description.

Connections are still useful in the film sector. A course in photography at a college of further education and a knowledge of electronics is an asset for a prospective trainee. A BTEC Higher National Diploma in an appropriate area, such as lighting or optics, is another plus. Many film schools and art colleges have courses in cinematography, and it is included in a few media studies courses. If you specifically want to become a film camera operator, it is probably best to follow a college course in photography or cinematography and then try to get into a film company as a runner. From there, go for one of the assistant camera operator posts such as a clapper-loader. Working your way up on the basis of proven competence is still the best method.

The BBC still trains its own camera operators and there are also a few traineeships in some ITV companies. Both the BBC and ITV take their pick of applicants, so your credentials have to be good.

Camera operators are increasingly freelance. Film camera operators are accustomed to freelance work, but the decline of union power has made the job more competitive. Today there are many more inexperienced (and unemployed!) camera operators around than ever before.

The best route in is probably via video companies or television. If you have a proven knowledge of video cameras, through working in a workshop for example, a small company might take you on. With experience in television, some camera operators move on to film camera work, although in the past many were not prepared to risk this because television camera operation was a 'secure' job and film camera work was less so. This is no longer the case. Television camera operators nowadays might do a short course in film (and vice versa), so that they can work as freelances across all sectors.

With the N/SVQs more completely in place camera operators will be able to earn qualifications on-the-job and this should improve the present rather confused situation. Highly skilled, experienced camera operators will always be in demand.

Camera work can be quite stressful, so temperament is important. Camera operators are responsible for getting a number of details correct, such as the exposure, colour balance, filters, the choice of lens and film, the camera angle and so on. The need to remember everything can cause anxiety. Physical fitness, stamina, good eyesight and hearing are also essential.

There are short courses available in camera operation, but these are usually open only to people with experience in the industry. Camera operation used to be a job area which was almost exclusively male, but this, like everything else, is changing.

SOUND CREW
SOUND OPERATOR/TECHNICIAN/RECORDIST
BOOM OPERATOR
SOUND SUPERVISOR
GRAMS OPERATOR
SOUND DUBBING EDITOR/MIXER

Sound technicians record and mix sound during shooting and recording. On location with film or on a television outside broadcast they usually work with portable equipment (unless the OB van is used); in a television studio a sound technician operates a sound desk in the sound control room next to the gallery (and is then sometimes referred to as sound supervisor, see below). In the past sound technicians who worked in the studio rarely worked out on location and, in turn, location sound crews were hardly ever studio-based. Multi-skilling, however, is having an effect in this area as in others, and it is now more common to find sound technicians who are prepared to tackle both aspects.

Sound technicians aim to obtain the best possible quality of sound and interpret the director's wishes to find ways of creating an 'atmosphere' appropriate to the style of the film or recording. They have to be aware of acoustics and problems with echoes. Sound has developed a great deal in the last decade with the advance of stereo and digital recording and, clearly, sound technicians have to be up to date with new technology. On pop videos sound supervisors are very important indeed.

Recording sound on location can be difficult: the sound crew has to ensure that the sound is authentic and that there are no inappropriate noises. It is surprising how often this presents a problem. Everyone else on set tends to be concentrating on the picture quality and only the sound technicians actually listen to the sound. If a police siren can be heard faintly in the background it is the sound recordist who has to notice (especially if the film is an eighteenth-century costume drama!). On location, after a scene is shot, the director asks the sound recordist if the sound quality is 'okay'. Everyone holds their breath at this point because, if the sound team is unhappy, there often has to be a retake. This can make the sound crew very unpopular indeed and diplomacy is an essential, but often unmentioned, aspect of the sound recordist's job.

On location, sound operators will also often record 'wildtrack', or sound which is not in synch with the camera but is intended for background. Wildtrack will later provide necessary atmosphere ('atmos') over shots, for example, which do not include dialogue. Sound technicians on location make notes about the sound which are then passed on to the editor to help him or her in the task of editing.

The *boom operator* is a junior member of the sound team who controls the boom, a long arm with a microphone which pivots and responds to sources of sound. In a drama, for example, the boom operator will have to swing the microphone between the speakers, so he or she has to know the dialogue and be ready and alert when different speakers come in. The job looks easy but requires considerable skill; inexperienced boom operators can make the jobs of more senior members of the sound crew very difficult. Boom operators cannot thump around in hobnailed boots! They have to wear quiet shoes and clothing. Boom operators must have good hand-to-eye co-ordination and possess some understanding of camera angles and lighting.

Sound technicians can sometimes be seen in outside broadcast interviews holding the gun mike, which is usually covered with a fuzzy woolly protector. Gun mikes are directional, which is very useful when there is a great deal of extraneous noise. Mikes are sometimes attached to performers' clothing; this often requires tactful handling because female interviewees are sometimes disconcerted by the prospect of male technicians fixing microphones to their chests!

Sound has to be compatible with the picture, or, in other words, quiet for distant shots and louder for close-ups. If two supposed spies are whispering secrets in the background, and the voices boom out, it subliminally destroys the scene for the audience. Sound and image have to be synchronised so that they match exactly. In film that is the whole purpose of the clapperboard (which is such a symbol of the film-making process). In post-production the editor synchronises the loud bang on the soundtrack (as the top of the clapperboard hits the bottom) with the exact frame of the film which shows the clapper making contact. This is to ensure that sound and image are 'in synch' and is the reason why each scene in a film should begin with the clapperboard.

With ENG and PSC cameras the sound is recorded onto a strip on the videotape: sound and image are not separate entities as they are in film. Sound quality still has to be monitored, however, and the sound operator works in conjunction with the camera operator, carrying the recorder which is connected by cable to the camera. In the Betacam system the actual sound recording equipment is incorporated into the camera (just like the home video camera). Again, however, the sound person is attached to the camera operator so that he or she can monitor sound quality. The sound operator does not have heavy equipment to cart around as in the past, but often has only the mixer to transport.

Sound technicians often begin as trainees on the studio floor. Trainees learn about the various types of microphones (how to place them correctly) and are responsible for making sure that communication systems such as 'talkback' and loudspeakers work well. They also have to become familiar with the work of the sound supervisor in the sound control room.

The *sound supervisor* or *sound mixer* supervises programme sound and monitors and adjusts sound during a studio recording. He or she is responsible for the operation of the audio-mixer console or sound desk. This consists of a vast array of buttons each representing a sound source. The sound mixer has to fade the sound sources up or down and balance them to provide the right mix. This can be complicated: in one scene, for example, there may be people talking, the sound of rain falling and then the theme music in the background. They all have to be balanced correctly or the rain will drown out the voices and the music overwhelm everything. The job requires experience and an artistic sense of which sound is appropriate at a given moment.

One of the feed sources into the sound desk is from the *grams operator*, who has a library of sound effects and music. The grams operator plays in on cue sound effects and music which are mixed with, for example, an actor's dialogue on the studio floor.

Sound dubbing editors, or mixers, are concerned with post-production and are highly skilled and experienced sound technicians. They work on the edited soundtrack and mix dialogue and sound effects and add the music for the final soundtrack. Sound editors sometimes have to re-record parts of the track to fit in with the pictures.

The soundtrack of almost any film or television programme is made up of a variety of sounds which were recorded in different acoustic conditions. The dubbing editor must blend the sounds in such a way that the audience accepts the track as completely natural to the film. Changes of levels have to be ironed out or varied (to give the illusion of depth). The music must be added so that it contributes to the dramatic impact of the programme or film without overwhelming it.

There are all sorts of problems for sound editors to sort out in post-production, from dogs yapping in the background to a narrator whose voice in one scene sounds oddly different from his voice in other scenes (possibly because he had a cold and sore throat on one day of filming). It is a real skill to be able to cope with these problems without shifting the viewer's attention from what is being said to how it is being said. The bugbear of many television interviews in offices is the telephone which rings when the interviewee is in mid-sentence. For news, if the phone is picked up quickly, the soundtrack is generally left as it is and the interview is not reshot, but this is an indication of how distracting extraneous sound can be. Viewers begin to wonder if the phone will be answered and they do not listen to what is being said.

On high-quality productions it requires considerable artistic flair to knit together the sound elements in a coherent and pleasurable manner.

How do you become a sound technician?

People enter sound with varied qualifications, not necessarily in science, although most television companies look for GCSEs or A levels in maths or physics. Television courses at college can be useful, as can a BTEC, a City and Guilds course or a degree in electronics, computer science, programme operations or communications. Proven flair in audio work is obviously helpful.

There is no particular pattern of employment. Some sound technicians stay in the job for life, but others see it as a first step towards camera operation, direction or production. People get into film sound either with experience in television or video or, again, through contacts. Beginning as a runner, and attaching oneself to a sound team (helping the boom operator, for example) is one way. Employers often look for someone who is interested in music and it is sometimes possible to get in by begging a sound operator in a video company to take on an assistant. Those with no qualifications but who have a passion for sound, who know a great deal about audio equipment and are very talented may be taken on by a small video company at very low pay and then work their way up. Some sound recordists begin by working voluntarily with amateur rock bands and go on from there.

The crisis in training has meant that there are untrained sound recordists around. Again, however, the NVQ system may help to encourage training and retraining in the future.

In addition to further education courses there are also privately funded short courses available for sound technicians. These have to be paid for by the individual and are usually open only to those with experience.

VISION MIXER

Television and Video

Vision mixer is a profession specifically associated with television/video technology. Vision mixers assemble the visual elements of a television production so that the images flow in a realistic and logical order. The expression 'vision mixer' is used to describe the person who operates the equipment and the equipment itself. A vision mixer sits in the gallery, on the other side of the director from the PA. The vision mixer equipment consists of a large electronic console panel with buttons, faders and knobs and the vision mixer's job is to ensure a smooth transition from one shot to the next.

Each camera in the studio has its own input into the mixer, as have telecine machines (which transfer films into a television tape format), digital video effects units, computers, electronic caption generators, colour bars, colour matte generators, slide photographs and so on. Outside broadcast materials from abroad via satellite may also have to be fed in at the appropriate time.

The vision mixer, under instruction from the director, cuts (perhaps a 'mix' or a 'wipe') between vision sources. The vision mixer can add captions and provide special electronic effects, in this sense having much in common with an editor in film. He or she must be able to respond instantly to the director's wishes.

The director may decide to start a programme with a presenter on Camera 1, followed by shots of a pop group in the studio on cameras 2, 3 and 4 (light entertainment, in particular, involves much directorial imagination), then there may be a call to 'run VT', perhaps a recording of the pop group touring America by bus. The viewer watches a collage of images from the American tour and hears in the background the band playing in the studio. Then the director may order a 'wipe' of the American tour image so that it slides off the screen in one direction, the image of the band in the studio following behind until it again fills the screen. Finally a slide photograph of the leader of the group with his girlfriend may appear as the band plays their hit love song. The permutations are endless; the vision mixer must make all these cuts from one source to the next at the right moment. As the vision mixer operates the controls the end result is recorded on videotape, or transmitted live: it depends on the programme. Live transmission can be harrowing.

Some modern vision mixer consoles are extremely sophisticated and can produce a multiplicity of technical effects, such as dividing the screen into multi-images or creating rapid zooms in which a small dot appears on the horizon and becomes larger and larger until it dominates the whole screen. This, however, is moving into the world of special effects and there are certain companies and artists who special-ise in this area (see Chapter 13).

A vision mixer must be able to anticipate when the director will give a cue because exact timing is important from a creative point of view. In music programmes the cuts must be made on the right beat: a cut at the wrong time can spoil the mood of a light entertainment sequence. Some experienced vision mixers have a more developed artistic sense than many directors, and it is not unknown for the vision mixer to carry along an inexperienced director.

It follows from the above that the job requires good visual and artis-tic sense, quick reactions and manual dexterity. For light entertainment a sense of rhythm and a feel for music are essential. For drama, vision mixers have to be sensitive to the exact moment when an image must be changed to suit the mood of the piece.

Temperament again is important. Vision mixers work long hours in darkened control rooms. They have to concentrate for long periods and work under immense physical and mental pressure – eye-strain and fatigue are quite common. There can also be a curious restlessness, the result of sitting in the same place for hours. Vision mixers have to be capable of a hair-trigger response to any change in the overall pro-gramme plan. They must never panic – even if the director does! All of which can provoke high stress levels in all but the most confident and competent.

OB units have their own vision mixers; this is reasonable since an OB unit is basically a mobile television studio.

How do you become a vision mixer?
Occasionally some television companies do take on trainee vision mix-ers, but they are mostly recruited from existing staff. Video companies take on recruits from recognised college media courses. Some colleges also offer production courses that are a good preparation. Video mixers are usually young and there are just as many women as men. Again, vision mixers today are mainly freelances.

ELECTRICAL TECHNICIANS (technical)
GAFFER
BEST BOY

Film, Television and Video
Lighting or *electrical technicians* (often referred to in Britain as 'sparks') are responsible for the electrical safety of the lighting equip-ment and the supply of power to it. Lighting technicians wire and set up the lights used for illuminating the studio or location set. Lights come in

various shapes and sizes and can be tilted at many angles. Lights may also be placed on portable stands at the side of the set. Sometimes electricians may have small hand-held lights for an interview on an outside broadcast. Electricians rig the lights under the direction of the chief lighting technician who, in film, is called the gaffer. The best boy is the traditional name of the second electrician working under the gaffer in film. (Be careful! Some people confuse electricians with lighting directors. They are not the same at all: the lighting director is part of the camera crew and he or she decides *where* the lights should go.)

In television studios the brilliance of the lights can be altered from a lighting console in the control room. The operator of the console may be an electrician. Most studios have a lighting grid: a criss-cross structure of metal bars, overhanging the studio space from which the brackets holding the lights are hung. Some grids can be lowered, but often electricians have to work on the grid many feet above the ground. Sometimes lights are attached to a specially built scaffolding or to a gantry (a framework rather like the arm of a crane, from which lights, and sometimes cameras, are hung). Electrical technicians should therefore have a head for heights. Electrical work can be very hard physically and electricians have to be strong. It was, and remains, very male-dominated, but there are a few female electrical technicians and their number appears to be on the increase.

How do you get to be an electrical technician?
For film and video the main route is to be a qualified electrician and have contacts. Electricians usually have a City and Guilds qualification from a further education college and then apply to the company (either film, video or television) of their choice. Some move into the industry from theatre and stage lighting and there is also movement in the other direction.

Case Histories

JANE ROUSSEAU

Jane is 29 and works as a freelance camera operator and lighting camera operator.

I was interested in science and arts at school and I went to what was then the Leeds Polytechnic (now Leeds Metropolitan University) to do

185

graphics because I was interested in the technological side of things. At the time Leeds had a film option as part of the graphics course and there were seven of us on the option, six blokes and me. None of us had any idea about how to handle the camera, we didn't have a clue. We were supposed to shoot a film but it was the first film we'd ever shot. The other students discussed who would be the camera person, which nobody knew how to do, but no-one asked me because I was a woman I suppose. I was so annoyed that I lied and said I could handle a camera and then I stayed up all night learning how to load the mag! We shot the film, and I found that I loved it. I'd found what it was I really wanted to do. After that on the course I shot all the film which required an extra camera person.

After I finished my degree I took a year off to travel and went to Australia hoping for a job in the Australian film industry. But this was around 1988 and they had just removed the tax incentive for making films in Australia. The industry took a nose dive so back I came to Britain. Richard Woolley, who was setting up the Northern Film School at Leeds, wanted me to do their course but I didn't want to be a student again. Instead I got a job on a deferred payment film which means you don't get paid until it's finished and makes some money (as it turns out I didn't get paid at all). Anyway I went to Nantwich with the film crew and we sat round the table. I knew about lighting because of my science background, I knew the physics of electricity and how to wire up a plug and so they said: 'Right you're the gaffer'. I didn't really know what a gaffer was but I went ahead and did everything, night shoots, going down mines etc. Looking back it was extremely dangerous and I wouldn't do any of that stuff now, not without proper training.

I seemed to be getting stuck doing the electrics. I'm fairly strong so I thought, 'Well, I'll do it for a while.' But then people persuaded me to go on the Leeds film course after all because I was desperately keen to stay in the north and it seemed a good thing to do. I trained as a camera lighting operator, the only woman again. The course lasted a year and I got to shoot a science fiction drama and a film set in the Lake District. I wanted to do the science fiction because it offered all sorts of lighting and shooting opportunities and I did not want to get stereotyped doing women's films. In fact, I like filming nature and now live in the Lakes.

After leaving the course I carried on sparking because there were no camera opportunities for me. Then I was asked to work on a science fiction film called *Shadow Chaser* being made at Pinewood studios in London. I really still didn't know the job properly, although I kept it quiet, because I had not been properly trained but it was the time when union power was collapsing and newcomers could get in. The experienced people were very suspicious – not surprisingly. I didn't know anything about union rules or safety or anything. I was a bit raw. I really didn't know much about how the industry worked or about the rules and regulations and I was questioning myself all the time. The money was low and I had not been taught how to pitch my price or how to ask for a decent wage. I am a bit cross about that, looking back. No one at college had taught me about pricing my work fairly.

When I was first in London I was also worried about being ghettoised into women's film-making. I always wanted to be part of the mainstream industry – sometimes I felt I was only doing lesbian movies or tampon adverts. Every now and again, however, some one would ask me to light something really interesting and again I would stay up all night making sure that I could do the job. Gradually I made more and more contacts which are very important in this industry. The Director of Photography on *Shadow Chaser* was Alan Trow. He is very helpful to young people and encourages them. He asked to see the films I'd made at college and he said that he was rethinking my job. He said he wanted me to do some camera operation. He waited until I got more experience and then eventually offered me jobs as the camera operator!

In the meantime, I was freelancing as a sparks and I got to know a lot of women in the film industry down in London. It was very unusual for a woman to be doing electrics and so people were curious about me but I still did not know anything about pricing my work properly. I suppose I was too timid to ask. It was only when I met Nuala Campbell (who is a sort of legend in the industry because she is a well-established female gaffer in a very macho world) that I realised that I was being underpaid. She asked me how much I was getting on one film that I was working on and, when she found it was only £50 a week, she made the most enormous fuss on my behalf. She told me never ever to accept work for less than £100 a day. I still find it difficult to ask for a decent rate but I am learning and, in fact, after Nuala's advice I started getting better jobs because I suppose I valued myself more. I now have an agent, Vicki Standeven, who is brilliant.

As time went on, thanks to Alan Trow, I began to get more and more jobs as a camera assistant. I am presently working for Mersey TV as camera operator on the new soap *Hollyoaks*. I think I am the first woman at Mersey TV to touch a camera. The Head of Camera had never had a woman operator in thirteen years, and, at first, people kept turning up to look at me. This was very stressful because if I messed up it would vindicate all the prejudices against women on the technical side of the industry. However, I have to say that some of the best working experiences I've had have been with the older, more traditional men. They make things tough for me for about the first three days, then, when they find I can do the job, they are very supportive and extremely helpful. Sadly, it is sometime young males of my own age or women on the production side of the industry who can be the most hostile. They seem to resent women on the technical side of the industry. Women within the camera and lighting areas, however, can be very supportive of each other.

Ninety per cent of this job is getting on with people. I've begun to realise that the sexism in the industry is not an immovable mountain; you have to push with the grain rather than fight against it. At the moment life is wonderful after being totally hideous. Getting where I am has been soul-destroying at times because you do encounter a lot of prejudice. You've got to really want to do it. It has to be a passion. I know now I never want to do anything else.

RICHARD SPOONER

Richard Spooner is 27 and works as a First Assistant Dubbing Mixer with a post-production house in Soho

After I did A levels I went to Art College to do an audio-visual course but it wasn't very good. It had only been in existence for a year and there were real problems with it. I knew about sound because my father was in the film business as a dubbing mixer and I'd worked round him in the summers and was given a few small tasks – 'fade-ins' and so on. Anyway I left the course (which actually closed down later so there must have been problems with it) and got a job as a runner, for John Wood Studios in Soho where my father worked. He helped me get in initially but after that you are on your own. I worked for three months as a runner making tea and coffee.

Then I was moved into what was called the Transfer Bay. This was in 1987 and we dealt mainly with film transfers. It was pretty basic technology looking back and I was given jobs like making copies of sound effects, and so on. After six months I moved to Camera Operator in the 'Machine Room' behind the studio where the final product was mastered from all the play-off machines. Part of my job was to monitor the sound on the master film and listen for any discrepancies or what are called 'drop-outs'. This was fantastic training. I would be in the 'Machine Room' listening all day and acquired knowledge, almost by osmosis ... picked up so many things intuitively. As I said, the technology now seems quite crude – the new digital sound systems were just beginning to come in – but you did learn the basics. Your ears were trained. Computers, however, were then just beginning to change everything.

The John Wood Studio specialised in adverts and eventually it closed down, but I moved on as a Sound Camera Operator to the Video London Sound Studio which did documentaries for television. The studio had been started by someone who had realised the potential of video very early on. I spent two years there as well as camera operating doing what is called 'shooting footsteps' which basically means the process in which location sound effects are redone in the studio. Video London Sound was redoing the sound on old Korda films for the international market and we would mix the music, the 'atmos' and 'the footsteps'. Then the new version would be sent off, for example to Germany, for the voices to be dubbed.

I left in 1990 and travelled round the States for six months, working at summer camps and when I came back I went to work for another company called Hackenbacker Sound, again in a Film Transfer Bay. Eventually I went back to Video London and started track laying and working on the sound for television documentaries.

By this time what I call the 'hard disc' systems were coming in for dubbing – in other words computers – I began working with them. The technology has gone mad since then. Computer editing is so versatile. The software is all designed to be as user-friendly as possible, you're just cutting and pasting with sound the same as you do with words on a word processor. A lot of the digital systems came from the music industry. One was called Synclavier Post-Pro and had been designed for musicians from programmes which had supposedly been used initially for one of the Space Shuttles. The CIA was supposed to be still monitoring the users! You could really manipulate sound and even concoct and 'make up' sentences out of scattered words.

What really changed with digital technology was how the post-production studios worked. Many of the picture editors began to convert to systems such as Lightworks and they could do much more for themselves. Even old-school feature film editors were using computers. The programme designers incorporated features of the Steenbeck into the design! This affected the whole working situation in post-production. Assistant film editors were not so necessary. There was no need for large teams of assistant editors working with the editors. They no longer had to 'catch' and collect the film 'trims' and put them in order. Nowadays, if there is an assistant, he or she digitises the rushes and does general 'housekeeping' for editors. Editors on simple, straightforward television shows can do everything themselves, including sound, so this began to have an impact on jobs in sound editing and dubbing.

I was working in track laying but eventually I became assistant mixer on bigger drama and documentary productions which is what I work in today. I'm familiar with several computer systems. It's essential because everything today, including the mixing desk, is almost always computerised and totally automated. All the sound-camera-operation-type work that I used to do in the 'Machine Room', that's all gone.

Many productions in television now use BETA SP to record rather than film. It's all new technology. In a way, in post-production, people who still use film do so for romantic reasons. Although still, when there is a lot of footage, film works better because there can be too much footage for the hard disc system to handle (although this will change soon enough). I worked as assistant to Colin Martin doing the mixes for Philip Agland's documentary series about China called *Beyond the Clouds* which won a BAFTA award. It was post-produced on film because work on it went on over a long period of time: there were lots of rushes. But most documentaries nowadays use Avid or Lightworks because film is a nightmare in comparison. The whole dubbing process is now so much less painful. There is a generational thing, however, my dad still works in dubbing and mixing sound for film and the older generation are not really into computers in the same way (sorry Dad!).

I now mainly operate with computers which means that everything can be left until much later. After a production is shot on location with the sound linked to the camera or DAT, the tracks are digitised into Avid or Lightworks. After the picture cut the EDL (Edit Decision List) is sent to us and a copy to the on-line picture house. The disc goes into the machine and the computer assembles the sound as cut for the programme. Today the whole dubbing and mixing process is so much easier.

As I say, its so easy that some picture/film editors do it themselves but it means that the sound is not monitored in the same way as it used to be. It's a great shame because no-one is really being trained anymore. The newcomers can manipulate the computers but they don't have the 'ears'. All that time I spent in the dubbing theatre listening for 'drop-outs' – it taught me a lot. That slow process of acquiring a skill just doesn't happen anymore. The whole process is speeded up. Line-ups which used to take ages now take a minute; film reels which used to take half an hour to change can now be done on your own in one minute.

I'm glad I experienced the old technology. The new entrants coming in behind me just don't have that background of knowledge. They know about computers but they don't know about sound. Also the industry atmosphere is changing. At the same time as we had all the changes in the technology, the institutional side of the industry shifted dramatically, television companies were floated on the stock market. The emphasis was all on profit and doing everything fast and quickly to make money. Directors who, in the old days, would make a fuss about standards and insist on things being done right (and again and again!) now have to worry about bringing things in on time and on budget – almost to the exclusion of everything else.

I'm only 27 but already I've seen so many changes. It's not as much fun as it used to be. Before when you had so many people working together in a studio it was great to go out after work to the pub. There was a camaraderie. Now there are just fewer people needed and they are much more uptight. However, even if it is not as much fun as it was, it is still a hell of a lot better than most jobs! In the dubbing theatre everyone joins in and you're all there casually dressed in your jeans, stars included. You meet lots of famous people, so there's lots of tales to tell your friends. I went out with Bob Hoskins for a beer and I've met Anthony Hopkins, Joan Collins, Jeremy Irons and loads of television people. My friends think that it's very glamorous but after three days or so it is just normal.

I am quite optimistic about the industry bouncing back. The computers came in at the wrong time in that broadcasting was changing with the Broadcasting Bill. Television companies became concerned about the franchises so they were looking for ways to cut back. I think things will settle down and get better now.

Note

1. *See* Sue Davis (ed.) *The Official ITV Careers Handbook*, (London: Hodder and Stoughton, 1989), p. 62.

13

DESIGN/CRAFTS

Design jobs in the industry include set design, wardrobe and costume design, make-up, graphic design and animation. Skillset is finalising standards of competence in Make-up, Costume and Animation, and more N/SVQs in other areas are being developed to come on stream in the near future. New recruits and those already employed should note that there is an Industry Lead Body for Design which is also establishing broad 'performance criteria'. A specific section of the Lead Body for Design (ILB) is concentrating on television and film (as well as theatre) in terms of sets, props and costumes. New recruits and those who wish to retrain should be aware of the work of this organisation (its address is listed in the Appendix).

SET DESIGN
PRODUCTION DESIGNER (creative)
ART DIRECTOR (creative)
SET DESIGNER (creative)
DESIGN ASSISTANTS
SET DECORATOR (creative/craft)
PROPERTIES (creative/technical/craft)

Film, Television and Video
The designer of a film set is usually referred to as the *production designer*; in television the term *set designer* is more common. *Art director* is a term also used, mainly on feature films, to indicate the person with overall responsibility for sets and properties and everything related to the film's design 'look'. There is a certain overlap between art director and production designer jobs: indeed, they can be indistinguishable. In any case, whatever it is called, set/production/art design is one of the most creative jobs in the industry and increasingly designers work as freelances across all three sectors.

192

The set/production designer is usually involved in a production from the initial planning to, and through, production. If the programme or film is a historical drama, the set/production designer will research the period in detail to make sure that the design and props are authentic. If the film or programme is to be shot on location, the designer will go out with the location manager to find appropriate sites and settings. The design team for a series like *Poirot*, for example, would have to scour the country looking for examples of 30s architecture unaltered by 'modernisation'. Designers are also often asked to attend actual filming in order to keep an eye on what is going on.

In the pre-production period the set/production designer draws a floor plan, constructs a working model and decides the content of the set. Set/production designers work in close co-operation with producers and directors. The director and the set designer discuss their ideas in detail and then the set designer will draw a 'storyboard', rather like a strip cartoon, which describes the progression of the story, and what the set will look like, scene by scene. (Storyboards of famous films are collector's items for real film 'buffs'.)

The next step is the production of simplified architectural drawings of the sets, which are then 'costed'. Designers have to have a fairly good business sense, especially if they are freelance, because extravagant designs are unlikely to win approval at times of financial stringency. Nowadays designers often have training in computer graphics, and they may plan the sets with the aid of a computer (Computer-assisted design – C.A.D.).

Once the sets are agreed upon, the designer may construct scale models to be used in liaison work with the costume designer, lighting director, sound supervisor, and so on. Designers must ensure that sets are practical for the equipment and this is where scale models come in. It is important that sets do not impede the cameras, throw malign shadows or sound hollow if they are thumped. On a recent sitcom, the author noted an actor putting a plate on the draining-board of a sink unit. The whole unit shook unconvincingly and its flimsiness was immediately apparent. This distracts and annoys most viewers.

During the pre-production period designers tell the craft and workshop areas what they want constructed. They discuss with the properties department which cushions, plants, rugs and so on are required to 'decorate' the set and, in some cases, they go out to select and buy those furnishings which the props department is unable to produce.

Designers are crucial to the atmosphere of a film or programme. Television and film are visual media and the images which impinge on the viewer are important because they produce an emotional response. Set design can involve massive tasks, such as the creation of a medieval castle or a spaceship, or it can concern simple projects such as the choice of desks and furniture for a news programme. The latter, however, can be very important: chairs which look uncomfortable or bizarre can make the interviewer and interviewee look ill at ease. This can subconsciously alienate the audience and break down the feeling of confidence in what is being said. Television design, in particular, involves a wide variety of work, from the complexity of a major historical drama to the set for a chat show or a mobile for a pop music programme.

Many film and television designers have a background in theatre design, but some come from architecture or interior design, or even from landscape architecture. Film or television design is more complex than theatre design because the audience sees the set from all angles and in close-up. Film and television screens produce images of great clarity and the set has to stand up to close scrutiny as the camera moves in and even lingers. Sets, of course, are illusions: they are not what they seem. The cold eye of the camera, however, can reveal the smallest inaccuracy and anachronism. This can jar the viewer's sensibilities and, at one blow, destroy the atmosphere which the director or scriptwriter has sought to create. Attention to detail, and an understanding of the cinematographic art, are therefore essential to the set designer's job.

Designers on complex productions are usually aided by *design assistants* who help with the research and the preparation of drawings and models. In film the production designer is usually also assisted by the *set decorator*; the latter is responsible for the selection of props and also supervises the 'dressing' of the set. The set decorator works from plans or sketches provided by the designer and prepares prop lists. He or she works closely with the Props Department in organising the dressing and striking (taking down) of the sets.

How do you become a set designer?
Most designers in all areas of the industry have degrees in some aspect of design. Set designers have BAs in Interior Design, or Art and Design, or Architecture, or Stage Design or Sculpture or Industrial 3-D design. Many art colleges provide specialised courses in set design. Prospective stage or set designers usually have an interest in furniture, fashion design and architecture.

The design area of the industry is probably the one where raw talent is most at a premium. It takes time to suss out an untalented director or camera operator, but people who cannot draw or design are easy to spot. Consequently, designers, in all areas of the industry, are often very young.

It is quite common for a designer to start in the theatre and then move to film or television. Some very fortunate young people may get taken on as assistants by television or video companies straight from college. In film some young people start in the properties department, move on to become set decorators and move up from there. Most designers now work across all sectors as freelances.

WARDROBE DESIGNER (creative/administrative)
COSTUME DESIGNER (creative/administrative)
DRESSERS

The *costume* or *wardrobe designer* is appointed during pre-production to assess costume needs. After consultation with the director, costume/wardrobe designers plan, design and fit costumes in keeping with the look and spirit of the production. They are assisted by wardrobe staff who remain throughout the production to maintain the clothes and ensure that performers are dressed properly (buttons and zippers are closed, stockings are unwrinkled, for example).

The costume designer begins by reading the script and identifying the period in which the production is set. Designers must have a sound historical sense and know about the class and social details which are intimately connected with how people dress. If gentlemen in nineteenth-century England never wore brown suits in town; if society ladies in the Edwardian period always changed into 'tea' dresses in the afternoon; if contemporary middle-aged British men wear socks with their sandals but sophisticated Frenchmen never do: then wardrobe designers must know about all these details, which provide clues to a character.

Wardrobe is also connected with an intuitive understanding of personality. If the leading female character has a flamboyant personality, she will not be dressed like a governess in lace collars and long black skirts. Costume designers have to be alert to the emotional tone of the drama. Clothes are intimately connected with confidence and costume designers must therefore have considerable psychological insight. An English middle-class lady will probably wear chainstore underwear while the sophisticated, international business woman may like hand-made lingerie from an expensive French couturier. When an actor undresses for the camera the underwear must look 'right'.

Costume designers also have to know about lighting and lighting plans. At times directors and cinematographers may want to create a mood which lighting and costumes should enhance. If the production is to have a pale tone, with sepia overlays reminiscent of an old photograph, then a designer who produced costumes designed in vivid scarlet would likely be thrown out of his or her job, unless perhaps a single costume in the colour served some dramatic purpose. If the director wants to convey the style of an impressionist painting, the costume director must look at the clothes in those paintings and check that the materials are in the correct style, textures and colours.

In a film or programme with a contemporary setting many of the clothes are simply purchased from ordinary shops or hired from theatrical costumiers. On the other hand, historical drama means a great deal of research in libraries, museums, art galleries, print shops and similar sources. Designers do not usually make the clothes themselves, but they do supervise their construction. They should understand tailoring and dressmaking and they will buy accessories (for example, stockings, tights, gloves, hats, belts, ties, scarves, shoes, earrings and leggings).

Actors themselves can be very involved with wardrobe. Most of them are sensitive about their appearance (their face is truly their fortune) and they can be obstreperous when it comes to wearing garments which they don't believe suit them. If the leading female actor does not like her costume and thinks it makes her look ugly or fat (when she is supposed to be young and beautiful), her unhappiness can affect her performance and the quality of the production. The costume designer has to be aware of such pitfalls and deal tactfully with sensitive feelings. Costume designers usually have to keep control of the department budget and, in addition to 'people skills', they ought to have both, administrative talent and business acumen.

During the production of a drama wardrobe designers will be assisted by staff (*dressers*) who help dress the actors and wash, clean and iron the garments. Washing and drying facilities can present a major headache on location; a costume can get torn and covered in mud one day and be required for the shooting of another scene on the next.

Dressers help performers in and out of their costumes. This is a job which calls for real empathy and human concern. Actors can become very tense during filming and they may let off steam with their dressers. Many dressers are retired actors or young would-be actors who enjoy working in film and television and understand how actors feel. They often provide a sympathetic ear for a tirade against an insensitive director and boost the ego of the actor, stressing how good they look in a particular costume. Dressers frequently carry out minor alterations to the costumes during filming or recording, so they should be able to sew quickly and do small repairs. They are also responsible for the care of the clothes, including the washing, cleaning and pressing.

How do you become a wardrobe or costume designer?
Today costume designers often come into film or television from the fashion industry or from art school. Many of them have degrees in

Fashion Design, History of Art or even Museum Studies. Some have a background in textiles; some costume designers have taken degrees in drama with a special emphasis on costume or wardrobe. They must possess a knowledge of fabrics and style and an understanding of dressmaking. Many costume designers come in via the theatre, where they may have come up through the ranks after gaining experience in a theatre wardrobe department. Increasingly, however, wardrobe designers do receive specific training on courses in the new universities (mainly the former polytechnics) and art colleges. Nowadays wardrobe designers are often freelance and work in all sectors of the industry.

How do you become a dresser?
Dressers are usually mature people with experience of the industry who wish to keep working in an environment which suits and interests them. They have to have the right temperament.

MAKE-UP ARTIST (creative/technical)

It used to take them hours and hours in make-up to give me character. Now I've got character they take it all out. (Roger Moore)

The *make-up artist* on feature films or a television drama can have a very complex job indeed. They may have to make actors look older, younger, bald, hirsute, dowdy, ill, or attractive. Make-up has come a long way since the old Hollywood films in which female stars in a six-teenth-century romance about pirates pranced happily aboard ship in the heavy 'pancake' make-up of the 40s. Today make-up must fit in with the 'look' of the production. Fashionable women in the 60s wore heavy eye-liner, false lashes and white lipstick but no blusher; in the 70s eye-shadow and blusher came into fashion; lip-gloss was the rage in the 80s; certain coral and pink colours were not available in lipsticks prior to the Second World War, when the fashion was for a bold red: all this the make-up artist must know. They have to study the fashion plates of the periods in magazines like *Vogue* and incorporate them into their work with a subtlety that will not offend contemporary taste in beauty.

Science fiction, horror or war movies call upon the creative resources of the make-up artist. There are some highly specialised make-up artists who make a great deal of money creating, for example, terrible facial or body wounds for war films or, at the other end of the scale, the fantasy make-up for the Addams family. Highly skilled technicians work with latex foam and other materials to recreate or change the shape of a face. The more specialised make-up artists have to know about the chemical composition of plastic substances: they cannot put a chemical that eats away at the skin on the face of an actor. They also have to be aware of the dangers of fungal diseases which can be one of the side-effects of being encased in foam rubber! In America film and television make-up is dominated by men, and this used to be the case in the film industry in Britain. However, the BBC and the independent companies trained large numbers of women in make-up and it is now a much more evenly balanced profession in this respect.

Much of the work of the average make-up artist in television, on the other hand, is not so dramatic. It is usually described as 'corrective', which means making people look better by 'correcting' their worst features. Make-up artists will apply powder to shiny noses, cover up acne or 'white out' areas which will look shadowed under the studio lights. Make-up artists in television usually also have responsibility for hairstyling and for keeping wigs and hairpieces cleaned. They may have to wash, set and brush hair out and colour it in period and modern styles.

Once again it is important for people who want to become make-up artists to have a rapport with others, with some of whom, after all, they will work at very close quarters. They often deal with actors on an early call, which can be at six o'clock in the morning, when few people are at their physical best and when many can be very bad-tempered. The actors may be depressed about their appearance, they may fear that their looks are going, that their eyes are baggy and their wrinkles showing, and they may blame it all on the hapless make-up artist, who will, therefore, have to tread very carefully indeed.

Make-up artist and client are often in one-to-one situations. One of the hazards of the job for female make-up artists may be sexual harassment in the form of propositions and fondling. This has to be handled in a mature manner so that it is clear that such behaviour is unacceptable. Timidity and shyness are not useful attributes for a make-up artist!

Make-up artists on a film or major drama production work closely with the directors, costume designers and lighting personnel. Lighting is particularly important where make-up is concerned: the wrong make-up can be disastrous on a brightly lit set.

How do you become a make-up artist?
The BBC and the independent companies used to train make-up artists but now they are freelance. Some trainee make-up technicians take up the career after a training as a hairdresser or beautician, but others have degrees in Drama or Art and Design from art colleges and film schools. Art schools provide training in sculpture which can be important for some of the more skilled areas. The City and Guilds and BTEC, both provide recognised courses in Make-up and Hairdressing and Beauty

Therapy, and these can help candidates to get jobs when they are advertised. Very specialised make-up artists have sometimes received a training at Madam Tussaud's. Make-up has been badly hit by the decline in training provision in the industry and it is quite difficult for students to secure the necessary financial support to follow courses.

GRAPHIC DESIGNER

The work of the *graphic designer* in films or in a television company is extremely wide-ranging. It includes typography, lettering, doing simple credits, designing mobiles and weather charts but it can also involve the creation of cartoons and animation. Graphic designers might also be employed making props for special programmes: passports, foreign money, ration books and other historical ephemera, for example.

Graphic design really arrived in television in 1974 when ITN revolutionised General Election coverage with the introduction of computer graphics rather than handwritten results. Today Silicon Graphics, Softimage and Quantel are all engaged in a technological battle to increase the speed and sophistication of the hardware and the software.[1]

Graphic design is continuously being upgraded by continuing developments in computer technology. Graphic designers now have instant access to over 16 million colours through digital paint systems; they can construct 3D animation in real-time; and manipulate images, frame by frame, through non-linear editing techniques. This is such an expanding, rapidly changing area of the entertainment business that students should consult a more specialist book for detailed information.[2]

Graphic designers are most usually associated with the opening (the 'titles') and closing credits on films and programmes. Titles have to be eye-catching and original and the price reflects this. A film title sequence can cost many thousands of pounds. In the future new developments in computer technology will require graphic designers to be extremely flexible in their skills; they will have to be prepared constantly to retrain on new equipment.

The production of credits for feature films is a particularly specialised craft and there are companies which work only in this area. The graphic designer could well be part of a company team that consults with the producer, director and set designer on a film to establish a continuity of theme and mood for the credits. Most cinemagoers and television viewers accept the credits unthinkingly and do not appreciate the great ingenuity and effort that goes into them. Yet they can be crucial in preparing the mood of the audience for what is about to follow.

In television the 'titles' of a long-running series can cue the audience in to a meeting with 'old friends'. Graphic designers today do not,

199

as they sometimes used to, prepare captions (the identification of a speaker in written letters at the bottom of a television screen). These are now usually the responsibility of a caption generator operator, who uses specialised equipment similar to a word processor. (Caption generator operators might have secretarial training or be assistant floor managers who have been roped into the job.)

How do you become a graphic designer?
Graphic designers are usually art college trained, with degrees or diplomas in Graphic Design. Alternatively they may have a Licentiate of the Society of Industrial Designers. Some of them come into television via commercial art studios or have been trained in computing where they find they have a talent for designing with computer graphic systems such as Paintbox. Others work with special effects video companies. Highly talented art students who are trained in computer graphics should not lack for job opportunities.

GRAPHIC DESIGNER/SPECIAL EFFECTS TECHNICIANS/OPERATORS/ARTISTS

A few years from now if you can still portray a human being, you'll be quite a valuable commodity. (Jack Nicholson)

Special effects are currently the glamour area of film, as one film after another tries to outdo rivals in the scale and imagination of its special effects. Every kid with a computer dreams about creating special effects. Film used to present problems for special effects because essentially it is 'wet, chemical, messy and more organic than mechanic'. Today, however, when even film images can be digitised, special effects are an increasingly significant element in most blockbuster movies.

Traditionally, before computers, *special effects artists* were highly specialised freelances for whom there was no set career pattern. Nowadays they tend to be divided into *physical* and *computer special effects* artists. Physical usually means sets that are constructed, sometimes in miniature, specifically to be set on fire, blown up or whatever the script calls for. There are all sorts of techniques associated with this type of work, many of which are handed down by word of mouth (although books about special effects are available). Pyrotechnic experts need to have a special licence from the Home Office because the work is dangerous and can affect the safety of others. *Physical special effects operators* come from a wide variety of backgrounds – electricians, explosives experts, inventors, ex-soldiers and the like; they may be scientists with an interest in robotics or may have worked at Madame

Tussaud's. There is simply no particular background that can be said to be typical: special effects people 'emerge' by being fascinated with the problems presented, 'having a go' and proving that they can do it. Temperament, however, is important: physical special effects experts have to be inventive, ingenious and scrupulous about safety. There are also specialist *special effects camera operators* who invariably have a camera background.

In the last decade special effects have been revolutionised by computers. Today there are video effects companies which, usually as part of post-production, provide a specialised effects service to films, television programmes, television commercials, independent pop video companies, and so on. The Computer Film Company provided a number of effects for the Mel Gibson film *Braveheart*. For scenes of huge armies lining up for battle, the same scene was shot with a small group of warriors in a number of different positions across the battlefield. The groups were then seamlessly 'patched' together. The Computer Film Company also removed offending pylons from the skyline and replaced them with more picturesque mountains. One of the producers, Alison O'Brien, commented: 'At first sight the cost of digital effects in movies may seem high, but in a case like this one [*Braveheart*] where the production was able to avoid making hundreds of costumes, hiring thousands of extras and searching for exactly the right landscape, it makes a lot of sense' (*Broadcast,* 13 October 1995).

Digital Film was the company which worked on the Bond film *Goldeneye*. The Chief Executive, Matthew Holben, described how the company worked on three major sequences for a total of fifty-six shots:

In the pre-title sequence our work was all tied up with the opening stunt where a plane goes diving over a cliff and James Bond has to try and save it. It was tricky to get the look right – blending in models shots with live action. The whole thing was about trying to make the sequence believable. We also created scenes for another sequence where Bond's plane is flying through the jungle – including the backgrounds that can be seen through the plane's windows – using green screen and compositing techniques. The other big sequence was the final confrontation – a big fight between Bond and the baddie which takes place on the Arecibo Dish, a big satellite telescope in South America. The fight takes place on a cradle perched 300 feet above the dish, so obviously they didn't use real actors. The fight was shot against a green screen and then we replaced the background and generally blended the two together. (Quoted in *Broadcast* 13 October 1995)

201

Advertisements are particularly innovative in their use of post-production special effects and there still tends to be a split between the facilities houses which do special effects for commercials and those who work on feature films. Increasingly, however, the dividing line between film and video effects work is becoming blurred. This field is developing very rapidly and young people who combine technical ability with artistic talent are in a very strong position indeed in terms of employment.

How do you become a special effects specialist?
Aside from studying computer special effects, no career path can be specified. People certainly do not leave school or college and go into physical special effects. They have usually worked elsewhere in the industry first.

People who work on the computer side of the industry often have a passion for new technological techniques and a flair for design, a relatively rare combination.

ANIMATORS

Film, Television and Video
It's verging on insanity. I spend all my time talking to characters who are not there, fighting weasels and being thrown out of clubs by gorillas. (Bob Hoskins on shooting *Who framed Roger Rabbit*)

Animation is now closely associated with special effects and graphic art and computing and yet true animation is still, as one commentator described it, the 'Holy Grail'. According to the purists, the best animation is still done by hand. In the traditional method of animation the *animator* breaks down the action of the proposed cartoon character into very small movements which are drawn on individual sheets of paper and photographed. When the film is projected, it seems as if the characters are alive and moving – 'animated'.

In most animation companies there is usually a key animator, the *animation director*, who will do most of the creative work. He or she comes up with the idea, designs the scene, decides how the action will happen and the expressions and appearance of the characters. This role is equivalent to the director on an ordinary film. Animators will draw the characters and *assistant animators* will tidy up the initial drawings and do the minor characters. Assistants may also prepare instructions for the camera operator (sometimes known as 'dope sheets') saying how a scene should be shot and how many frames of each drawing are required. There may also be assistants known as 'in-betweeners', who

202

do the drawings in-between the important actions (increasingly this is done by computers). Generally animation studios also had a 'paint and trace' department which took the completed drawings and copied them on to 'cells' (sheets of transparent material) before they were photographed.

Animation studios are increasingly dominated by computer technology. The software can take the drudgery out of animation and it is easy to add special effects. It is now possible for the animator to produce a cartoon character's major 'poses' and then the computer can fill in the drawings 'in-between'. The computer does the connecting movements and the colouring.

The feature film *Toy Story* made animation history because it was entirely generated by computers. It took the director John Lasseter and the Pixar/Disney crew four years to make the film and a few more years to develop the software and the script, but *Toy Story* took over £100 million pounds at the American box office in the first few months of its release. According to Leslie Felperin, in an article in *Sight and Sound*, the photo-realistic quality of the rendering on the toys and surroundings in *Toy Story* is 'breathtakingly sharp and fine-grained ... Ordinary *cel* animation can not achieve the same density of colour or the believability of the lighting effects' (*Sight and Sound*, March 1996).

Most animation studios make their money through commercials rather than features. Full-length animation feature films are extremely time-consuming and very expensive. One of the most interesting examples of animation in recent years was Robert Zemeckis's *Who Framed Roger Rabbit?*, which combined live actors with animated cartoon characters. Most of the animation for this film was prepared in studios in London.

Britain is increasingly a centre of first-class animation as the three Oscars to Nick Park for the *Wallace and Grommit* films testify. Channel Four has provided a showcase for the work of young animators in recent years, and this has given a boost to the profession. The British seemed to have evolved an approach to animation which acts as a bridge between the United States and Europe.

Hand-drawn animation is so very costly because it is labour-intensive. The best animation is still done by hand and, although much research is being done on computer animation by companies such as Disney and Cambridge Animation, the problem of creating really natural movement in drawn figures has not yet been conquered. No computer software yet designed can render the muscles in a human face that express nuance of feeling and emotion. Artists do this instinctively and this is why the best animation is still hand-drawn. Human communication skills are infinitely variable and modern technology simply cannot mimic the slight changes in gesture and movement that are necessary if cartoon characters are to appear really 'animated'. Computers, which are an extremely expensive initial investment, do not have the elegance and naturalness of true animation. They can, on the other hand, produce and colour images very quickly and efficiently and, once the investment has been made, they are obviously cheaper in terms of wages and manpower. It really all depends on the type of image the producer of the film or programme wants to convey. Most animation studios use hand-drawn animation for the main characterisations and movements, and computers for the essential in-betweening tasks that are time consuming and somewhat tedious.

How do you become an animator?
Mainly by going to art college and being good at rapid drawing and sketching. There are independent animation studios that make animated films for commercials and features. The would-be animator should take a video which illustrates their own work to the studio and try to get a job as a 'runner'. Studios will be looking for originality and creativity as well as artistic ability: there are many more people who can draw than there are those who can draw and come up with original ideas.

There is some controversy in the animation sector today over whether it is better to hire computer graphics technicians and teach them how to be picture makers or train artists and traditional animators to work with computers. Most people favour the second option because the artistic eye is still important.

Although the most famous animation studio of all is Walt Disney, most commentators believe that Britain now has some of the best animators in the world. Animators in British commercial studios working on cartoons for advertisers can make a great deal of money. The European Community's CARTOON scheme provides funds for young animators to produce pilot videos, and this has been a positive contribution to the development of the skills of European animators.

Summing Up
Design areas encompass some of the most creatively exciting areas of the industry. The design industry has expanded in Britain in the last ten years largely due to the high quality of education and training in British art colleges and universities. It is a strange anomaly that Britain, which is somewhat philistine in its approach to art and design in daily life, produces some of the best commercial artists and designers in the world. The British film and television industry has benefited from this.

Case Histories

ALASTAIR FELL

Alastair Fell is 32 and Key Animator and Designer for Cosgrove Hall Films, the BAFTA award winning studio, based in Manchester

When I was at school I loved art and I did A level Art as my main subject. All I wanted to do was draw. After school I did an Art Foundation course at Chester Art College in Art and Design and then went on to Salford College, more or less by accident because I came across a reference in the *Guardian* to a diploma course in Graphic Design at Salford. My real interest was in drawing but I decided to do the course anyway and in the final year I specialised in Illustration because my interests and abilities lay more in that direction. Graphic Design people tended then to go into advertising but I wanted to do something which was freer.

After Salford I took a year out to redo my portfolio, and this is where serendipity comes in to play, because one day I went back to Salford with my portfolio to see one of the lecturers and he happened to have a friend there who worked for Cosgrove Hall. It was a case of the right place at the right time because the friend asked to borrow my portfolio saying that someone would be interested in it at Cosgrove. Anyway I was interviewed for a job but then they turned me turned down! What I did then was to keep writing to them at decent intervals just to say 'I'm still here'. I tried to take a light approach and not overdo it. Anyway eventually there was a second interview and I got a job with this Company in a grade called 'newcomer-to-grade-in-betweener'.

Ten years later I am still here but now I am key animator which means I have overall charge of a scene working within the limitations of the overall layout and the storyboard. As far as the drawn creative side is concerned, I suppose the construction of the storyboards is the first part of the whole process and then the key animator has responsibility for creating all movement.

When I started I was plunged straight in at the deep end. The company was right in the middle of producing a feature film called *The B.F.G.* My job was to clean up an in-betweener's 'roughs' because at that time the process was 'rough animation to cleaned-up keys' and 'rough in-betweens to cleaned-up keys'. There were effectively four people working on one particular piece of animation. It was excellent working in a group like that. It created enthusiasm, you learned from the others and we all made the tea! You moved up the system as the people above

205

were promoted so you were really very well trained all the way at every level. Cosgrove has always been a good training company.

I went from 'newcomer-to grade-in-betweener' to assistant and I was assistant for about three years working on films like *Dangermouse, Count Duckula, Victor and Hugo.* Each film was a spin-off in terms of names from the film that had gone before.

I really like my work. Ultimately it's fun to be paid to draw. If you love to draw, you draw. In fact I'd draw even if I wasn't paid to do so. Anyone going into animation should draw and draw and draw. You have to be able to do it quickly but speed comes with practice and experience. When I first started I would take an hour to do an in between drawing but I've speeded up an awful lot since then! Most animators, you find, also enjoy watching animation of all sorts to see what works. I really like Disney and the old Tom and Jerry cartoons. You can learn such a lot from them. They are brilliant.

It is not necessary to do a college course to get into animation. I don't know of anyone who got a job through a degree in Animation. What you need is an ability to draw and you have to go to life classes so you intuitively understand human movement and facial expression. You also have to have a logical mind and an eye for timing because humour is vital. Eventually timing becomes second nature. You know how to make the drawings snappy to make people laugh.

It is also important to get on well with people and be able to work as part of team. It is no use being a prima donna in this business. It just doesn't work because you have to work with other people as a team in a small studio. The prima donna types usually move out of animation and do something else. You have to be able to cooperate and not get on other people's nerves. The type who can't compromise can be very tiresome.

Of course, computing has taken the drudgery out of animation but I can't see computers replacing animators completely because you need that human dimension. Computers are simply another tool. They are enjoying a honeymoon period at the moment when computer genera-tion is all the fashion but eventually they will be absorbed and become part of the accepted mainstream. Probably the puppet side of animation will suffer more from the presence of computers – much more than hand-drawn animation.

You have to learn to be realistic about financial things in this busi-ness because you can't spend acres of time on each piece of animation. You do have to make decisions about which parts to spend lots of effort on and which parts allow you to take a few shortcuts because you are always working under time pressure. I should also say don't go into animation for the money. If you want to make a fortune then don't think about animation for a career.

JILL SWEENEY

Jill Sweeney is 31 and works as a freelance make-up artist.

I went to the Abraham Moss College in Manchester and studied Hair-dressing and Beauty Therapy. I got my first job working for the Royal Ex-change Theatre in Manchester doing wigs and make-up. I worked on many productions including *Great Expectations, An Inspector Calls, Ridley Walker*. It was great experience and I worked with many artists – Amanda Donahoe and Hugh Grant – in fact I once cut Hugh Grant's hair!

Then when I was 21 I got a job with Opera North in Leeds and worked there for eighteen months while applying to the BBC. I was keen to get into the Beeb because once you got a job there they gave you three months intensive training after which you were a trainee for a year. I really wanted that. I got in eventually and the Beeb certainly gave you a stiff training! We did everything. If your attitude wasn't right, or your work wasn't good enough, you were thrown off the course and you could lose your job. The BBC doesn't have the same internal train-ing system anymore; only Granada and Yorkshire still train in the old way. Now people pay the Beeb to go on their training courses, it's gone commercial, so it is not quite the same as it was.

Working in make-up is 50 per cent skill and 50 per cent psychology. You have to have insight into people because you are working under pressure; sometimes it can be a fourteen-hour day and the actors and artistes get tired. Also everything can change at the last minute. If you are on a drama and the weather changes you might have to change the hair and the make-up at the last minute when everyone is tense. You really have to be able to walk on eggshells and you have to know how to juggle your time so you use it to the very best advantage. You can't afford to waste time and you always have to be aware of how much time you've got left. You really have to be able to cope with the per-formers. I think getting older helps because you have to learn to listen and when you are young you don't listen very well.

In January 1995 I left the staff job at the BBC and went freelance and since then I've worked on a number of programmes. At the moment I am working on *Frost, The Beat Goes On* and *Cuts* for Yorkshire, which is a drama about the television industry.

It was part of my plan to go freelance eventually. You are better off making your own employment deals but you have to be self-sufficient and not nervous. Being freelance is an exciting life although you have to be prepared to go anywhere. If you are the type that doesn't like, or is frightened of, driving all over the place – over hill and dale – this is *not* the job for you.

207

I often work on my own so I have to be resourceful. Usually when you get to the set or on location you are the new girl on the block and no-one knows you. Mind you, you do get to know people and make friends everywhere but initially you can't afford to be shy.

If it's just a job you want then forget about being a make-up artist. You have to really enjoy the work and put your heart into it. It's not just about earning a living. I love the fact that it is not routine and that I don't have to go into the same office everyday. But if you are the sort who likes to know what you are doing all the time then you won't like this type of work because there can be a real atmosphere of chaos and confusion – a production schedule can alter and change very suddenly.

The next step for me, I suppose, would be to get into make-up design, to design the 'look' of a whole programme, to read the script, design the right approach, envisage what the producer wants, hire the make-up staff and so on. I don't know where exactly I will end up. In this business you make many contacts and contacts lead on to many things. You never know where the opportunity may come from and which contacts will take you in a new direction.

I know I have to get more into networking but I've only been in the business mode for just over a year. Working at the BBC I was protected; working as a freelance is different. You have to learn the hard way to negotiate fees for yourself. I'm only a novice business woman. I think it is important to be a member of the make-up union and know how to charge properly for a job. You have to protect the profession and other people in it and realise that you have to make sure that other people are not enticed by the glamour of the job into working for very little.

Notes

1. See Andy Fry, 'Character Building', *Broadcast*, 15 December 1995.
2. One of the best books in the area is Douglas Merritt, *Graphic Design in Television* (Oxford: Focal Press, 1995).

14

RESEARCHERS, JOURNALISTS AND WRITERS

There are many jobs associated with writing in film and television despite the fact that they are essentially visual media. Television is a great consumer of journalists who are required in many different staff grades. Films and programmes also employ scriptwriters for the dialogue or commentaries. Many journalists begin their careers as researchers.

RESEARCHERS

Television
In television the *researcher's* job is extremely varied and the post tends to be the catch-all grade for graduate entrants. The term 'researcher' can be confusing because it implies study of a rather academic sort; people tend to think research means delving into matters deeply. In fact there is little of this in a television research job. Researchers spend a great deal of time on the phone making contacts, setting up programmes and finding interviewees. Most researchers work in current affairs and have the same time constraints as journalists. In other words, they have to put items together quickly and work under pressure.

Researchers are expected to come up with programme ideas and they can help write scripts and news reports. They act as the producer's right hand. The nature of the job really depends on the producer to whom the researcher reports: some producers have a great deal of confidence in researchers, who then gain a great deal of experience; other producers like to do everything for themselves and give researchers very simple tasks. Most researchers want to become producers and indeed many of them do, or they move into journalism in the news room.

The job is immensely varied. Researchers can be based in the television offices one day and out finding people and locations the next. They sometimes do the preliminary preparation for a programme and talk to members of the public to decide if they have anything to contribute and whether they will be able to cope with the interview situation.

Researchers therefore meet the public a great deal and must be able to win people's confidence and put them at their ease. If someone is researching for a programme on Aids, for example, they must know something about the disease and deal with people in a sensitive and understanding way. Getting a good interview will depend on coaxing people along, especially if they are under severe emotional pressure.

Researchers also go out on recordings and they assist the director by setting up interviews and chatting to people beforehand about what they are going to say. Research may involve finding people to form the studio audience for light entertainment or audiences to participate in controversial debates, for example representatives of the pro- and anti-smoking lobby. When the tabloid press was having a field-day with the story of men being able to have babies, the present writer was given twenty-four hours notice to find a man who wanted to get pregnant so that he could participate in a studio debate! It is not a job for the shy or the easily embarrassed.

In some cases researchers will actually help with the editing, particularly if a director has only been hired to do the actual recording and is not interested in the subject of the programme. This is most appropriate if the researcher has had the original idea for the programme.

There are specialised researchers for specific types of programmes. Researchers will be hired for a science series or a series on anthropology or music and so on. A fair number of researchers are employed in educational programming. Film research for television is also a more specialised area, and especially so if it involves archival film. Researchers who work on series which cover the Second World War, for example, will probably have a detailed knowledge of old newsreels and a good historical knowledge of that War.

Programme research is the area where ambitious recruits are supposed to show their potential. Increasingly people are taken on by television companies on three-month contracts and have just that time to prove they can do the job. Nowadays many researchers are hired on these very short-term contracts and only a few will ever secure more permanent employment.

Film

Researchers in the film industry are usually experts recruited for particular films. Thus, if a feature film is set in revolutionary Russia, the company could well hire a researcher to check up on particular facts. If a real person is being portrayed, the film company might want to know if he or she smoked, or was a vegetarian or was fond of children, all of which might be incorporated into the actor's performance.

210

How do you become a researcher?

Most researchers are graduates because intelligence, ingenuity and flexibility are important and a degree is taken to indicate this. In general, it is the first job which is hardest to get. Once you have experience in television research, you do usually get other contracts, even if these are mainly very short-term.

One way in is the obvious one: apply for the researcher jobs that are advertised. They do crop up in the trade papers (see listings at the back of this book), but remember there will be probably hundreds of other applicants. Many graduates think of programme research as a dream job and the competition is very intense. Another way is to target a programme that interests you. Watch it, try to think up ideas for the programme and then send these to the producer, care of the programme and the company. Finding research jobs demands the sort of initiative which the job itself calls for. Again, send in letters, even though most of these will go directly into the wastepaper bin. Knock on doors and say you will do anything. Many researchers only get jobs in television after they have worked in newspapers or radio. Some people quite brazenly cultivate contacts and not a few researchers have found jobs through 'knowing' the right people. Once in, you will be expected to work long hours. There are very few old researchers. It is a young person's job and most researchers aim to be producers by the time they are thirty.

JOURNALISTS
NEWS WRITERS
REPORTERS
CORRESPONDENTS
NEWS READERS
NEWS EDITORS

Television

Journalism has been discussed in some detail in the section of this book that dealt with media education (Chapter 6). *Journalists* can work on-screen or off. They can work on news or current affairs programmes and can also be very important in documentary programming. Many producers in current affairs are journalists.

One of the main focuses for journalists in television is television news. News journalists can work behind the scenes in the studio putting together news bulletins, they can appear on-screen in the studio as newscasters, or they may go out on location and send in 'filmed' reports.

News is a high-pressure area. Programmes have to be up to the minute and, if a major news story breaks, items can be changed even as the news goes out on air. Hours too can be awkward: if there is a major air crash at four in the morning, then reporters will have to go out and cover it and journalists on call will have to come into the studio to put the story together. News stories come from a wide variety of sources. Journalists always have a fat 'contact' book in which they list useful names and numbers: politicians, police, doctors, 'experts' in all areas.

Most television journalists start behind the scenes as 'researchers' or *news-writers* in the news room. They will try to find stories, check up on the accuracy of information received and write news bulletins. They might then graduate to *reporter* level, usually in local news, and be sent out with a camera operator or a camera crew to report on a local event.

The best way to learn about local news reporting is to watch it over an extended period. Journalists will report on hospital shortages, visits by politicians, a local row over the police, complaints about rubbish in the streets, football hooligans, the first new babies of the year who have turned out to be triplets, the old lady who has reached the age of 105 and still has all her own teeth, and so on. Notice what shots are used to establish a scene. If it's the baby story, is there an outside shot of the hospital? Is there a shot which links in with the New Year theme (fireworks at midnight perhaps)? Local news reporters do not have much time for setting up, original or beautiful shots and their viewers are not likely to be interested in the avant-garde. Reporters usually only have only an hour or two to assess the story on the spot and decide how it should be presented. They may do one or two interviews with the people involved and then a 'piece to camera', in which he or she reviews the situation and gives background information.

Once reporters are satisfied there is enough material, they go back to base so that the video editor can put the story together in sequence. At this point they might record a 'voice-over' as the camera pans across, for example, the rubbish-strewn streets. The reporter is his or her own producer and director, makes most of the decisions and also writes the script.

The job requires intelligence, quick-wittedness and an ability to get on with people. Not everyone welcomes the reporter with the camera and there can be tricky encounters. After one of the so-called 'race' riots in the early 80s, local reporters in an inner-city area were often met by indignant residents shouting, 'We're not animals in a zoo. Get out of here.' People had been annoyed by bad publicity and insensitive reporting mainly by the national tabloids. It took months of patience and tact to restore the feeling of goodwill which is essential if a local reporter is to do his or her job properly.

212

After overcoming all obstacles, the story might be dropped at the last minute because something more important has come up. This is annoying to the reporter and it can be embarrassing if the interviewees have gathered all their relatives together to watch themselves being interviewed on the local evening news. Great diplomacy is required in this situation, especially if one of the 'dropped' interviewees is the obstetrician who has given half an hour in a very busy, highly pressured day to the interview.

The aim of most local reporters is to graduate to the national news, BBC, ITN or Channel Four, or to a prestigious news programme such as *Newsnight*. These news programmes have special *correspondents* who report from Washington, Moscow, the UN, or Brussels or have a specialist area of responsibility such as social affairs, parliament, industry, the law or the media.

News editors have a very senior job. They make the final choice on the content of the news programme and bulletins, as well as deciding the 'running order': that is, which item should lead, which should come second, and so on. This is a very important decision and news editors can be subject to enormous political pressure, particularly in an election period. Political parties complain vociferously if their point of view, on the National Health Service for example, is not the lead item. Editors also have to deal with decisions about content – whether an item is libellous, for example – and they are also responsible for long-term planning, management of staff and budget control (in association with others).

Budgets are a very sensitive issue at the present time because television news costs have been escalating. Covering the Gulf War, for example, was very expensive. There has been some concern expressed that, since the privatisation of broadcasting, television companies are less prepared to send news crews to record and report on foreign stories. Unlike public service broadcasting, private companies are interested in profit and there is a suggestion that concern for the interests of shareholders prevents news editors from sending crews to follow up issues in far flung corners of the globe. News people themselves, of course, instinctively want to cover everything just in case a big story breaks. A news editor who decided not to cover the Prime Minister's political sortie to a regional city might lose his or her job if someone made an assassination attempt during the visit and there were no pictures available!

News readers, *news presenters* and *newscasters* have the most glamorous jobs in news and can be very highly paid. They must have a pleasant appearance, good diction, a pleasant manner and be able to remain calm when chaos is breaking out all around them. In the past it was felt that only men had the *gravitas* to read the news and that women did not have credibility. Newspapers used to run articles about how the 'lightness' of women's voices made them unsuitable for serious newscasting. Fortunately this has changed dramatically in the past ten years and women journalists are on screen more frequently. Some newscasters are experienced journalists and write their own copy but some have their scripts prepared for them by back-room journalists in the news room.

People tend to confuse announcers and news presenters. News presenters are invariably journalists, while announcers are men and women of pleasant appearance and voice who provide links between, and information about, programmes (see Chapter 15).

How do you become a journalist?
It is estimated that there are over 30,000 journalists in the United Kingdom of which about 21,000 are paid-up members of the National Union of Journalists. Nearly 4,000 NUJ members work for the BBC and about 4,500 work as freelances. About 6,500 work for newspapers and just over 2,000 for magazines. Journalism has always been an insecure profession and the Thatcherite onslaught on the unions did have a significant effect on the NUJ, which, for a while, lost members. The union did weather the storm, however, and in 1996 is gaining members even as (or perhaps because) managers are abandoning collective agreements and negotiating individual short-term contracts.

As explained in Chapter 8, the education of journalists presents a complex picture, with a bias towards workplace training. Many television journalists begin their careers in newspapers or local radio where a patchwork of different types of training is available. Increasingly, despite a traditional antipathy towards academic training, most new journalists are graduates and more of them today have degrees in journalism. There are also very well-established courses in journalism at postgraduate level for people who have a first degree in another subject.

Journalism training which is specifically geared to television is hard to find. The BBC has trained television journalists for many years on a variety of schemes but its in-house training of journalists tends to be for people who already work for the Corporation. One interesting trend is the 'multi-skilling' courses on which, in addition to training in journalism, BBC employees are provided with training in production, camera operation and other areas. This is an indication of the changes in the industry which have been discussed at length in this book.

In terms of broadcasting in general, the BBC also runs a Radio Trainee scheme, the aim of which is to recruit reporters for local radio. The idea is to bring in 'new blood' and applicants must have no formal training and no experience on a newspaper. It is an open scheme for which there are no formal entry qualifications, although about three-quarters of applicants are graduates. Trainees receive a two-year contract and a training salary. They have an initial training period in London and then three different placements in local radio, after which they go on the local radio reporters' reserve list. Trainees must be prepared to move at a moment's notice. The scheme applies to trainees in England and the Channel Islands and is not confined to younger applicants. People who have worked in jobs outside the industry for many years are eligible. It is, however, extremely competitive.

ITV was criticised for many years for not providing training schemes but at one time, under pressure from the IBA, founded a National Broadcasting School. Unfortunately it went bankrupt after two years. However, many people enter journalism through independent local radio, which provides excellent experience. ITN also has a few traineeships available which are sometimes advertised.

Skillset is establishing standards of competence in journalism and writing.

SCREENWRITERS
SCRIPTWRITERS
SCRIPT EDITORS
SCRIPT READERS

Film, Television and Video
I don't like reading scripts. It's a real effort for me, which is not very good – I might throw something good out like 'Platoon'. (Nicholas Cage)

Screenwriting is the specialist term used for writing scripts for the cinema. *Screenwriters* in the past rarely worked in television, but today writers find themselves working in film, television and the non-broadcast video sector. The former clear distinction between screen and scriptwriting is, as in other jobs in the industry, becoming increasingly blurred.

Script Formats
Despite this, however, scripts still fall into two main formats, depending on whether they are intended for film or television. The film (sometimes called the Hollywood) format uses the whole page and there are very precise rules to be observed in layout which allow the length of the script to be judged immediately. It is not unknown for a producer to weigh a film script in his or her hand to estimate its length.

The film format will set out the script scene by scene, with an across-the-page description of where the scene is set and what the characters are doing. The actual dialogue, however, is set out down the centre of the page, with plenty of room on each side for the continuity marks.

For a television script the page is usually arranged in two columns. In the left-hand column are the instructions which relate to visuals (shot numbers, camera instructions – pan, zoom, VT inserts, Colour Separation Overlay and so on). The right-hand column contains everything associated with sound, including the narration or the dialogue. This format is now used for television drama as well as for non-fiction, studio-based shows because of its great flexibility. News operations today often use elaborate computer software that produces scripts for news rooms in this format. Computerised news rooms can quickly produce scripts already cued to a particular performer's speaking pace.

Both film and television formats are relatively easy to produce, once writers have had experience with them. Sophisticated scripts, however, perhaps for a television drama, can take a long time to reach a final version. Drama production on television has to be extensively pre-planned, because studio time is very expensive and must therefore be used to its maximum potential. The director and production team meet during pre-production and, with a copy of the script, plan camera angles, shots and so forth, which are then listed in the left-hand column and linked by a line across to the dialogue. There are not many opportunities for a change of mind on the day of recording.

The Writing Process
As discussed in Chapter 10, screen- and scriptwriters can either approach a film or television company with their own idea or, more frequently, they are given an idea and commissioned by film or television producers to develop a script from it. Sometimes they may be asked to 'adapt' a book or a play for the screen: the BBC's extremely successful production of Jane Austen's *Pride and Prejudice* was one such adaptation. If the screen- or scriptwriter initiates the idea, he or she will produce a synopsis or summary (as brief as two pages), and then approach commissioning editors, script editors, producers, agents, directors, production companies, in order to sell them the concept.

Presentation is important. If an idea wins favour, the commissioning agency will ask for an extended outline or 'treatment', which can run from ten to forty pages or more. The treatment will usually include a description of the setting and style of the film or programme. If the treatment is accepted, then a shooting script is developed. Sometimes

216

the director and the screen- or scriptwriter work on the shooting script together and there may be a number of rewrites.

Television producers who commission a script might only want a 'rough script', or they might want a complete script. Writers can be commissioned for one or two episodes of a serial or for a complete set of scripts – it all depends. Different scriptwriters can be hired at different stages of a script (this is very common in film) or there may be a stable of writers on an extremely popular television soap opera. Comedy writers tend to work collaboratively, although most other creative writers prefer to write on their own. The writer gives an estimated date for delivery, but writers, as a group, are notorious for missing deadlines and a certain amount of bullying by producers can go on at this stage.

Most writers are freelance and on occasion directors assigned to a film will work with them. In television, producers often write the scripts; this is especially the case for documentaries, when the producer might have a personal point of view to convey. Also, if a programme is low-key and low-budget, there may simply be no money available to hire a professional writer.

Permanent positions for writers in the industry are few and far between. The only posts which are really staff-based are those for so-called *script editors* or commissioning editors employed by drama departments or by series. Script editors on soap operas often need good memories, because they have to remember what the characters did three or four or twenty years ago. If they make a continuity mistake, if they forget the long-lost child or husband, the audience will soon make them aware of the error.

Script editors have the difficult job of acting as mediators between producers and writers. Writers are often very sensitive and dislike having to make changes to suit the demands of the small or large screen. When a famous author is hired to adapt his or her own work it can require great resources of tact on the part of the script editor. Writers have maternal feelings towards their 'children' and they can be outraged by an unsympathetic producer or director who decides to kill characters off because 'they make the story too complicated'. Older, revered writers, who are not overfond of television, often find the whole process very unpleasant, especially when faced by young directors who are, from the writer's viewpoint, 'wet behind the ears'. Smoothing over such personality clashes is the very stuff of the script editor's job.

Script readers are sometimes employed by the established film and television companies, some of which might receive dozens of scripts each week. They handle submissions and report if any might be significant or useful.

How do you become a screen/scriptwriter or a script editor?
Screen- and scriptwriters usually have some experience in the theatre, film, journalism or television, or they may have written novels or other books. Some start by submitting a play for radio transmission and move on into other areas such as television or film. The BBC Radio Drama Department has a distinguished record in encouraging new writers and many people receive their first break in this way. A few people manage to get directly into film or television by writing a particularly original piece.

Some writers seek out a reputable literary agent but agents are very choosy and it is quite difficult to register with one for the first time. If an established scriptwriter does not have an agent, then he or she can join The Writers Guild of Great Britain, which is basically the trade union for writers. The Guild negotiates minimum terms and conditions for writers in the industry and has an agreement with PACT covering higher and lower-budget feature films, single television movies, television series and serials. It also has agreements with BBC and ITVA. Similarly the BECTU writers' section can provide useful help in negotiation.

Script- and screenwriting are not particularly lucrative unless the writers are very well-known and experienced. One of the major complaints associated with all forms of moving pictures is that insufficient attention is paid to the script. There is certainly a tendency for the industry to be so visually oriented that it forgets the importance of a strong story-line. The worth of a good script is immediately apparent. An award-winning series such as *Cracker* owes a great deal to its writers.

Most screen- and scriptwriters work freelance from home and this can be an advantage for women with children. In general the industry can be hard for people in this category because of the unstructured working hours and the need for location work away from home. Writing avoids these problems.

In the past there has been little training of any sort for writers in the industry, but increasingly there are courses springing up, such as those provided by the National Short Course Training Programme of the National Film and Television School, CYFLE and certain universities. The Moving Image Development Agency (MIDA), which was established in 1993 in Liverpool, has initiated a project to foster new screenwriting talent in the region and documentaries have developed from this.

Script readers, who assess scripts for radio, television and film, are few and far between and are also often badly paid but, like scriptwriting, script assessment has the advantage that it can be done at home. Here again, experience of the industry is a tremendous advantage.

Case Histories

GWENNO HUGHES

Gwenno is 24 and did a degree in Welsh Literature and Media Literature at the University of Wales, Bangor. She works for BBC Wales as a scriptwriter/assistant script editor for Pobl Y Cwm (People of the Valley).

After my degree I stayed on at Bangor to complete an MA in Welsh TV Drama and Theatre. I then saw an advert in a magazine called *Golwg* which was looking for trainee scriptwriters, researchers, second assistants and camera persons for a one-year CYFLE course. I thought it worth a try and I was fortunate enough to be picked for the script writing course. Oddly enough they selected all girls on that intake.

In the first three months CYFLE gets you to do the works – script writing, presenting, camera work, floor managing, directing, and so on – so you are not totally clueless about the whole programme-making process. I then specialised in scriptwriting for nine months. I was sent to different independent companies for experience. I spent about four months working with Norman Williams as a trainee with his film company *Ffilmiau Eryri*. He threw me in at the deep end and it was either sink or swim. I worked with him on three very different projects and the experience I gained was invaluable. He taught me the importance of always keeping cool under pressure.

During the seventh months of the course, I wrote a try-out script for the daily Welsh soap opera *Pobl y Cwm* and they liked it. Then, soon after I'd started writing for the programme I saw an advert in the national press for a script editor at the BBC. I didn't think I'd get it, due to lack of experience, but thought I'd give it a whirl anyway. It's important that they get to know your face. Anyway I got lucky because I was offered an assistant script editor's post. There are people with a wealth of experience at the BBC and I'm fortunate enough to have some of them to teach me the ropes. I am currently working for *Pobl y Cwm* and I am loving it. We have about twenty authors, who all write an episode in turn and since we're broadcasting daily, our job is to make sure that the continuity of the story-line is right and that there are no repetitions or contradictions. The dialogue has to be genuine South Walian dialect and we have to make sure that each episode keeps to its nineteen minutes, forty five seconds time slot. We record in studio and on an OB on Monday, Tuesday and Wednesday. Then on Thursdays and Fridays the following week's episodes are rehearsed. I do some researching as well, especially for the big stories, and therefore get to go to places and meet people I'd never meet otherwise.

My advice for anyone wanting to get into television is to go for it. If you want it bad enough don't let anything stop you.

JOHN RILEY

Jon Riley is 27. He read English Literature at Leeds University from 1987 to 1990 and is now a BBC researcher with Youth Programming in Manchester.

When I was at university I was heavily involved in music, mostly jazz. I had a life outside the university. I ran clubs, was involved in promotion, had my own band. Because of the music I got to tour round the country, met lots of different people in different parts and really enjoyed that. Although I had no hard and fast career plan at that time and the experience had no bearing on getting into television – I wasn't thinking about that then – it all did pay off later. I got some self-confidence about dealing with all sorts of people in all sorts of places.

When I left Leeds I happened to meet a theatre director and as result got involved in Theatre in Education. This particular group was a three-person operation so I did everything – script writing, set designing, acting. It wasn't especially glamorous going round Bradford schools but it was fun and excellent experience. Again, I met people and had a million different experiences and tried my hand at anything. The group was a fairly successful and we went to Paris and a festival in Denmark. We were all working for pittances of course.

Then, after a year, the group split up and I decided to go to Edinburgh just because it was a city I liked. I knocked on doors looking for a job and eventually ended up working for something called the Broadcast Monitoring Company which I suppose could be described as a 'cuttings agency' for television and radio. I learnt a hell of a lot there about all sorts of things. One of the things I would emphasise to anyone wanting to get into this business is to have what I call a 'dust-bin' mind. It's vital. You have to be interested in everything and read everything from *Hello to* the broadsheets and watch lots of television. You must really enjoy acquiring information. It can really pay off because you can come up with ideas. You may half-remember something interesting, mention it to someone and it turns out to be useful. You can check up on the detail later.

The problem with the Edinburgh job was that the company was owned originally by Robert Maxwell and there were financial problems because of that. Suddenly the whole operation went bust and I was fired. So then I came back to London and I did not know what to do, although by now I was interested in getting into television. I began to write off to the BBC, answered adverts in the *Guardian* and kept trying to think what new letter I could write that would be different from the other 5,000 applications. I quickly realised that I was getting nowhere. Then, round Christmas, I had a conversation with my brother who was just starting out writing comedy and knew a bit about the business (he's pretty successful now) and he mentioned that it was important to get known, to get my foot-in-the-door as a runner. I hadn't really thought about this. At the time I was either on the dole or working at all sorts of different jobs including teaching English as a foreign language. In fact, the last job which I had before working in broadcasting was in a cat flap factory. It's all experience!

Anyway over Christmas I watched television most of the time and noted the names of producers of series I liked and rang them up. One of them said, 'Come and see me on Monday', and so I did. She asked me what I wanted to do and I said that I was interested in everything and that I would be prepared to work for nothing. She said: 'Start in a couple of days.' And that was it. It was real luck because once I had decided on an approach strategy then 'getting in' came quite quickly.

This first job was as a runner and researcher and I would do anything. I was working very long hours and I did everything for everyone. These particular programmes used a lot of music which I knew about. I realised then that I could create a niche for myself so I rang up record producers and got hold of original and new material. People began to realise that they could rely on me, that I knew about music. I would help the directors choose new music which meant they noticed me.

All this time I was sleeping on floors and living with friends. In the end, I went to the producer and said, 'Look I can't do this anymore', so they paid me £100 a week and I was off. You're not supposed to work for nothing anymore but it was how I started.

Then I heard through the television grapevine that BBC2 was commissioning a programme called *The Ronson Mission*. Jon Ronson is an ex-columnist of *Time Out* and writes for the Saturday *Guardian*. This was right up my street so I talked to the producer over lunch and basically said: 'I know lots about music.' In two weeks I was up in Manchester working for the BBC on a runner contract.

I have never learnt so much. I was with the *Ronson* programme from inception, through to the end. I had to find locations. Some of the 'set-ups' were very difficult. I used the archives, did research, did music interviews. Then when all that was done, at nine o'clock in the evening I would go and chat to the programme editors. I did a hell of a lot but I learnt a lot and I made contacts. The people I worked with on the

221

Ronson programme went on to do lots of things. You have to put yourself about in this business and get yourself a reputation for hard work. It is no use sitting around or resenting it if someone asks you to do something.

Now I am a researcher mainly on Youth and Entertainment programmes. I have worked on *Weird Night, The Living Soap* and have just done a documentary about *The Carpenters* so I got to go to Los Angeles. One of the things which I think is very important is finding out about everything, asking people what they do. You mustn't badger them but most people like being helpful if you ask and that way you can learn. If you talk to the camera operator about what this does and what that does they will tell you. You have to ask questions if you want to learn and you have to work hard. It is incredibly hard graft.

15

EDITING AND ENGINEERING

EDITOR (craft/creative)
ASSISTANT EDITOR (craft/technical)
PROJECTIONIST (technical)

When a great actor says the line, you can put the scissors precisely at the point A and it's wonderful. When the star says the line, you hold for four frames longer because something else happens. (Sir David Lean talking about Michael Caine)

Editing is one of the key creative elements in the process of film- and programme-making. In the last few years it has been one of the areas most affected by the impact of new technology as computers have come to play an increasingly significant role in post-production. In video, in particular, the introduction of, what is called, non-linear editing has had a dramatic impact but in film too computing technology has brought about significant change. As a result, the way film and television programmes are 'constructed' and working practices in the post-production sector altered profoundly during the 90s.

This chapter can only sketch out the significance of what has been part of a broader trend towards convergence in the film, television, video, telecommunications and computer industries (discussed in more detail in Chapter 4 which deals with the multi-media revolution).[1]

Where Do Editors Work?
Television companies used to carry out most of their editing in-house. Along a certain corridor visitors would find rows of small film-editing suites where *editors* worked away on different programmes. Usually quite separate from these, in another area, there would be a VT or VTR Centre where video editors (and also engineers, see below) were located. These still survive, but in recent years there has been a rapid growth of what are called 'facilities' houses or post-production companies,

which exist independently of television and film companies and specialise in various technical services including editing. An editing job today, therefore, is likely to mean working in a facilities house, rather than in a broadcasting company and also working, in some cases, with both film and video interchangeably. The Producers' Choice initiative at the BBC, the growth of the publisher/broadcaster model at ITV and the development of the independent sector have all promoted the development of the specialist facilities houses.

The Editing Task

Film and video editors take decisions about the picture images which have been shot in production. They decide what should be retained and what should be discarded, so that the film or programme can 'come together' in a visual and stylistic narrative that audiences find appealing and that expresses the vision of the whole creative team.

Editors have to understand the techniques of telling a story and know how to create a logical and coherent narrative. Editing techniques for both film and video are fairly simple to learn, but editing is much more than technique. The way a good editor puts together the images (and sounds) is the crucial final stage in the whole creative process. It takes talent and a great deal of experience to become really expert in this very demanding profession.

Film Editing – The Traditional Way

Editors on feature films and filmed television programmes (such as high-prestige drama) are often hired at the beginning of the production period. They work on the film on a daily basis, doing a 'rough assembly' of the day's shots which the director and members of the lighting and camera crew can look at and assess each evening. This viewing of the day's rushes makes final editing much easier, since the editor is aware of the day-to-day progress of the film, and is also able to draw the director's attention to poor material (and even, in exceptional circumstances, suggest reshooting a scene). If the editor is associated with the film from the beginning in this way, he or she is a key player in the creative team and acquires an intimate knowledge and understanding of the director's intentions.

The 'rushes' theatre may be a specialist dubbing or viewing studio or a very small private cinema with an experienced specialist *projectionist* to lace up the film and prepare the reels for the crew to view. A company in production may book such a preview cinema each evening for several weeks and the projectionist sees how the film evolves and how the editor cuts the film down to the final product. Not surprisingly, therefore, projectionists in this type of work often want to move into editing and they try to make the contacts that lead to assistant editor jobs (although today there are few of these around – see below for the reason why).

The luxury of the preview theatre, however, is not the lot of most editors, but only of those who have very distinguished reputations and are engaged on major films. Most film editors have no input at all at the production stage, but are faced with a *fait accompli* when the copy of the developed film arrives in the editing suite from the laboratory. There are no opportunities for second thoughts or reshoots, except in cases of dire emergency. Camera operators will have been dispersed, performers are working on other productions and the editor is faced with the relatively lonely task of 'crafting' the film into an acceptable finished article. Much grumbling and cursing about directors and camera operators can be heard emerging from the depths of the average editing suite as editors come to grips with this task.

In the first stages of editing, the editors and assistant editors work on a copy of the film (workprint or cutting copy) and the original picture negative is stored away secure and unmarked so that it is in prime condition for the final edit. The workprint, however, is still treated with great care: no dirt or grit must gather on the surface because this could damage the print. Editors often work with thin white gloves to keep the film as clean as possible. A film does not arrive in the editing suite in complete isolation. It is usually accompanied by a copy of the script and the notes which camera and sound assistants have made on location. There are also laboratory report sheets including technical comments.

Traditionally, the initial handling of the film is the task of *assistant film editors*. Assistant film editors have to be meticulous and highly organised. They do the preparatory work with the rushes. Picture rushes came from the laboratory, while sound rushes often came separately from a sound transfer facility. Rolls of rushes could be anywhere from 400 to 2,000 feet in length. The assistant 'synchs' them up, which means synchronising the sound with the picture. When in synch, the image and sound coincide properly; when out of synch, they are mismatched. (The appearance and sound of the clapperboard, as explained earlier, was the 'synch' point for both sound and picture.)

During the process of 'synching up', the assistant breaks down the film into manageable units of usually around 1,000 feet and each unit is clearly labelled with the name of the production, the roll number and other relevant information. Every shot has to be 'logged' in this way, because accurate written records are essential to keep track of the shots. This is as true for rejected shots as it is for shots that are included, because there are always frequent changes of mind at the editing stage. Nothing must be thrown away because, at some point, the editor might decide to use scenes which were initially rejected. Scrupulous record-keeping is an essential feature of the traditional film editing process; film editing suites have hundreds and hundreds of strips of film hanging around the cutting room, and without proper records the whole process can quickly descend into chaos.

Once the basic picture and sound footage have been synched up by the assistant editor, the editor takes over and, sometimes with the director's assistance, begins the process of editing the film. Scenes are viewed carefully and arranged in the proper order. Good shots are included and poor shots are taken out. The scenes are put together in a 'rough assembly', which is then tightened into a 'rough cut' and then into a 'finished edit' or 'fine cut'. The soundtrack is also cut to coincide with the picture and the sound editor puts together ('mixes') several different tracks (dialogue, music and sound effects) to make the final soundtrack of the film.

The edited picture and sound then goes back to the laboratories for so-called 'combined' or release prints to be made for distribution to cinemas. 'Combined' prints are exactly that: the sound and picture combined on to the same piece of film. The magnetic soundtrack is translated into an optical one which run alongside the picture at the edge of the film. This the film projector converts into sound when the film is projected onto the screen in a cinema.

As we can see from all this, film editing has always been very much of a hands-on process: film is actually physically cut and reassembled. Until recently, film editing technology had remained very much the same as it had been for about seventy-five years with the basic film viewing/editing table changing little over that period. Then, suddenly, in the early 90s, this was no longer the case: accepted procedures and techniques began to shift and change under the impact of digital technology, especially in the area of animation and special effects. In the past, for example, it was very difficult to create special effects for film because film, in the words of one editor, was essentially 'wet, chemical and messy and more organic than mechanic'. Special effects could only be accomplished by using complex and expensive techniques in the lab. Once a scene was shot the actual pictures could not easily be altered and, if a really drastic mistake occurred, the only solution was to reshoot. Today, film images can be digitised (i.e. converted to a digital format on a suitable matrix, readable by computer hardware and software) and then edited by non-linear editing computer technology. This means that in post-production, images (copied without any loss of quality thanks to high-resolution digital technology) can be manipulated, altered and moved easily and reliably. Visual and special effects technologies, which have remained more or less the same since the inception of film, have now been supplanted by digital techniques.

Some film-makers believe that digital technology has allowed film-making to get sloppier because problems can be removed and mistakes fixed digitally.[2] Forecasters predict that in the future all film will be transferred to computers for the editing process, returning to the negative only for the final stages, perhaps not even then if high-definition video copies are taken immediately after initial processing. There is also the possibility that cinemas of the future will not project from film at all but will receive a digital signal from a remote distributor via broadband cable. The cutting room will have gone and the mechanical skills of the film editor will have been completely replaced by the computer, leaving visual judgement as the main characteristic of the editorial craft. Not surprisingly this has produced some angst among traditional film editors.

Film Editing: Summing Up
Film editing is a creative, prestigious and satisfying occupation. It is a highly skilled, craft job which still requires physical dexterity and excellent visual judgement, and, since film editors deal with large amounts of raw film, they have almost always required assistants who, from their close day-to-day contact, learn from the experienced professionals. Assistant editors gradually acquire editing skills and once they become fully fledged editors they, in their turn, acquire assistant editors – a process which has resulted in what has amounted to a highly effective apprenticeship training system. However, in the future, if computers do most of the work the need for assistants will disappear and a whole training process will evaporate.

Video
The *video editor* and the film editor basically carry out the same function but, in the past, the techniques they used were very different because the technology was not the same. As a result, film and video editing used to be sharply differentiated professions but today, with the introduction of non-linear editing, freelance editors work in both media and draw on similar reserves of creative talents and skills. This represents a profound change.

For broadcasters, one of the great advantages of video over film is its immediacy: once a scene has been shot it can be played back immediately and assessed. While film is highly flexible in its editing possibilities and produces images of a very high quality, one major drawback has always been the delay that occurs after a film has been shot and while it is being processed. With film, unlike video, there is always a lag between what was shot and what can be viewed and in the time pressured world of broadcasting this was very annoying. Before electronic news-gathering (ENG), news events were recorded by film cameras and cans of film had then to be rushed back to the labs to be developed and edited for the evening programmes. This was a cumbersome process and stories are still told of motorcycle messengers carrying vital film coming into collision with a car and seeing the precious item for the evening news unrolling along the road to be driven over and destroyed by heedless drivers.

Editing video usually consisted of retaining the original tape (the master), and then selecting the desired scenes and images, which were copied on to a blank cassette on another machine. In the past, however, the great drawback with videotape editing was its rigorously linear format. A scene would be electronically marked and then replayed on to a recording machine. A second scene was similarly marked and copied onto the end of the first and so on until a complete programme was assembled in linear, sequential order. Unlike film, where different shots could be spliced in virtually at will, video did not easily allow for any shot changes. Removing a shot left a blank space and if a replacement shot was not exactly the same length as the one it replaced then spaces were left at the end and beginning of the shot. A programme could be recopied until the section to be changed was reached and then a new 'master' made but there was always a loss of quality when tape was copied to tape – never mind the time which was wasted in duplicating previous work!

Over the years, of course, video editors and programme-makers adjusted to the problems and developed various techniques to counteract the difficulties inherent in the electronic medium, but video editing was always regarded as being less artistically satisfying than film editing because it was less flexible. Film editing was an art and a craft while video editing, although it was fast, was thought to demand more trickiness and cunning of its editors who had to learn how to circumvent difficulties posed by the medium's linear format. In addition, film editing took time but its technology was cheap. By contrast, video editing equipment was extremely expensive and was often rented on an hourly basis which also tended to work against any over-leisurely exploration of artistic picture creation for which the film medium was so highly regarded. Videotape editors in the past often began their careers as electronics engineers and technicians, because it was useful to know something about the equipment which, in the early days, often broke down. This also tended to emphasise a practical, nuts-and-bolts type of attitude rather than the visual or imaginative skills that characterise film editors.

To summarise, film editing required a specific manual dexterity that video editing did not. Video editing was done electronically: the editor did not cut anything, but instead pressed buttons on a console. However, with video, unlike film, soundtracks could be mixed and synchronised with the pictures during the actual editing process. It was also always easier to try out special effects with video (according to the capacity of the video equipment). All of this made video popular with broadcasting institutions.

The persistant problem with video, however, was the inflexibility of the linear format and the loss of quality in the image every time the tape was copied. By the late 80s, as computer power grew, programme-makers began to experiment with computers, videotape and film-style editing and the eventual result was the emergence of non-linear editing systems such as AVID and Lightworks. Non-linear editing systems use computer technology and have a user interface similar to those in use for personal computers. The best analogy is to compare non-linear editing to word processing, only with moving pictures and sound recording instead of words. It is now, thanks to computers, as easy to move a complete edited sequence within a programme as it is to 'cut and paste' a paragraph within a document.

Freelance editors in broadcasting companies and in facilities houses increasingly work across all sectors of the industry. People who initially trained as film or video editors quickly acquire non-linear editing skills which they 'perceive as an extra string to their bow in the increasingly competitive field of television post production.'[3] Because it is quite easy to learn to operate the non-linear machines there is some concern that in the future directors will simply do their own editing and the separate, defined profession of editing will disappear. This is attractive to broadcasting institutions because it will cut down on editing costs, but ultimately it could affect picture quality. People without experience or training in the visual grammar of programme production will find the technology accessible to them but the quality of what they produce will probably be rather poor. This is part of the multi-skilling or de-skilling process which critics believe is the negative fall-out of digitisation.

The Editing Experience

Editors usually work on more and more complicated films and programmes, gaining experience as they go. As we have seen, they must have organisational ability and they must be systematic. They must also have an aesthetic sense, a quality which is difficult to describe. Editing may be an innate talent, but it also develops through practice. Editors acquire an instinctive 'feel' for what will create the right effect and they have a sixth sense for when a shot should be cut or held. They will decide if a close-up is better in one scene than a long shot. They will know when to cut from one shot to another and when to slow the

229

action down and when to speed it up. The pace of edits can have an enormous effect on the mood and emotional temperature of a scene. A jump-cut, for example, is a cut which takes place abruptly and draws attention to itself, and yet it may be appropriate in certain circumstances.

Sometimes editors work on a film or programme almost entirely on their own; at other times the director sits alongside the editor and is very dominant. Editors have to be ingenious, because the very shot which would have been useful as a bridge between scenes may not exist or may not have turned out. Problems must be overcome in such a way that the audience is not aware that editing techniques have been used to cover them up. This is where experience comes in.

Really experienced editors can cut a film in such a way that essentially unpromising material is put together in a manner that is appealing and unique. This is a rare talent and such editors are much sought after and highly paid. The decline in the need for assistant editors in both film and video has raised concern about how, and where, a future generation will acquire the necessary visual and imaginative training which can make a great editor.

How do you become an editor?
Most people become editors by being taken on as trainees or assistants by broadcasting companies or as runners in post-production companies and facilities houses. Some students from film schools and colleges who have been trained in editing techniques may be taken on directly as fully fledged editors in the non-broadcast sector (or they might be if the recession had not hit the industry so badly), but this is still relatively rare. Film people tend to believe that editors are born not made and that they have particular imaginative and creative gifts which cannot really be taught; that the best training for new recruits, therefore, is to be taken on in the humblest of jobs, where the favoured few with latent talent, gradually acquire the necessary skills through watching the experts and through hands-on experience.

There is much truth in this, but aptitude can be developed. Also there is a danger inherent in the industry's anti- formal-education bias. Technological hardware is becoming ever more complex, and in future there will be a need for editors who will understand and keep abreast of developments and who will be prepared to train and retrain as new technology comes along. Although deep technical knowledge is not necessary for editing, it does have a place, particularly in an increasingly technological world and especially for those who wish to reach the top.

One commentator (Mark Bishop in *Televisual*, June 1990) has suggested that it is more correct to compare the post-production business in film and television in the 90s to the computer industry, rather than to the film industry of the 50s. This makes sense: film and television are intimately connected with technological developments and the workforce has to be aware of the significance of this.

In the past, educational qualifications have not been important for editors, although, to be taken on by a broadcasting company in the first place, trainees had to have a good general education with respectable GCSE passes. The most important qualifications were, and are, a passion for film and television and an obsessive interest in editing, together with a willingness to work long hours for miserable pay in order to acquire the necessary experience; successful editors can then command a more than adequate remuneration.

There has always been considerable competition for jobs as assistant or trainee editors and this is even more the case today. Many people with editorial ambitions learn the basic skills and practice by joining workshops or community groups which make films and videos. They also attend colleges and courses. They may then edit their own film or tape, which they take round with them in the search for jobs. On feature films, editors have a big say in who they have as their assistants, so they are best approached directly.

ENGINEERS (scientific/technical/administrative/operational)
TECHNICAL ASSISTANTS (technical)
TECHNICAL OPERATORS/TECHNICIANS (technical)

Broadcasting

Broadcasting depends for its success on its *engineers*. Without the technology, broadcasting and video would not exist. Service and research engineers not only keep everything running but also running smoothly.

As has been discussed often in this book, we live in an ever more technically oriented society. Broadcasting has witnessed extraordinary advances in the past decade, thanks to, among other things, the microchip. As the technology of the industry has become more complex, there has been a greater tendency to employ more qualified people on the engineering side and graduates have become more common. This is especially so in specialist research areas especially within the BBC. In the past the BBC or ITV would recruit would-be engineers with A levels and then train them. Today graduates in electronics, electrical engineering and applied physics are increasingly taken on for direct appointment as engineers as BBC training, even in this area, has declined.

There are many categories of engineers in broadcasting and they often have different titles in different companies. One the whole, however, *operational engineers* look after the technical facilities that make

231

broadcasting possible. Operational engineers can be found in studios, on location with outside broadcast vans, or at transmission sites. They are concerned with the operation and maintenance of the networks, with radio links for outside broadcasts, with actual recording, with news-gathering, and with transmission.

One of the most important areas of operational engineering work is vision control. Very precise standards are demanded of broadcasters in Britain and engineers are necessary to make sure these are enforced. Vision control or video engineers sit in control rooms and ensure that each camera in the studio is correctly adjusted so that it matches the others and that the exposure settings and the colour balance are right. It is no use for the presenter's face to have a green tinge on one camera and a red tone on another. Every camera should produce pictures of a consistent quality or viewers will be distracted. In the past the job of matching cameras to each other was complicated, but this function is now largely computerised. Nevertheless, video engineers still need to adjust and align cameras during operation. In some companies vision-control staff also carry out maintenance work on the cameras, while in others this is the responsibility of maintenance engineers.

Engineers are also required to monitor and correct the technical parameters of all video and audio sources within the station and are responsible for incoming signals from other centres.

Outside broadcast engineers carry out many of the above duties, but their job is more varied and they frequently have to deal with emergencies that call on their initiative and ingenuity. They often have to repair malfunctioning equipment at very short notice and with highly agitated production staff breathing down their necks. Outside broadcast engineers meet the public much more than ordinary engineers in television stations.

Engineers are also required for maintaining, servicing and repairing equipment. Microtechnology has resulted in more complex equipment with built-in automatic correction circuits, so there is less hands-on repair work but instead a greater need for expert technical knowledge of electronic circuitry. Increasingly, engineers who join the BBC are involved in the maintenance and operation of the diverse and complex digital and analogue equipment of broadcasting. In the future, as digital technology replaces analogue, the traditional engineering tasks will shift to accommodate to this.

Senior experienced engineers are also required to plan new technical developments and to develop new systems. These *administrative engineers* play an important role in assessing the new equipment and new technology that constantly come on to the market and they provide advice and make decisions about purchase and installation. Engineers in these areas also require financial acumen and must be able to write technical reports that communicate difficult scientific information succinctly and clearly.

Engineers are helped by *technical assistants* or trainee engineers and *technical operators* or technicians. Assistants set up, align and maintain broadcasting equipment and in some cases operate it. Technical operators are more junior members of the team who help with the preparation and operation of equipment.

Engineers and trainee engineers may be responsible for recording programmes being made in the studio, replaying recorded inserts into live programmes (such as news), replaying completed programmes for transmission and using the telecine machine to transfer ordinary cine film or slides to tape so that they can be viewed on the television screen. Cine film is not easily adapted to the television screen, and telecine staff, with the help of sophisticated electronic processors, have to overcome many problems posed by, for example, the variety of film gauges and different screen widths.

How do you become an engineer?
Trainee operational engineers usually have Maths and Physics at A level or a BTEC Higher Certificate or Diploma in Electronics with Television and Communications, or a City and Guilds or Higher National Diploma or Certificate in Engineering or Electronics or Telecommunications. Sometimes they have a degree in Engineering, or Electronics or Telecommunications. Specialist engineers almost invariably have a degree in Engineering, Electronics or Telecommunications. Technicians must have good general education and usually Maths and Physics at A level. They may also have a BTEC or City and Guilds in Electronics or Computer Science. Virtually all technical people are now expected to be able to use computers and, in certain cases, to carry out computer programming.

Case History

ALEX BLAND

Alex Brand is 29 and is working as Assistant Editor on Bait *a drama for BBC Scotland.*

I started quite late in the industry which isn't a disadvantage because you have more experience which is a real help. The people I was on

233

courses with were three or four years younger than I was. When I was at school, I didn't know what I wanted to do; when we had interviews about career options I had no idea. Going into the film or television industry didn't occur to me until later because I didn't know what it was all about.

Initially I decided to do Graphic Design and went to Plymouth Art College. It wasn't for me, so I left and worked for Exeter City Council as a part-time photographer. I'd done photography at the college as one of the options and found that I really liked it.

After Exeter I was unemployed but I did become interested in broadcasting and did a one-year training course in Radio Production but again it was difficult to find a job so then I did a year on the Edinburgh video training course because it seemed ideal. I really got into it while I was there and the editing side really stuck out as something I wanted to do. I was pretty much determined by then to try and become an editor. After I finished the course I got work sporadically, editing community videos and the like, and I wrote off to a number of film and video companies in Glasgow and Edinburgh, basically saying that I was keen to work. This drew a blank.

The problem is that editing has changed with the new technology and assistant editor posts are fewer and farther between and I really did not have too much knowledge of the industry at that time. I did not know the big picture or how would-be assistant editors like myself fitted in to the whole scheme of things. I think young people who want to go into the industry should try and find out more about what working in the industry entails. I kept applying for jobs but, although I did not really realise it, I was competing against people who had edited film and television programmes and my experience of editing community videos was not very impressive at that level of competition. People were very nice and wished me good luck in the future and that sort of thing but I really began to wonder if I could make it. It was disheartening.

Then I saw an advert for the Scottish Broadcasting Film Training Course (SBFTC) and that looked very interesting. I phoned up and heard a bit about it, that it was for people who had an idea about the industry and some competence but couldn't really get their feet in the door. The SBFTC is a different kind of course because its industry funded and you have access straight into the industry through the work placements. When eventually I went out on placements I found that you were taken more seriously because you came from the SBFTC. Anyway I had an interview and was accepted on the strength of what I'd edited. I was eligible because I'd done so much community stuff. I think it's important to edit as much as you can for practice.

I started with the other trainees. They came from all across the board and so were their interests: make-up, editing, camera, and so on. It was great. I was taught about non-linear editing and, as I said, was sent out on editing work placements where I could observe and learn. The course is very good but the competition to get on it is fierce. There were eight places and four hundred applicants!

When I finished I went straight into this job on *Bait*. Big features like this usually do have an assistant editor to help with the manual work and the paper work – information and rushes are coming in all the time, far too much for one editor to cope with. The editor has a lot to do and you can learn such a lot. At the present time there is a lot of worry in editing circles because with non-linear editing systems such as the Lighthouse and Avid there are fewer opportunities for assistant editor jobs. It is relatively easy today to learn the technique of editing but the craft of senior editors takes time to acquire and its difficult to see how this will happen in the future if a new generation of assistants are not trained up. Anyone can be taught to operate a computer but the visual literacy – the eye – can't be developed overnight – it takes years. There are things that you can't learn except by working with, observing and sitting in on, editors as they work.

I do meet people who were in the position I was in two years ago and I think my basic advice is to keep chipping away. It is obviously very tricky because you have to keep justifying yourself when you're trying to get a job in an area where no-one seems to be interested in employing you. I almost gave up but then my luck changed. There is a certain etiquette in the editing business and the film industry in general. You must not be too gabby and throw your weight around and yet you must know the jargon so that you can talk about it competently and produce information that may be useful.

I think it is important to make contacts but there is a very fine line between being persistent and annoying busy people. It is not a good idea to pester. Personality counts a lot. If people like having you around then they want you to do well and will help but even when you've got a job you still have a lot to learn about getting on with people. New situations still keep coming up. Its difficult, you have to be open and admit what you know and don't know honestly otherwise you would never learn and most experienced people are sympathetic and willing to share their knowledge with you. On the other hand you have to be careful because there are some people who will go for the jugular if you show any weakness. This is a very competitive industry and it is always important to learn to read the situation accurately and see and know who you are dealing with.

Notes

1. For a more thorough analysis of the revolution would-be editors should see Chris Thompson, *Non-Linear Editing* (London: Skillset and BFI, 1994) and Roy Stafford, *Nonlinear Editing and Visual Literacy* (London: BFI, 1995).
2. Phil Tippett, in *Resisting the Virtual Life,* ed. by James Brook and Iain A. Boal (San Francisco: City Lights, 1995), p. 260.
3. Chris Thompson, *Non-Linear Editing*, (London: BFI and Skillset, 1994), p. 24.

16

PERFORMERS

'The Talent'

Most of the people we see on the small and large screen can be described as performers who exercise their professional skills in the provision of entertainment. In feature films virtually everyone we see is an actor by training and by profession. On television, however, the 'faces' which appear on the screen include actors, musicians, dancers, singers, stunt performers, as well as journalists, newsreaders, presenters, announcers and members of the public. Television viewers often do not distinguish between the various categories, but lump everyone together as 'stars'. This is incorrect: there are sharp distinctions between the various categories.

News readers, as we have seen, are not actors, but journalists who appear on-screen. Announcers are usually not journalists, but instead are personable public relations-type people employed by television companies to provide links between programmes and inform the public about the station. In this chapter we will look briefly at the jobs that make up the various aspects of life in-front-of-camera.

PERFORMERS (creative) including
Actors
Musicians
Stunt Artists
Dancers
Singers

As a person, I'm not very interesting. As an actor, I hope I'm riveting.
(Willem Dafoe)

Very few *performers* ever have permanent jobs. Acting, dancing and making music are not very stable professions. On the large screen major stars, and indeed all *actors*, are contracted for a particular film during the production period only, and are sometimes referred to as 'the talent'. In the old days Hollywood studios kept a 'stable' of actors under contract. Contract players were paid a regular salary, for perhaps a seven-year period, and were drafted into films as the studio bosses saw fit. In this system actors had little control over the films in which they appeared. If they did kick up a fuss about an inappropriate role, they would find that they were not given any further parts and, when their contracts came up for renewal, they would be dropped. This system, which did offer something in the way of guaranteed employment, no longer exists. Today film actors are freelances who work on a film for a certain length of time and then move on. They usually employ agents to help them find work and to negotiate their fees. In the United States actors can make a living solely out of film, but in Britain most actors need to work in the theatre and on radio and television if they are to survive.

In every sector, as already mentioned, they are usually employed for the period of performance only. Actors in a feature film or a television drama are hired only for the number of days for which they are required. Television companies do not employ performers on a staff basis. Even if actors are important characters in a long-running soap opera, their contracts will be regularly subject to renewal, perhaps every year. Indeed it is not unknown for a character to be written out of a series if the individual actor makes a fuss about money or is perhaps involved in a real-life scandal that may 'reflect' negatively on the character in the drama.

As a result there is little financial security. The only possible exceptions are certain categories of *musician* working for the BBC. The Corporation continues to maintain orchestras and, although these are constantly threatened with extinction and are always subject to cut-backs, they do provide a form of regular employment for musicians. Also, because music and light entertainment are an important feature of television (and radio), the BBC, and some independent television companies, employ Musical Directors or Heads of Music to advise on the musical content of programmes, the arrangement of music and the contracting of composers. These are experienced people with vast knowledge of performance and management. Musicians employed by film, television or video companies are generally members of the Musicians' Union.

In the past it would have left a false impression to include a description of performers in a book about 'careers' in British television because, despite their vital role, they were never part of the career structure of television, nor part of the core of employees who earned their living solely in film. They were rather 'hired in' as necessity demanded, often from the theatre, and they moved in and out of the entertainment industries as opportunities opened and closed. As film, television and video have drawn closer together, however, and as freelancing has become the more common pattern of employment across all sectors, the experience of actors and performers is not so different from that of all employees on temporary, short-term contracts.

In general, all actors in film, television or video are members of the British Actors' Equity Association, the actors' union. Although the reality is that most actors spend far more time unemployed than working, acting is a very attractive and glamorous profession and new recruits therefore constantly clamour at the door. If everyone who wished to act were allowed into the profession, it would be swamped and many newcomers would be willing to work for very little pay. As a result, Equity tries to protect its members from too much competition by imposing limits on the numbers who may enter the profession in certain areas each year. The quota system that sets the limits is heavily criticised for its exclusivity. On the whole, however, the criticism comes from outside the profession rather than from within. The simple fact is that there are not enough jobs round for all the people who wish to act; if the doors were opened to anyone and everyone, the acting profession would be overwhelmed by amateurs wanting to 'have a go'. Salaries and fees would fall and standards would drop.

It is in order to avert this danger that Equity has made special agreements with many employers who agree to employ only 'professionals'. Newcomers, therefore, cannot enter the profession through West End theatre, the National Theatre, films, television, commercials or radio. Only artists who already have professional experience can be employed in these areas. Equity does, however, grant recognition to a certain quota of new entrants each year in certain sectors and jobs. Newcomers can qualify for union membership by securing jobs as performers or assistant stage managers in a subsidised repertory company or in theatre-in-education or a young people's theatre company. They can also join pantomimes, small-scale theatre companies and summer season companies, all of which make them eligible for Equity membership. The Royal Shakespeare Company at Stratford-upon-Avon and the Chichester Festival Theatre can take on a certain quota of new recruits, but competition for these places is extremely fierce.

Ambitious young actors who come in via these routes serve what amounts to an apprenticeship, learning their trade. Drama graduates, or those who have done courses in stage management, usually find their way in by this means.

Most actors and *dancers* obtain further work by signing a contract with a theatrical agent. The agent then seeks work for the performer. When film or television producers or casting directors want actors they usually approach agents or scan through casting directories such as *Spotlight*, which includes a photograph of the performer and a description of their work to date. If a producer is looking for a 'type' or a look-alike (in a historical drama, for example, casting directors might want someone who looks like Churchill), the photographs can help in the search.

Singers and dancers are usually granted Equity membership once they have secured employment, as are directors, designers and choreographers employed in the theatre. Professional broadcasters in television or radio can also sometimes obtain membership of Equity on the basis of their experience in non-acting areas. Thus a presenter might wish to become an actor and his or her experience on television may help to gain Equity membership.

There is no easy or classic route to becoming an actor or dancer in film or television. People with ambitions in this direction should follow a drama course at a college or university, or go to one of the leading drama or ballet schools. Training, talent, hard work and luck are all essential requisites. Performers have to be versatile, and those who are successful will work on the stage, in film, in commercials, on video, on television and on radio as opportunities arise. It is no use thinking 'it would be nice' to act in *EastEnders* and writing to the BBC to apply. Acting is a hard profession to enter and an even harder profession in which to make a living. This is particularly so for women: Equity has been criticised recently because women actors generally earn less than men, even when they are better known.

There is a common belief that would-be actors without a union card can start work as an 'extra' or 'walk-on' in television or as 'background', 'crowd artist', 'double' or 'stand-in' in films and commercials, and that such work will be considered as professional experience by Equity. This is not the case. Equity does not recognise that such jobs amount to a 'professional' portfolio and, in any case, such work is usually given to professional performers first. Only when sufficient professional performers are unavailable are 'walk-on' jobs offered to amateurs. It is virtually impossible, therefore, to break into serious professional acting in this way. On the other hand, working as an extra is one way to find out about the profession of acting and also how film and television work. It can provide insight into the way the industry functions and what the various people do. Advertisements sometimes appear in the journal *Stage* for these types of jobs.

One of the in-front-of-camera jobs that always attracts interest is that of *stunt performers*, artists or 'arrangers'. Stunt performers in film and television must also be listed on the Equity Register of Stunt Performers. Only professional actors or performers can join the Stunt Register. This is because many stunt people in the course of their work actually double other artists, so they have to be able to act.

There is a variety of expertise under which stunt performers can register, including Fighting, Falling, Riding and Driving, Agility and

240

Strength, Swimming and Sub-Aqua. In most of these categories there are many subdivisions. In Falling, for example, stunt artists can be qualified in Trampolining, Diving or Parachuting. They must have achieved, for instance, the elementary Gold Award in Trampolining; or a Silver Standard in Highboard or Springboard Diving from the Amateur Swimming Association to qualify for inclusion in the Diving subdivision; or a Category 8 from the British Parachute Association with a 'c' license (minimum of fifty jumps) for the Parachuting subdivision (full details can be obtained by writing to Equity).

It is not easy to become registered as a stunt performer, which is sensible since doing and arranging stunts can be very dangerous. As we have seen, very high standards of physical and sporting skill are required.

To qualify for the Stunt Register it is necessary to be a full member of Equity and to be aged between eighteen and thirty. Stunt performers have to serve a probationary period of three years on the Stunt Register, during which time they can only work under the supervision of a Full Member. After that time they qualify as an 'intermediate' member and are free to take work performing and arranging their own stunts, but they cannot arrange and supervise stunts for other people. Only after another two years are stunt performers fully registered, at which point they are then free to arrange stunts for fellow performers or actors. Interestingly, stunt performance is increasingly experiencing the impact of new technology since it is now possible to manipulate stunt performances digitally. It is easy, for example, to impose an actor's head on a stunt performer's body. Many stunt performers expect that the enhanced versatility that computing technology permits could ultimately damage their professional standing and working conditions – stunts which used to be performed in 'real life' can now be concocted on computer screens.

Standards of competence for actors, dancers, musicians, performers and stuntpersons are being developed by the Art and Entertainment Training Council in association with such bodies as Equity, the Musicians' Union, the National Council for Drama Training, the Council for Dance Education and Training, and the Association of British Orchestras. For further information see the addresses of the Arts and Entertainment Training Council and Equity at the end of this book.

PRESENTER
ANNOUNCER
CONTINUITY ANNOUNCER

Television

Presenter is the term used for people who 'front' programmes. They act rather like a host or 'Master (or Mistress) of Ceremonies' within a

241

programme. Presenters introduce programmes and often provide the verbal links between items. They sometimes also interview guests. On very popular programmes the presenter *is* the show, which may be named after them. The programme is then a vehicle for the presenter's own personality.

Presenters are frequently well-known personalities who have come into television after winning a distinguished reputation in another sphere of activity. In other cases, television has 'made' them. In North America personality presenters tend to have a relatively short public life, but in Britain an innate conservatism has ensured that some presenters have been around for many years.

Personalities 'emerge' and there is no way of predicting who will end up a success and who will not. Producers searching for new faces will sometimes seek out presenters. A television company will sometimes hear of an athlete who is attractive, articulate and quick-witted, and who is on the point of retirement, and offer them a job in sports presenting. A producer planning a new show on cookery will contact various well-known chefs and ask them if they would like to front the programme. In the same way, academics are sometimes asked to present programmes such as *Timewatch* and scientists may, on occasion, be invited to introduce *Horizon*. Presenters of documentaries are often distinguished journalists: in 1996 the veteran journalist, Charles Wheeler presented a highly regarded series of programmes on the United States, a country which he had covered as a television journalist over many years. Political programmes are sometimes hosted by ex-MPs. Quiz shows are often presented by actors or comedians who have had a career in clubs.

In other words, presenters often have a notable career apart from broadcasting and very few people actually set out to be television 'presenters'. If they do, they are unlikely to succeed. Presenters are important because they can make or break a programme. *Blind Date*, for example, is identified with the personality of Cilla Black but then she too made her reputation first in another area, pop music.

For all the above reasons there can be no description of a presenter's typical career path. It is a matter of chance, but being a celebrity in other fields is probably an advantage. In any case, presenting is not, for the most part, a long-term job. Many presenters only appear on television for one series. Presenters who do become identified with a long-running show, however, are often able to earn considerable amounts of money from public appearances, opening garden parties, supermarkets and the like.

Announcers are employed by television stations to provide the link between programmes. They are sometimes called continuity announcers because they provide the atmosphere which ensures that the programmes flow smoothly and continuously one after another. In recent years on-screen announcers have been a feature of the commercial sector rather than the BBC, which has tended to use voice-overs. ITV companies use announcers to gave a 'face' to the station. They may have a touch of a regional accent so that viewers can identify with the personality, who should never appear remote.

Announcers inform viewers about the evening's schedule. They announce the next programme or programmes and any changes or delays. It all looks very easy, but there is more skill than first appears. What the announcer says may influence the viewer's decision to continue watching or to change to another station. They therefore have to deliver their material (and many of them write their own scripts) in such a way that viewers are persuaded that the next programme will be exciting and interesting. In this sense the announcers are part of the sales team of television. Their aim is to keep the viewers watching the station.

They can also play a very serious role. One of the strengths of local and regional television (and even more so of radio) is that it can respond quickly to an emergency and often has a highly respected profile within the community so that viewers trust what it says. If a major catastrophe happens in the region, the station will interrupt programming and an announcer will appear to provide information in a news flash. If there has been a major road crash, for example, and the police wish motorists to avoid a certain area, it is the duty announcer who will appear on-screen to relay the police information. If there has been a leak of poisonous fumes from a chemical factory, and the police want an area to be evacuated, they will inform the local television station. Again it is the duty announcer who will appear on the screen to tell residents what to do. At such times announcers have to be calm and sensible: they have to keep the viewer from panicking and ensure that accurate information is conveyed so that the emergency does not become blown out of all proportion.

Announcers, therefore, have to remain calm in a crisis. They also have to be able to *ad lib*, since there may have been no time for a script to be written and they have to provide correct information without benefit of notes or an Autocue. In some areas announcers are also journalists and participate in local news and regional programmes as presenters.

Announcers represent the public face of the local television station. They can become very well-known and instantly recognised on the streets. As a result they are often asked to help with local charities or, like presenters, to open local supermarkets, and this can earn them considerable sums of money in addition to their salaries. Since announcers represent the station, they have to be careful about their public image and must not offend viewers by cantankerous behaviour in real life. This 'always being on show' can be quite a strain for some temperaments.

Announcers work very difficult hours, since many stations broadcast seven days a week, twenty-four hours a day. This is not conducive to a normal social and private life. They must also be well-groomed and keep themselves looking smart and alert no matter what pressures they may be under. Most announcers are good-looking and dress in a conventional way, since most television viewers are not yet ready for alternative clothes styles. Television stations want to woo, not alienate, their audiences.

How do you become an announcer?

Advertisements for trainee announcers do sometimes appear in the press and the television company is then snowed under with applications. Most television stations are actually looking for people with experience and newcomers are rarely employed. It is the sort of job that looks easy and glamorous, and people who dream of fame think that they could do it just as well as the person on-screen. In fact, most announcers have had some form of drama or speech training and they may even have acting experience and be members of Equity. Most importantly, they must have an ability to get on well with people in all walks of life and genuinely enjoy meeting people. They must not be hostile or aggressive, but have warm and expansive personalities. They are usually intelligent and well-read and are able to talk easily on any subject. Announcers have a natural charm and pleasant voices so that people are both interested in them and enjoy listening to them speak.

If you feel that you have all these rare qualities, and you still have a burning desire to be an announcer, it might be an idea to write a script and prepare a videotape of yourself as a 'mock' announcer. This would provide you with the opportunity to spot the verbal mannerisms or facial ticks of which you may not be aware, but which would be a constant irritation on-screen. Only when you think you have a professional 'look' should you send the tape to a television station.

Announcers, as we have pointed out, are part of the sales team of television. The whole marketing side of film and television has become increasingly important in recent years and in the next chapter we will take a brief look at this side of the industry, where opportunities are currently burgeoning.

Case History

STEVE RYDE

Steve Ryde is 24 and works off-camera as a presenter for Children's ITV.

Basically I am an actor. I started work at the age of 14 mainly through joining Central Television's Junior Television Workshop. This was a really innovative idea. The company got together groups of young people in drama workshops. They advertised for members in the local papers in the Central region and also sent out a mail shot to schools. There were workshops in Nottingham and in Birmingham and it was my cousin who saw the advert and told me about it and I joined the Nottingham one. The company cast workshop members occasionally in productions and we were also used as a resource by producers who would talk over programmes and programme ideas with us. The idea has really paid dividends. Over the past ten years other workshop members have gone off to drama school and film school and ended up working in the industry.

Through the workshop I auditioned for a show called *Your Mother Wouldn't Like It* and I got the job and the programme won a BAFTA award in 1987. Since then I have never looked back. In this business you get to know people and that way you build up your CV. I've really learned the acting craft through experience.

I've been extraordinarily lucky because I've managed to find work for ten years. I've had at least one sizeable acting job a year and, alongside that, I've done other things. I went to college to do A levels and since I was 18 I've done other sorts of jobs, such as working in a warehouse, behind the bar (my mother's a publican) and even worked for a debt collection agency, but not collecting debts I have to say! I think it is important for an actor to do 'other things'. Its a good idea for would-be actors to take a year out after A levels and do something unconnected with acting or school.

I am a member of Equity. Since I started before I was sixteen on a professional contract I was entitled to a Junior Temporary Membership if I worked for thirty weeks cumulatively. Then between sixteen and eighteen I was entitled to a provisional Equity membership and then after working a certain number of weeks I got full membership.

In December 1992 I got this job. Children's ITV was looking for a presenter. I love it. I provide the links and the promotions for the entire Children's ITV network. I had not done any presenting before because

I had mainly worked as an actor but the acting experience and voice-overs for commercials help in presenting.

I work 'live' every weekday from 3.30 to 5.15 pm. After three and a half years I've relaxed into it. I provide the voices for the characters and the presentation links. I write all my own material and I try to bring something original and daring to the job. I've got a fairly wild imagination. You really have to hone the material because sometimes you have to get the message across in exactly twenty-five seconds and you have to make it entertaining and informative at the same time.

We prepare for the afternoon show everyday. I design and invent characters and conceive promotional on-screen ideas. To me it is an acting job as much as a presenting job although I like the anonymity of voice-over because it means that I am not pigeonholed or typecast too early. I am quite happy to be in front of camera.

Without question I enjoy this. It's great, it gives me the opportunity to be inventive and appeal to a large audience – Children's ITV has the largest audience ratings in the country. When I think about how I got in, it frightens me, talk about a back door into the business. It was all so unlikely and yet here I am. That Junior Workshop was the real turning point. I'm learning all the time. My rule is not to impersonate other children's presenters or even other presenters. Be myself but not play safe. I try and bring something new all the time to what I do.

My working hours are as long as they need to be. Sometimes I'll be in at 11.30 am but other days I can start at 7 am and still be here at 3 am if it's necessary. It just is not a nine-till-five job. You get so excited about what you are doing you don't want to leave the building or do anything else. You want to be at work twenty-four hours a day especially when, as I do, you have a free reign to create.

17

SALES AND MARKETING

The entertainment industry is audience-related. Theatre and film have always been concerned with the 'bums on seats' factor: customers keep the industry working. Film, especially, stands and falls by the profits accrued from tickets sold at the box-office.

It was never quite the same for European television. Heavily regulated, public-service broadcasting monopolies delivered programmes to captive audiences. In the UK, BBC viewers paid the Licence Fee which provided the money for radio and television, but licence holders had little control over what they were offered. They must have been fairly content because there were never any mass demonstration against the programmes. Only a very few people refused to renew their licences, perhaps because anyone who did not pay was not only deprived of the BBC but also of ITV.

It was true that the ITV companies had to make money by selling airtime to advertisers, but ITV managers also had to please the Independent Broadcasting Authority (IBA). Independent television was obliged by law to abide by certain fairly rigorous public-service obligations which meant that market forces and audience tastes were never the sole determinants of the programmes which were made. As far as Channel Four was concerned, its minority programming was guaranteed by Parliament, and it too was protected by the simple expedient of having a large part of its income derived from a subscription paid by the ITV companies to support Channel Four via the IBA. In return the ITV companies were allowed to sell advertising space on Channel Four in their own regions.

The 1990 Broadcasting Act, however, pushed ITV and Channel Four out into a colder, more competitive economic environment. Part of the intention of the Act was to put the ITV companies on to a more level pegging, as far as revenue was concerned, with satellite and cable TV. Today, in the commercial sector, television is about delivering audiences to advertisers. What that has meant in practice is that the selling, marketing and retailing of programmes have become very important elements in the economics of television, just as they always have been for film.

The film industry has always had to cope with the market-place. Costs are only recovered by effective distribution, and distribution depends on marketing and advertising. Today television too is becoming more dependent on people with selling, retailing and financial skills.

SALES AGENT (administrative/legal/ financial)

Film

Once a film has been made, it has to make money to recoup its costs. The transfer of film from the production phase to the market-place is often the work of the *sales agent*. Sales agents represent film producers and negotiate sales agreements with distributors. Sales agents are usually people with vast experience of, and enthusiasm for, the film industry and who understand finance and contracts. Some sales agents are lawyers, but even those who are not, must have some legal knowledge, even if it is only gathered second-hand. Sales agents are very important people indeed because, if it is difficult in the first place to raise money for film, this second phase of the money-making process is even more crucial. Sales agents must recover costs and make a profit for the backers, otherwise the film industry would collapse.

DISTRIBUTORS (administrative/financial)
SALES, MARKETING AND PUBLICITY

Film

Distributors are specialists in the exploitation of film in a particular territory. Most distributors in this country deal with American film because that is where the big money is made and many distribution companies are in fact American-owned. In the eyes of supporters of all European film-makers, this is one of the main problems facing the home-grown industry. The distribution system is very effective in delivering mainstream Hollywood films to British audiences. It is less effective in distributing British or European films to the same people. Critics of the distribution system are also irritated that marketing is mainly directed at audiences in the big metropolitan areas. As far as European or minority films are concerned, the small-town cinemagoer is very badly served (unless there is a local film society), since many of these films are never released on video. The whole system, say the critics, is so geared to American film that audiences cannot broaden their tastes and develop an interest in other types of film. They are restricted to consuming the 'Hollywood diet'.

Distributors negotiate the rights to show a film in cinemas and now, increasingly, for television and video screens. Distributors also orchestrate the number of prints required and the advertising campaign to promote the film. Film advertising is becoming increasingly expensive (especially for blockbusters), but it is very important to a film's success. Producers can feel betrayed by distributors who do not market a film effectively. Sales agents, of course, should make sure that they extract guarantees about the way the film is advertised before they sell the rights, but problems can nonetheless develop. Sometimes distributors have put up part of the cash to help a film to be made and they then do a deal ensuring they receive the film at a cheaper price. Escalating advertising costs have led some distributors to believe that eventually producers themselves will have to pay a share of the advertising and marketing costs.

There are five major distributors in the UK market: United International Pictures (UIP), which distributes films from Paramount, Universal and MGM/United Artists; Warner Bros.; Columbia TriStar; Buena Vista; and Twentieth Century-Fox. In addition, there are others such as Entertainment, Guild, Rank and smaller independent distribution companies such as Oasis. A full list can be found in the BFI's *Film and Television Handbook*. The small independents tend to concentrate on non-mainstream and foreign productions, and they often have great difficulty finding cinema spaces for their films (between 1989 and 1992 an average of 28 per cent of British films failed to gain UK distribution). For this reason several of the independents also own their own cinemas.

A job in distribution means working in sales, marketing/advertising, or publicity. There is also a great deal of administrative work of a routine type. A public relations qualification is often a help on this side of the industry, as are financial and accountancy skills, sales, marketing and business diplomas and degrees. Sales and marketing people are usually extroverted, self-confident and thick-skinned. They have to be: distribution is a tough business.

The distribution sector of the film industry is very open and there is none of the emphasis on 'family contacts' that exists on the production side. Once in, however, the new recruit will find that distribution is a rather close-knit sector and people know each other very well. There is much toing and froing between rival companies as jobs come and go. There used to be little chance of moving from distribution into production but today there is more contact between the two areas and people have moved from one sector to the other.

Anyone with sales, marketing, organisational or public relations skills who has a burning desire to get into film distribution should look out for advertisements in the trade press. They could also look up the names and addresses of distributors in the BFI *Handbook* and write a letter of enquiry.

EXHIBITORS (financial/administrative/marketing/retail)
SALES STAFF

Film

Exhibitors are the owners or operators of cinemas and they negotiate terms with distributors for the exhibition of films. Distributors generally receive about a third and exhibitors two-thirds of box office receipts. Over the years there has been much concern about British cinema attendance but during the 90s box-office receipts have grown. This may have been connected with the recession. One of the traditions of the film industry is that it does well when times are bad because people want to escape from the depressing facts of life into the fantasy world of the cinema. This was certainly the case in the Depression of the 30s. However, the situation is not quite the same in the 90s, since cable and satellite television now provide round-the-clock movie competition for the cinema.

One of the major developments in exhibition in recent years has been the spread of multiplex cinemas. This really seems to be responsible for the revitalisation of cinema attendance. Over 37 per cent of all cinemas in the UK now have five screens or more and they account for 50 per cent of revenues which include bar and kiosk takings and the revenue from cinema advertising which is very popular with advertisers who wish to reach a young audience. Multiplexes are proving very popular, especially with women, perhaps because of the brightness and cleanliness of the foyer and the unintimidating character and comfort of the smaller-scale auditoriums. Jobs in exhibition include directors of operation, theatre managers, box-office managers, ushers, kiosk attendants, concession and box-office *sales staff*. These posts are usually advertised in local newspapers.

Increasingly, exhibition staff are trained in presentation and good customer relations. Most multiplex cinemas have in-house training courses. Box-office and retail staff are also trained in the use of computers, since advance-booking is an important part of modern cinema exhibition.

PROJECTIONIST

Film

Traditionally the most sought-after 'technical' job on the exhibition side is that of *projectionist*. *Cinema Paradiso*, an Italian film, beautifully illustrated the romance of the job in the days when the cinema was the only moving-image mass medium. Modern projection is increasingly automated and 'high tech'. There is also no longer the fire risk associated with the use of nitrate film which, in the early days of motion pictures, used to give the job its rather daring image. Large exhibitors train their own projectionists, and again advertisements appear in the local press.

Anyone interested in this side of the industry who wishes to pre-empt advertisements in the local press should write to the exhibitors listed in the BFI's *Handbook*.

SALES CO-ORDINATORS/NEGOTIATORS/EXECUTIVES
(financial/retail/administrative)
MARKETING EXECUTIVES (managerial/financial)
MARKET RESEARCHERS (research/administration)
TRAFFIC/MAKE-UP STAFF (administrative)

Television
The main activity for *sales* and *marketing* staff in television used to be interesting advertisers in the programmes on offer. Advertisers naturally like popular programmes, but in the past they were not allowed to associate the name of their product with a particular programme. They could say where they wanted an advertisement placed but, for most of the history of independent television, direct sponsorship of particular programmes was strictly forbidden. Such rules helped to protect programme-makers from too much interference by advertisers and this probably helped to promote more experimental, adventurous, innovative programming than conventional advertising agencies would initially have liked.

Developments in technology, however, have ended the era when the air waves were viewed as a limited resource, protected and watched over by governments. Cable and satellite TV have meant the multiplication of stations and channels and television has moved briskly into the market-place. The satellite and cable businesses stand and fall on their ability to sell their equipment and services to subscribers who are 'customers': the viewer pays for what he or she watches. Satellite and cable also derive revenue from advertising and they now compete with ITV in this area.

In the past decade ITV and the BBC have acquired considerable additional revenue from the sale of their programmes overseas. High-quality British programmes are in demand, especially on so-called 'public' television channels in the United States. Overseas sales have become a lucrative source of extra finance and BBC Enterprises, for example, employs marketing and sales staff in this area. Some ITV companies run similar 'Enterprise' organisations to exploit their programmes. There is in addition considerable money to be made from marketing the spin-offs of popular series through video and book sales.

All this has contributed to the expansion of the sales side of television. There are many more jobs than ever before for people who have been trained in accountancy, retailing, public relations or marketing. Moreover the development of the European dimension in television (and film) has also led to greater demand for people with skills in foreign languages. This is particularly so in the era of co-production.

What Do Sales People in Television Actually Do?

In ITV and cable and satellite TV advertising *sales co-ordinators/executives/negotiators* (they can have different names in different companies) negotiate the sale of air-time. They take bookings and see that commercial breaks are filled so that there is no empty space within or between programmes. They spend a great deal of time on the phone talking to advertisers and refer constantly to computers which display details of available air time.

In principle, working in television advertising sales is similar to working in newspaper advertising, in that the aim is to recruit clients. The actual details of how television advertising is bought and sold, however, are more difficult to grasp, because of the problem of peak and off-peak viewing. Advertisers have to decide where to place an advertisement so that it is most effective. They have to determine which spot in the schedule gives the best value for money for their type of advertising. Off-peak times are cheaper than peak viewing times and very cheap spots are often 'pre-emptible'; that is, an advertisement can be withdrawn at the last minute to be replaced by one paying a higher rate. Costs increase the more precisely an advertisement is placed. If an advertiser wants to place an advertisement in the break between the two halves of the ITN News, this is certainly possible, but at a price. If the advertiser is content with a 'scattergun' approach, by which the advertisement is shown many times but randomly at the station's discretion, then costs can be reduced considerably. This is because the television company prefers to retain flexibility over the scheduling of advertisements. Sales staff have to be familiar with all these details and they discuss the problems and the opportunities with the clients.

Sales staff have to know their company's schedules. They also have to know which advertising companies will be interested in particular types of programme. Computer manufacturers might not want to advertise during a game show, but they may be interested in a programme on a scientific topic because it will attract viewers who are likely to be customers for the product. Certain seasons of the year appeal to

252

some advertisers more than others. Companies selling lawn mowing and gardening equipment may not, for example, find November a particularly attractive month.

Sales staff have to be articulate, outgoing and also good at numbers, because they have to calculate very quickly the different rates of advertisements. Most companies train their own staff according to their specific demands and needs.

Marketing staff are responsible for attracting new business. They are top-level management people who usually supervise sales staff. They visit customers and manufacturers all over the country and try to persuade them that television is an effective advertising medium. Increasingly, marketing staff are concerned with the sponsorship of programmes. Linking an advertisement with a popular character in a series used to be considered somewhat immoral and illicit, but this point of view now carries little weight. The increase in sponsorship means that marketing people have to know much more about the content of programmes in order to know what will appeal to potential sponsors.

In addition to marketing and sales staff, there are also *market researchers* who do market research into the effectiveness of an advertising campaign. They produce data about the audience's reaction to advertisements on television and interpret it for clients.

Researchers also play an important role in examining the audience figures for particular programmes and in this case they are usually called *audience researchers*. Broadcasting organisations have always been anxious to find out how many and what kinds of people watch certain programmes. They want to know which programmes are popular so that they can repeat successful programme formats. They also want to discover the types of people the programmes attract: are they working-class, women, men, pensioners, young people? ITV, satellite and cable all need this information so that they can charge advertisers appropriately. The BBC wants knowledge to justify the licence fee.

The Broadcasters' Audience Research Board (BARB) is a company which carries out research into how many millions of people watch programmes and what they think about them. Audience research is an increasingly sophisticated profession and market researchers often have a background in statistics, computing or psychology.

So-called *traffic staff* monitor the composition (make-up) of commercial breaks and arrange for the receipt and delivery of advertisements, usually a few days before transmission. They also handle any last-minute bookings and number the advertisements in the correct order of viewing. It makes it easier for transmission staff if all videotape advertisements and all film commercials are collected together.

253

Anyone interested in the sales side of the industry should look up the addresses of the various television companies in the BFI *Handbook* and write to them for more information.

Case History

PAUL WRIGHT

Paul Wright is 30 and read Geography at University College, London. He is Group Sales Manager for BSkyB sales.

I came out of college in 1987 with a placement at Lloyds Bank as a graduate trainee which I applied for on the usual graduate milk round. I wasn't 100 per cent sure of what career I wished to pursue but I wanted some basic business skills, including sales and marketing. I became very keen to move into media and marketing, and through a friend who was working at Sky Channel I got in touch with their fledgling sales department. I started as a Sales Assistant but I knew nothing about the job – what it entailed, how advertising worked – but I decided to take the risk.

While I was at college I was interested in media jobs but I found the advice or information provided by universities was limited. Very few suggestions were made about how to even start finding a job in media. The only suggestion was to send letters to advertising agencies. This was quite discouraging because I knew the business was quite difficult to get into and the general impression was that advertising agencies were looking for 'wacky' creative types. My feeling was that tutors were not sympathetic to media and even when pushed had very little basic knowledge of the market.

Anyway, I started as a Sales Assistant and in February 1989 the company became Sky Television. After several years Sky merged with BSB and they became BSkyB. I have worked through all the changes and would not have swapped this job for the world. A company such as ours is always moving at a rapid pace into new markets and ventures.

During my years at Sky, I have met many people from my university, some even from my course who work in media or even in some cases at Sky. All of these people sort of 'fell into' media in the way I did, via contacts. Even my sister has spent five years in advertising.

I now run one of four main Sales groups and am responsible for 22 per cent of our advertising revenue. I have eight people working for me. As with all media sales jobs my team is allocated a set of agencies and their clients to sell to. This is on behalf of Sky's wholly owned channels but also channels such as Nickelodeon, CMT, Sci-Fi, the History Channel and the Paramount Channel.

I oversee all negotiations for these channels with my agency/client allocation and also look into other ways of selling Sky-related media such as the Sky Internet site, Fastext (our Text service) and Sky TV guide. These added-value packages are a key selling point for Sky this year.

You need to have a strong, sociable and out-going personality in media sales. A structured career path is unlikely to occur in a sales job like mine due to the rapidly changing environment we work in. The key to success is to have a natural interest in the business and to keep up-to-date with all developments. While we do train people some aspects are down to the individual. You have to have a natural interest and curiosity about technical developments about digital satellite technology and the Internet. I am really interested in all aspects of the media business so for me work is fun.

As the media market becomes further fragmented, media sales jobs will become more competitive so, unlike before, media sales people now need to understand other media. If you are selling TV you may need to understand cinema in order to win a pitch for an advertiser's money – so you have to keep an open mind.

Many students write to Sky about sales jobs, pretty average letters I must say. I am amazed how few press ahead after an initial approach. A lot of people working in this business are happy to talk, sales people are essentially a sociable lot and they would respond to a follow-up approach which might say 'Can you give me five minutes of your time?' I remember once I was looking for staff and I sent an advert to a university careers office saying: 'If you are interested in working for BSkyB – ring this number'. I only got one reply.

We like to see people. If students haven't got the initiative to see opportunities and follow through in looking for a job, they aren't going to be any good working in media sales.

My advice for applying to a company like Sky?

1. Send a typed letter, enclosing a CV (preferably with a photo).
2. Make sure that you are writing to the right person – this is often not the personnel department – each department in a media company is usually responsible for employing people so check the name and title of the person you are writing to – ring up the company to find out who is the right person if necessary.
3. Follow up your letter with a phone call – media companies are often more responsive to this form of communication. Check again you have the right person.

4. If there are no vacancies, ask if you can come in and see a member of staff for a chat. Most people have got into media via a contact and this may be a way of developing a contact. The person you are talking to might not have a vacancy but they may know someone who has.
5. If you do get an interview, research the company. This may sound obvious but I have seen so many interviewees who have done absolutely no background research. This will lose you an interview. You could ask the company for a media pack prior to your interviews.
6. This may seem obvious but TURN UP ON TIME! Media sales companies often have face-to-face meeting with clients – if you turn up late then they are going to assume that you may do this with clients and are therefore not right for the job.

Good luck!

POSTSCRIPT
Archiving and Film Research

There is a limited number of jobs available to people who are passionate about the preservation and history of film and television. The main area of employment is in the National Film and Television Archive (NFTVA), which was founded in 1935 to maintain a national repository of films of permanent value, but there are other archives around the country that also employ film archivists and at times there are jobs available with broadcasting companies (for more information about archives and collections see *The Researcher's Guide to British Film and Television Collections* published by the British Universities Film and Video Council). The NFTVA's moving image collection now comprises more than 275,000 titles dating from 1895. In the mid-50s the NFTVA also began to acquire television programmes, the recording and preservation of which are a major part of its work.

Archive work involves several stages: acquisition, preservation, cataloguing and dissemination. Since there is no law of statutory deposit for film and video production in the United Kingdom (in contrast to books), the acquisition of material for the NFTVA Collection is mainly through donation. The *acquisition* section is divided roughly into three areas: feature films, documentary and non-fiction films, and television. Keepers working in this area have to seek out possible donors and diplomatically persuade them to contribute to the *Archive's* holdings.

Preservation and restoration, which is a highly technical and specialised activity, is carried out at the J. Paul Getty Conservation Centre in Berkhamsted, which is the main storage site for safety film and video. Nitrate film is kept at a specially equipped site in Warwickshire. Nitrate film decomposes as it ages and becomes highly inflammable (there was a disastrous accident because of nitrate film at the Mexican film archives some years ago). The 140 million feet of nitrate film in the NFTVA's collection are systematically being copied on to modern safety film as part of the process of preservation.

257

Berkhamsted has an international reputation for film preservation and conservation and it trains people from all over the world.

The *cataloguing* section of the NFTVA is based in London and has the Herculean task of indexing, cataloguing and analysing all the films and programmes in the collection. Film cataloguing has to be very detailed, because it is not possible to scan a film as one can flick through a book. Film researchers are therefore very dependent on catalogues for information about a film. Also film can be damaged through frequent projection and it is important to protect material by restricting the viewing of film copies to bona fide researchers. The NFTVA is, of course, anxious to extend access to its collection to as many people as possible and, over the years, has greatly increased the number of films available for viewing on videotape in an effort to meet the ever increasing demand but, despite this, it is still sometimes necessary to explain that a film cannot be made available for viewing. Inevitably, this can cause annoyance in people who don't understand the fragility of film and those who work in the access sections often have to exercise considerable tact. The cataloguing section and viewing service provide an excellent service for film researchers and the production library provides film-makers and television producers with extracts of films for use in compilation films and documentary programmes once the necessary clearances have been obtained from the rights holders.

The training of film and television *archivists* used to be somewhat haphazard. Some keepers/curators had archival qualifications at postgraduate level, but many archive courses focus on documents and written material and do not include training in the preservation and archiving of the moving image. In the past, therefore, film archivists tended to be people who were passionately interested in the history of film, but who had to learn the techniques of preservation and conservation as they went along. As the work has become more technical and professional, however, the need for specialist training has increased. In response to this, the University of East Anglia established the first postgraduate MA course in Film Archiving in 1990. Based within the East Anglian Film Archive, housed at the University, the course lasts one year and is full-time and part vocational. Students do a placement in film archives in the UK or abroad. The course will provide fully qualified and competent recruits for this important section of the film industry over the next decade and will be one of the best qualifications for people seeking a career in film research. For further information contact: David Cleveland East Anglian Film Archive, University of East Anglia, Norwich NR4 7TJ.

APPENDIX
Applying for a Course or a Job

The basic rule in applying for a course or a job is to follow the instructions to the letter. When you apply for a position in film and television, or for a course in the media, the competition will be fierce. Therefore if the application form asks that you type your answers, do not write in pen, pencil or biro. One employer told me that for one job she had over 500 applications. Faced with so many letters and forms, she immediately rejected those that had failed to follow instructions. Into the waste-paper basket (unread) went all applications written in blue, red or green biro, because candidates had explicitly been told to use black.

Rule Number One: if you cannot follow basic instructions, you are of little interest to the industry.

Rule Number Two: do some research. Don't wait passively until you see a job advertised. Very few jobs are ever advertised, since most of them are filled internally. This is a very hard fact for newcomers to grasp. If you want a job, as a runner for example, you have to hustle. You have to find out about the employers: film and video companies, the BBC, ITV, satellite and cable companies. Ignorance will get you nowhere. Read the trade magazines so that you are well- informed about what is happening in the industry. Employers are impressed by people who have taken the trouble to find out about them. You must also have knowledge and awareness about the area you wish to work in. Saying vaguely 'I'd like to work behind the scenes' will not do.

Rule Number Three: make your own opportunities. When you feel you know something about the industry, then you should write to, telephone and visit the companies, again and again. Try to find the name of someone in a company who might be prepared to see you. Ask everyone for advice. And remember you must be able to take rejection: it requires persistence to get into this industry and there will be very many disappointments before you make any headway. Forget any nonsense about overnight success. Getting in will test your perseverance!

Rule Number Four: live and breathe the industry. In other words: watch films and television over and over again. Think about what you see constructively and analytically. What are the films and programmes saying? How do they get their messages across? Try to think up new approaches and ideas as you watch. Employers are looking for an enthusiasm and passion for the industry. The dilettante approach is fatal. Broadcasters want people who can present information concisely. They are looking for people who can think of a workable idea that has not been done before or that looks at the world from a new angle. However, it is no use having your own pet idea and writing a long emotional, meandering letter to the BBC in the hope that the Corporation may fulfil your dreams and offer you a job. They won't.

Rule Number Five: produce a portfolio of your own work. As explained earlier in this book, the advantage of formal coursework is that students are usually provided with the opportunity to make their own films and videos. They put together examples of their practical work to show prospective employers who, after all, need something by which to judge you.

Rule Number Six: construct an effective curriculum vitae (CV). A CV is a description of you, and should set out your skills, abilities, personality and experience. People are incredibly lazy about their CVs. Once they have done one, they send it out indiscriminately in all directions. In fact CVs should be tailored to suit each individual job. Companies specialising in corporate videos have different interests from companies specialising in pop or educational videos. Think about what the employer might be looking for. Emphasise that part of your experience which is relevant. For this reason it is always worth trying to put your CV on a word processor so that it can be easily adapted and updated. Make sure that there are no mistakes in grammar or spelling: employers can be very particular and some of them are insulted by poorly prepared CVs or letters of application. There is nothing charming about the casual approach.

Rule Number Seven: if you get the longed-for interview either for a course or a job, show your enthusiasm, but don't show off. As explained in this book, making moving pictures is a joint effort and employers are looking for people who can fit in with a team, especially at the beginning. When you are producing or directing the British film of 2001 you can afford to throw your weight around a little, but not before! The key personality traits that employers say they are looking for are: the ability to be a team worker, common sense, curiosity, good communication skills, attention to detail, a willingness to work long hours, the enthusiasm to keep a project going, commitment, physical stamina, tenacity, practical skills and lateral thinking. Employers today also like people with financial skills and sometimes those who have experience built up elsewhere, perhaps in areas which have nothing to do with broadcasting – working on environmental issues or abroad for a charity organisation or for the House of Commons.

Remember there are many more people than there are jobs!

Useful Names and Addresses

Broadcasting and Film Companies

There are now so many independent film and television production companies, in addition to the BBC, ITV and Channel Four, that the best advice is to buy the BFI *Film and Television Handbook* or the *Guardian Media Guide* (see details in the Bibliography). Both of these are excellent sources of information for anyone wishing to work in the industry.

Education and Training

Europe

European Film College
Dk-8400, Ebeltoft, Denmark
Tel: 45 86 34 00 55

The college runs a thirty-two week course starting in September. No special qualifications are required although students should be over nineteen years of age, and must be able to speak and write in English

Information about courses: Degrees, diplomas, short courses

There are many courses offering qualifications in film, television, video, communications and media. The British Film Institute publishes essential guides to university and college courses and to short training courses. These are:
Media Courses UK compiled by Lavinia Orton which includes sections on further education courses, undergraduate courses, postgraduate courses and short courses.
A Listing of Short Courses in Film, Television, Video and Radio, also compiled by Lavinia Orton. This is useful for those planning a professional upgrade as well as those wishing to learn a new skill. Entries are listed by geographical area and subject. The listing is updated three

times a year in January, May and September. For complete information on prices and how to order see the final page of this book.

Training Organisations (see Chapter 8)

CYFLE
Gonant, Penrallt Isaf, Caernarfon, Gwynedd LL 55 1NW
Tel: 01286 671000

ft2 – Film and Television Freelance Training
4th Floor, 5 Dean Street, London W1V 5RN
Tel: 0171 734 5141

Gaelic Training Trust
Urras Trèanaidh Telebhisean Gàidhlig
Sabhal Mòr Ostaig, An Teanga, An t-Eilean Sgitheanach IV44 8RQ
Tel: 014171- 844373

Moving Image Development Agency
Script Development Fund
109 Mount Pleasant, Liverpool 13 5TF
Tel: 0151 708 9858

National Film and Television Short Course Unit
Beaconsfield Studios,
Station Road, Beaconsfield, Buckinghamshire HP9 1LG
Tel: 01494 671234/677903

Networking
Vera Productions, 30-38 Dock Street, Leeds LS10 1JF
Tel: 0113 2428646

Scottish Broadcast and Film Training Ltd
4 Park Gardens, Glasgow G3 7YE
Tel: 0141 322 2077

Training Consortia

Skillset is developing Regional/National consortia. These are organisations that are industry-led and managed by the employers and the unions in their area. They are in regular communication with key trainers and educators in their areas. All have close relationships with Skillset and, broadly, their aims and objectives are to research training needs, to attract investment for training and to be involved in the development and implementation of vocational standard. Careers officers in schools and universities may find it useful to be in contact with the regional consortium. A full listing can be obtained from Skillset.

Vocational Qualifications

National Council for Vocational Qualifications (NCVQ)
222 Euston Road, London NW1 2BZ
Tel: 0171 387 9898

SCOTVEC
Scottish Vocational Education Council
Hanover House
24 Douglas Street, Glasgow G2 7NQ
Tel: 0141 248 7900

Vocational Qualifications: Awarding Bodies

The Business and Technology Education Council (BTEC)
Central House
Upper Woburn Place, London WC1H 0HH
Tel: 0171 413 8400

City and Guilds
1 Giltspur Street, London EC1A 9DD
Tel: 0171 294 2468

Royal Society of Arts
RSA Examination Board,
Westwood Way, Coventry CV4 8HS
Tel: 01203 470033

Industry Training Organisations

Skillset
c/o Channel Four, 124 Horseferry Road, London SW1P 2TX
Tel 0171 396 4444
Tel: 0171 306 8585

Skillset produces an excellent guide to the industry. It is entitled *Careers in Broadcast Film and Video* and is available by writing to Skillset.

Arts and Entertainment Training Council
Glyde House, Glydegate, Bradford BD5 0BQ
Tel: 01274 738 800

The Industry Lead Body for Design
(shortly to become a Training Organisation)
32-38 Saffron Hill, London EC1N 8FH
Tel: 0171 831 9777

Trade Associations, Unions, Guilds and Societies

Advertising Film and Videotape Producers' Association
26 Noel Street, London W1V 3RD
0171 434 2651

British Actors' Equity Association
Guild House, Upper St Martin's Lane, London WC2H 9EG
Tel: 0171 379 6000

BECTU
Broadcasting, Entertainment, Cinematograph and Theatre Union
111 Wardour Street, London W1V 4AY
Tel: 0171 437 8506

BKSTS (see The Moving Image Society)

Directors Guild of Great Britain
15-19 Great Titchfield Street, London W1P 7FB
Tel: 0171 436 8626

The Directors Guild is a union for directors in all media, including television, film, theatre and radio. Lower membership rates are available to students. The Guild issues an advised schedule of rates, codes of practice, model contracts and it gives advice and holds workshops. It also arranges an observer scheme and social events and publishes a magazine, *Direct,* and an annual directory of members.

Guild of British Animation
26 Noel Street, London W1V 3RD
Tel: 0171 434 9002

International Visual Communications Association (IVCA)
Bolsover House, 5/6 Clipstone Street, London W1P 8LD
Tel: 0171 580 0962

IVCA is the only European organisation which represents the users and suppliers of the corporate film, video and events industry. The association represents the varied interest of members including clients, production companies, facilities houses, freelances, rental companies and manufacturers

The Moving Image Society
(formerly British Kinematograph Sound and Television Society – BKSTS)
63-71 Victoria House
Vernon Place, London WC1B 4DA
Tel: 0171242 8400

The society organises regular meetings and demonstrations of new equipment and techniques. It also runs training courses and organises conferences and seminars on topics such as special effects and wildlife film making. It regularly reviews the relevant training offered to newcomers to the industry. Student membership is a way to make contacts in the industry.

National Union of Journalists (NUJ)
Acorn House
314 Gray's Inn Road, London WC1X 8DP
Tel: 071 278 7916

Many journalists working in the television industry belong to the NUJ and most broadcasters have agreements with the union.

New Producers' Alliance
9 Bourlet Close, London W1P 7PS
Tel: 0171 580 2480

The New Producers' Alliance sets out to educate and inform feature film producers in the UK and to seek creative partnerships with producers world-wide. It provides a forum for directing and writing talent to meet producers and share information and experience. From its beginnings in 1993 it has become a forum and focus for the new wave within the British Film Industry.

PACT
Producers' Alliance for Cinema and Television
Gordon House,
10 Greencoats Place, London SW1P 1PH
Tel: 0171 233 6000

PACT's role is to serve the film and independent television production sector and is the contact point for international/European co-production, financial partners and distributors. It publishes a magazine for members and is an organisation for established professionals.

The Royal Television Society
Holborn Hall,
100 Gray's Inn Road, London, WC1X 8AL
Tel: 0171 430 1000

The Television Society was founded in 1927 by a small group of enthusiasts who were determined to further the new scientific discovery of television. This was nine years before the first television broadcast from Alexander Palace. The Royal Television Society now has more 3,500 members from the whole spectrum of the industry. It is an independent forum where the art, science business, craft and politics of television can be discussed by representatives. It has regional centres and arranges workshops, master classes, conventions and symposia including the influential Cambridge Convention held in alternate years at King's College, Cambridge. It has a student membership which can provide excellent contacts and develop skills (see the case study of Rachel Wright in chapter 11) and publishes a journal called *Television*.

Writers Guild of Great Britain
430 Edgware Road, London W2 1EH
Tel: 0171 723 8074

The Writers' Guild of Great Britain is the trade union for professional writers in film, television, radio, theatre, and literature where it negotiates minimum terms and conditions. The Guild has an agreement with PACT covering higher and lower-budget feature films, single television movies, television series and serials. It also has agreements with the BBC and ITVA. The Guild has approved a new member category for students in writing classes. For more information contact the Guild.

Journals

The following are useful magazines and journals for information about the industry;

Audiovisual	*Stage Screen and Radio*
Broadcast	*Stage and Television Today*
IVCA Magazine	*Television*
Media Week	*Televisual*
New Scientist	*Time Out*
Stage and Television Today	*Wired*

The Media pages of the *Guardian* on a Monday are also very useful and the *European*, which comes out once a week, often has articles about the media industry in Europe usually from a business perspective.

Jobs are advertised in:

Audiovisual *Screen International*
Broadcast *State and Television Today*
Campaign *Sunday Times,*
Daily Telegraph *Televisual*
Evening Standard (London) *Time Out*
Guardian *The Times*
The Independent *TV Production International*
Manchester Evening News *UK Press Gazette*
Observer

Other useful contact points in higher education are:

National Association for Higher Education in Film and Video (NAHEFV)
London International Film School
24 Shelton Street, London WC2H 9HP
Tel: 0171 836 9642

The British Universities Film and Video Council
55 Greek Street, London W1V 5LR
Tel: 0171 734 3687

The Council promotes the study and use of television film and related media for research and higher education. It runs an information service which has viewing and editing facilities and it organises conferences and courses. For television researchers it publishers the *Researcher's Guide to British Film and TV Collections*, the *Researcher's Guide to British Newsreels Volumes I, II and III* and *Film and Television Collections in Europe: The MAP-TV Guide* which gives details of 1,900 film and television archives in over 40 countries. The Council maintains the Slade Film History Register which hold copies of British newsreels from 1896-1979. The Council publishes a database on audio-visual materials for higher education on CD-ROM which is entitled *Audiovisual materials for Higher Education* and contains the AVANCE database of 15,000 programme titles. The Council also runs one-day courses on topics such as: Copyright Clearance for Print, Broadcast and Multimedia Production; Archives and Footage Sources for Film Researchers. In addition, the Council holds copies of BBC Television Training Videos. These videos, which include such titles as *Creative Editing, Directing Interviews, Filming Action, Music and Sound Effects for Television* and many more, may be viewed and bought at the Council. The BBC unit which made these videos has now been disbanded so the BUFVC is the only available source. A full listing can be obtained from the Council.

BIBLIOGRAPHY

Alvarado, Manuel, and Edward Buscombe, *Hazell: The Making of a TV Series* (London: BFI, 1988).

Alvarado, Manuel and John Stewart, *Made for Television: Euston Films Limited* (London: BFI, 1985).

Angell, Robert, *So You Want to Be in Film and Television?* (London: BFI, 1992).

Bernstein, Steven, *Film Production*, 2nd edn. (Oxford: Focal Press, 1994).

Birtwistle and Conklin, *The Making of Pride and Prejudice* (Harmondsworth: Penguin Books, 1995).

David Bowne, Multimedia (London: Bowerdean Publishing Company Ltd, 1994).

British Film Institute, *Television Industry Tracking Study*, *The First Year Interim Report* (London: BFI, 1996).

Chater, Kathy, *The Television Researchers's Guide*, revised edn. (London: BBC, 1995).

Davis, Sue (ed.), *The Official ITV Careers Handbook* (London: Headway Books for the Independent Television Association, 1992).

Fraser, Cathie, *The Production Assistant's Survival Guide* (London: BBC, 1990).

Langham, Josephine, 'Inside the New Recruits', Paper presented to the Broadcasting Symposium in Manchester in March 1996; to be published by John Libbey, 1997.

Ostrov, R. *Careers in Film and Video*, 5th edn. (London: Kogan Page, 1996).

Merritt, Douglas, *Graphic Design in Television* (Oxford:Focal Press, 1995).

Negroponte, Nicholas, *Being Digital* (London: Hodder and Stoughton, 1994) in book and tape form.

Peak, Steve, and Paul Fisher, *The 1996 Media Guide*, a *Guardian* Book which is published every year and provides a wealth of information about the industry and names and addresses of useful organisations, available through the *Guardian.*

Ross-Muir, Anne, *Women's Guide to Jobs in Film and TV* (London: Pandora, 1987).

Rowlands, Avril, *The Television PA's Handbook* (Oxford: Focal Press, 1993).

Royal Television Society, *I want to work in television,* published by the RTS and available free from the RTS and Careers Offices.

Selby, Michael, Careers in Television and Radio, 6th edn. (London: Kogan Page, 1996).

Skillset, *Careers in Broadcast Film and Video* (London: Skillset, 1996); see above under Training Organisations for Skillset's address.

Stafford, Roy, *Nonlinear Editing and Visual Literacy* (London: BFI, 1995).

Thompson, Chris, *Non-Linear Editing* (London: Skillset and BFI, 1994).

Wasko, Janet, *Hollywood in the Information Age* (Oxford: Polity Press, 1994).

Watkinson, John, *Television Fundamentals* (Oxford: Focal Press, 1996).

Writers' and Artists' Yearbook (London: A. & C. Black) published annually.

Working in TV, Film and Radio, The Working In Series (no. 85); available from COIC, Room E455, Moorfoot, Sheffield, S1 4PQ (price: £2.95).

Yorke Ivor, *Television News;* an introductory book, aimed at journalists entering television from outside (London: Focal Press, 1995).

Source material for the quotations by the stars comes from Tony Crawley, *Chambers Film Quotes* (Edinburgh: W.R. Chambers Ltd, 1991).

BFI PUBLICATIONS

The British Film Institute's *Film and Television Handbook* published every year is an indispensable source of information on all aspects of the industry. In addition to annual reports on cinema, television and video, it also provides up-to-date information on courses, organisations, production companies, television companies, workshops, film societies, preview theatres, distributors, cable and satellite companies, studios, video labels, and so on.

The British Film Institute also publishes *Media Courses UK* which includes sections on Further Education courses, undergraduate courses, postgraduate courses and short courses. *Media Courses UK* is compiled and edited by Lavinia Orton and is available from the BFI (£8.99).

A Listing of Short Courses in Film, Television, Video and Radio also compiled by Lavinia Orton is useful for those planning a professional upgrade as well as those wishing to learn a new skill. Entries are listed by geographical area and subject. It is updated three times a year in January, May and September (£3.00).

The Handbook, Media Course UK and *A Listing of Short Courses in Film Television, Video and Radio* are available from BFI Publishing, 21 Stephen Street, London, W1P 2LN.

Teachers of the Media might find it useful to invest in the BFI *Screening Middlemarch,* edited by Cary Bazalgette and Christine James. The package includes a workbook, video and audiotape (£67. 25).

INDEX